# BELARUS

## IMMIGRATION POLICY, LAWS AND REGULATIONS HANDBOOK

### STRATEGIC INFORMATION AND REGULATIONS

**International Business Publications, USA**
**Washington DC, USA - Belarus**

# BELARUS
## IMMIGRATION POLICY, LAWS AND REGULATIONS HANDBOOK
### STRATEGIC INFORMATION AND REGULATIONS

**UPDATED ANNUALLY**

We express our sincere appreciation to all government agencies and international organizations which provided information and other materials for this handbook

Cover Design: International Business Publications, USA



**2018 Edition Updated Reprint International Business Publications, USA**
**ISBN 1-4387-8214-4**

For additional analytical, business and investment opportunities information,
please contact Global Investment & Business Center, USA
at (703) 370-8082. Fax: (703) 370-8083. E-mail: ibpusa3@gmail.com
Global Business and Investment Info Databank - www.ibpus.com

Printed in the USA

For additional analytical, business and investment opportunities information,
please contact Global Investment & Business Center, USA
at (703) 370-8082. Fax: (703) 370-8083. E-mail: ibpusa3@gmail.com
Global Business and Investment Info Databank - www.ibpus.com

# BELARUS

## IMMIGRATION POLICY, LAWS AND REGULATIONS HANDBOOK

### STRATEGIC INFORMATION AND REGULATIONS

## TABLE OF CONTENTS

**STRATEGIC AND BUSINESS PROFILES** .......... **7**

BASIC PROFILE .......... 7
*GEOGRAPHY* .......... *9*
*PEOPLE* .......... *11*
*GOVERNMENT* .......... *15*
*ECONOMY* .......... *19*
*ENERGY* .......... *24*
*COMMUNICATIONS* .......... *26*
*TRANSPORTATION* .......... *27*
*MILITARY* .......... *28*
*TRANSNATIONAL ISSUES* .......... *29*

**IMPORTANT INFORMATION FOR UNDERSTANDING BELARUS** .......... **31**

*PROFILE* .......... *31*
*HISTORICAL HIGHLIGHTS* .......... *32*
*GOVERNMENT* .......... *32*
*POLITICAL CONDITIONS* .......... *33*
*ECONOMY* .......... *37*
*DEFENSE AND MILITARY ISSUES* .......... *42*
*FOREIGN RELATIONS* .......... *42*
*U.S.-BELARUSIAN RELATIONS* .......... *44*

**BELARUS LEGAL SYSTEM BASICS** .......... **49**

LEGAL SYSTEM OF THE REPUBLIC OF BELARUS .......... 49
BUSINESS LAWS .......... 51

**IMMIGRATION SYSTEM AND POLICY - STRATEGIC INFORMATION AND DEVELOPMENTS** .......... **53**

BASIC INFORMATION ON IMMIGRATION TO BELARUS .......... 53
*PRINCIPAL LAWS ON IMMIGRATION* .......... *54*
CHANGES TO IMMIGRATION LAW .......... 54

**BASIC LAWS AND REGULATIONS AGGECTING IMMIGRATION AND MIGRATION ........ 56**

LAW ON IMMIGRATION ........ 56

*CHAPTER 1. General Provisions ........ 56*

*CHAPTER 2. Terms of Reference of Government Authorities in Controlling Immigration Processes ........ 57*

*CHAPTER 3. Obtaining Permission to Reside Permanently in the Republic of Belarus ........ 59*

*CHAPTER 4. The Procedure for Entry into the Republic of Belarus ........ 63*

*CHAPTER 5. Reunification of Family ........ 64*

*CHAPTER 6. Liability for Violating Legislation of the Republic of Belarus on Immigration ........ 65*

*CHAPTER 7. Deportation ........ 66*

ON CITIZENSHIP OF THE REPUBLIC OF BELARUS ........ 68

*Chapter 1 GENERAL PROVISIONS ........ 68*

*Chapter 2 ACQUISITION OF CITIZENSHIP OF THE REPUBLIC OF BELARUS ........ 71*

*Chapter 3 TERMINATION OF CITIZENSHIOP OF THE REPUBLIC OF BELARUS ........ 74*

*Chapter 4 CANCELLATION OF DECISIONS ON ISSUES OF CITIZENSHIP OF THE REPUBLIC OF BELARUS ........ 75*

*Chapter 6 COMPETENCE OF AUTHORITIES TAKING DECISIONS AND PROCESSING DOCUMENTS ON ISSUES OF CITIZENSHIP OF THE REPUBLIC OF BELARUS ........ 77*

*Chapter 7 PROCEDURE OF SUBMITTAL AND REVIEW OF APPLICATIONS ON ISSUES OF CITIZENSHIP OF THE REPUBLIC OF BELARUS ........ 79*

*Chapter 8 EXECUTION OF DECISIONS ON ISSUES OF CITIZENSHIP OF THE REPUBLIC OF BELARUS, APPPEALS OF DECISIONS OF STATE AUTHORITIES AND ACTIONS OF OFFICIALS ON ISSUES RELATED TO CITIZENSHIP OF THE REPUBLIC OF BELARUS ........ 80*

*Chapter 9 FINAL PROVISIONS ........ 81*

ON THE LEGAL STATUS OF FOREIGN CITIZENS AND STATELESS PERSONS IN THE REPUBLIC OF BELARUS ........ 83

*CHAPTER 1 GENERAL PROVISIONS ........ 83*

*CHAPTER 2 RIGHTS, FREEDOMS, DUTIES AND RESPONSIBILITY OF FOREIGNERS IN THE REPUBLIC OF BELARUS ........ 86*

*CHAPTER 3 ENTRY INTO THE REPUBLIC OF BELARUS, EXIT FROM THE REPUBLIC OF BELARUS, TRANSIT PASSAGE (TRANSIT) THROUGH THE TERRITORY OF THE REPUBLIC OF BELARUS OF FOREIGNERS ........ 91*

*CHAPTER 4 STAY OF FOREIGNERS IN THE REPUBLIC OF BELARUS ........ 97*

*CHAPTER 5 DEPORTATION. EXPULSION ........ 114*

*CHAPTER 6 Appealing against decisions and action (omissions) of State organs and officials of the Republic of Belarus ........ 116*

*CHAPTER 7 FINAL PROVISIONS ........ 117*

ON THE LEGAL STATUS OF FOREIGN CITIZENS AND STATELESS PERSONS IN THE REPUBLIC OF BELARUS ........ 122

*CHAPTER 1 GENERAL PROVISIONS ........ 122*

*CHAPTER 2 RIGHTS, FREEDOMS, DUTIES AND RESPONSIBILITY OF FOREIGNERS IN THE REPUBLIC OF BELARUS ........ 125*

*CHAPTER 3 ENTRY INTO THE REPUBLIC OF BELARUS, EXIT FROM THE REPUBLIC OF BELARUS, TRANSIT PASSAGE (TRANSIT) THROUGH THE TERRITORY OF THE REPUBLIC OF BELARUS OF FOREIGNERS ........ 129*

*CHAPTER 4 STAY OF FOREIGNERS IN THE REPUBLIC OF BELARUS* ..................... *135*
*CHAPTER 5 DEPORTATION. EXPULSION* ..................... *152*
*CHAPTER 6 Appealing against decisions and action (omissions) of State organs and officials of the Republic of Belarus* ..................... *154*
*CHAPTER 7 FINAL PROVISIONS* ..................... *155*
LAW ON IMMIGRATION ..................... 160
ON APPROVAL OF REGULATION ON STAY OF FOREIGN CITIZENS AND PERSONS WITHOUT CITIZENSHIP IN THE REPUBLIC OF BELARUS ..................... 160
*General Provisions* ..................... *161*
*Entry of Foreigners into the Republic of Belarus and Their Departure* ..................... *161*
*The Order of Temporary Stay of Foreigners in the Republic of Belarus* ..................... *163*
*Issuance of permissions for permanent residence and residence permits in the Republic of Belarus* ..................... *166*
*Responsibility for violation of this Regulation.* ..................... *169*
PROVISION ON ORDER OF DEPORTATION OF FOREIGN CITIZENS AND PERSONS WITHOUT CITIZENSHIP IN THE REPUBLIC OF BELARUS ..................... 171
*General Provisions* ..................... *171*
*Order of Making Decision on Eviction.* ..................... *173*
*Expenses related to the procedure of eviction* ..................... *175*

**BUSINESS TRAVEL TO BELARUS ..................... 178**

*Business Customs* ..................... *178*
*Travel* ..................... *178*
*Visa Requirements* ..................... *179*
*Telecommunications* ..................... *179*
*Transportation* ..................... *180*
*Local Time, Business Hours, and Holidays Return to top* ..................... *182*
*Temporary Entry of Materials and Personal Belongings* ..................... *182*
INFORMATION RESOURCES OF THE REPUBLIC OF BELARUS ..................... 182
*FREE ECONOMIC ZONES* ..................... *182*
*Government agencies* ..................... *183*
*REPRESENTATIONS OF INTERNATIONAL ORGANISATIONS* ..................... *185*
*OTHER BUSINESS RESOURCES* ..................... *185*
*MISCELLANEOUS* ..................... *186*

**SELECTED INDUSTRIAL AND BUSINESS COMPANIES IN BELARUS ..................... 188**

**IMPORTANT GOVERNMENT AND BUSINESS CONTACTS ..................... 229**

SELECTED GOVERNMENT CONTACTS ..................... 229
*SELECTED STATE COMMITTEES* ..................... *230*
IMPORTANT GOVERNMENT CONTACTS ..................... 230
MINISTRIES ..................... 230
STATE COMMI*TTEES ..................... 234
REGIONAL ADMINISTRATIVE BODIES ..................... 236
BELARUS CHAMBER OF COMMERCE OFFICES ..................... 237
*Minsk Branch* ..................... *238*
*Brest Branch* ..................... *241*
*Vitebsk Branch* ..................... *243*
*Gomel Branch* ..................... *244*

*Grodno Branch* ... *246*
*Mogilev Branch* ... *247*
*International Arbitration Court* ... *249*
*BELPATENTSERVICE* ... *249*
*Exhibition company "Belinterexpo – Belarusian International exhibitions" joint to the Belarusian Chamber of Commerce and Industry* ... *249*
*Representative office of BelCCI in Germany and countries of Western Europe* ... *250*
*Representative offices abroad* ... *250*
*Joint Chambers* ... *252*
OTHER USEFUL CONTACTS ... 252
*SELECTED BUSINESS CONTACTS FOR BELARUS* ... *253*

**SUPPLEMENTS ... 255**

BUSINESS LAWS ... 255
U.S. MERCHANDISE TRADE WITH BELARUS ... 256
*U.S. Imports from Belarus* ... *257*
BASIC TITLES FOR BELARUS ... 258
BASIC LAWS AND REGULATIONS AFFECTING BUSINESS ... 261

# STRATEGIC AND BUSINESS PROFILES

## BASIC PROFILE

| | |
|---|---|
| Capital and largest city | Minsk 53°55′N 27°33′E53.917°N 27.550°E |
| Official languages | • Belarusian<br>• Russian[a] |
| National language | Belarusian |
| Ethnic groups | • 83.7% Belarusians<br>• 8.3% Russians<br>• 3.1% Poles<br>• 1.7% Ukrainians<br>• 0.1% Jews<br>• 0.1% Armenians<br>• 0.1% Tatars<br>• 3.0% Other |
| Demonym | Belarusian |
| Government | Presidential republic |
| - President | Alexander Lukashenko |
| - Prime Minister | Andrei Kobyakov |
| Legislature | National Assembly |
| - Upper house | Council of the Republic |
| - Lower house | House of Representatives |
| Independence from the Soviet Union | |
| - Declared | 27 July 1990 |
| - Established | 25 August 1991 |
| - Completed | 25 December 1991 |
| Area | |
| - Total | 207,595 $km^2$ (85th)<br>80,155 sq mi |
| - Water (%) | 1.4% (2.830 $km^2$ or 1.093 sq mi) |
| Population | |
| - 2014 estimate | 9,475,100 ▲ |
| - Density | 45.8/$km^2$ (142nd)<br>120.8/sq mi |
| GDP (PPP) | 2015 estimate |
| - Total | $176.921 billion |
| - Per capita | $18,882 |
| GDP (nominal) | 2015 estimate |
| - Total | $81.627 billion |
| - Per capita | $8,711 |
| Gini (2011) | ▼26.5<br>low |

| | |
|---|---|
| HDI | ▲0.786<br>high · 53rd |
| Currency | Belarusian ruble (BYR) |
| Time zone | FET (UTC+3) |
| Drives on the | right |
| Calling code | +375 |
| ISO 3166 code | BY |
| Internet TLD | • .by<br>• .бел |

**Belarus** officially the **Republic of Belarus**, is a landlocked country in Eastern Europe bordered by Russia to the northeast, Ukraine to the south, Poland to the west, and Lithuania and Latvia to the northwest. Its capital is Minsk; other major cities include Brest, Hrodna (Grodno), Homiel (Gomel), Mahilyow (Mogilev) and Vitsebsk (Vitebsk). Over 40% of its 207,600 square kilometres (80,200 sq mi) is forested, and its strongest economic sectors are service industries and manufacturing.

Until the 20th century, the lands of modern-day Belarus belonged to several countries, including the Principality of Polotsk, the Grand Duchy of Lithuania, the Polish–Lithuanian Commonwealth, and the Russian Empire. In the aftermath of the Russian Revolution, Belarus declared independence as the Belarusian People's Republic, succeeded by the Socialist Soviet Republic of Byelorussia, which became a founding constituent republic of the Soviet Union and was renamed as the Byelorussian Soviet Socialist Republic (BSSR). Belarus lost almost half of its territory to Poland after the Polish-Soviet war. Much of the borders of Belarus took their modern shape in 1939 when some lands of the Second Polish Republic were reintegrated into it after the Soviet invasion of Poland and were finalized after World War II. The nation and its territory were devastated in World War II, during which Belarus lost about a third of its population and more than half of its economic resources. The republic was redeveloped in the post-war years. In 1945, Belarus became a founding member of the United Nations, along with the Soviet Union and the Ukrainian SSR.

The parliament of the republic declared the sovereignty of Belarus on 27 July 1990, and during the dissolution of the Soviet Union, Belarus declared independence on 25 August 1991. Alexander Lukashenko has been the country's president since 1994. Lukashenko continued a number of Soviet-era policies, such as state ownership of large sections of the economy. According to many countries and organizations, elections under Alexander Lukashenko have been widely criticized as being unfair, and that political opposition has been violently suppressed. In 2000, Belarus and Russia signed a treaty for greater cooperation, with some hints of forming a Union State. Belarus' Democracy Index rating continuously ranks the lowest in Europe, the country is labelled as "Not Free" by Freedom House, "Repressed" in the Index of Economic Freedom, and is rated as by far the worst country for press freedom in Europe in the 2013-14 Press Freedom Index published by Reporters Without Borders, where Belarus is ranked 157th out of an overall total of 180 nations.

Over 70% of Belarus's population of 9.49 million resides in urban areas. More than 80% of the population is ethnic Belarusian, with sizable minorities of Russians, Poles and Ukrainians. Since a referendum in 1995, the country has had two official languages: Belarusian and Russian. The Constitution of Belarus does not declare any official religion, although the primary religion in the country is Eastern Orthodox Christianity. The second most popular, Roman Catholicism, has a much smaller following, although both Orthodox and Catholic versions of Christmas and Easter are celebrated as national holidays.

After seven decades as a constituent republic of the USSR, Belarus attained its independence in 1991. It has retained closer political and economic ties to Russia than have any of the other former Soviet republics. Belarus and Russia signed a treaty on a two-state union on 8 December 1999 envisioning greater political and economic integration. Although Belarus agreed to a framework to carry out the accord, serious implementation has yet to take place. Since his election in July 1994 as the country's first directly elected president, Aleksandr LUKASHENKO has steadily consolidated his power through authoritarian means and a centralized economic system. Government restrictions on freedom of speech and the press, peaceful assembly, and religion remain in place.

## GEOGRAPHY

**Location:**
Eastern Europe, east of Poland

**Geographic coordinates:**
53 00 N, 28 00 E

**Map references:**
Europe

**Area:**
**total:** 207,600 sq km
**country comparison to the world:** 86
**land:** 202,900 sq km
**water:** 4,700 sq km

**Area - comparative:**
slightly smaller than Kansas

**Land boundaries:**
**total:** 3,599 km
**border countries:** Latvia 161 km, Lithuania 640 km, Poland 375 km, Russia 1,312 km, Ukraine 1,111 km
**Coastline:**
0 km (landlocked)
**Maritime claims:**
none (landlocked)

**Climate:**
cold winters, cool and moist summers; transitional between continental and maritime

## Belarus

Oblast boundary
Oblast center
Railroad
Road
Oblasts have the same names as their administrative centers.
0 50 100 Kilometers
0 50 100 Miles
C. I. S.
LATVIA
LITHUANIA
Russia
POLAND
Russia
Ukraine
Ostrov
Gulbene
Rēzekne
Daugavpils
Panevėžys
Ukmergė
Kaunas
Vilnius
Alytus
Suwałki
Augustów
Białystok
Biała Podlaska
Chełm
Zamość
Velikiye Luki
Nevel'
Zemtsy
Polotsk
Vitebsk
Postavy
Safonovo
Smolensk
Orsha
Molodechno
Borisov
Minsk
Mogilev
Roslavl'
Lida
Grodno
Krichev
Volkovysk
Slonim
Baranovichi
Osipovichi
Bobruysk
Slutsk
Soligorsk
Zhlobin
Klintsy
Rechitsa
Gomel'
Brest
Kobrin
Pinsk
Luninets
Zhitkovichi
Mozyr'
Dneprovsko-Bugskiy Kanal
Chernigov
Konotop
Kovel'
Sarny
Ovruch
Chernobyl'
Nezhin
Novovolynsk
Korosten'
Kiyevskoye Vodokhranilishche
Lutsk
Novograd-Volynskiy
Rovno
Priluki
Kiev
Zhitomir
Neman
Viliya
Sozh
Berezina
Dnyapro
Pripyat'
Zapadnaya Dvina
Dnepr
Desna
Volga
Nemunas
Bug
Final boundaries of Estonia, Latvia, and Lithuania with the former Soviet Union are expected to be confirmed by agreement. Other boundary representation is not necessarily authoritative.
802085 (R00098) 10-92

**Terrain:**
generally flat and contains much marshland

**Elevation extremes:**
**lowest point:** Nyoman River 90 m
**highest point:** Dzyarzhynskaya Hara 346 m

**Natural resources:**
timber, peat deposits, small quantities of oil and natural gas, granite, dolomitic limestone, marl, chalk, sand, gravel, clay

**Land use:**
**arable land:** 26.63%
**permanent crops:** 0.59%
**other:** 72.78% (2011)

**Irrigated land:**
1,150 sq km (2003)

**Total renewable water resources:**
58 cu km (2011)

**Freshwater withdrawal (domestic/industrial/agricultural):**
**total:** 4.34 cu km/yr (32%/65%/3%)
**per capita:** 435.4 cu m/yr (2009)

**Environment - current issues:**
soil pollution from pesticide use; southern part of the country contaminated with fallout from 1986 nuclear reactor accident at Chornobyl' in northern Ukraine

**Environment - international agreements:**
**party to:** Air Pollution, Air Pollution-Nitrogen Oxides, Air Pollution-Sulfur 85, Biodiversity, Climate Change, Climate Change-Kyoto Protocol, Desertification, Endangered Species, Environmental Modification, Hazardous Wastes, Law of the Sea, Marine Dumping, Ozone Layer Protection, Ship Pollution, Wetlands
**signed, but not ratified:** none of the selected agreements

**Geography - note:**
landlocked; glacial scouring accounts for the flatness of Belarusian terrain and for its 11,000 lakes

## PEOPLE

**Nationality:**
**noun:** Belarusian(s)
**adjective:** Belarusian

**Ethnic groups:**
Belarusian 83.7%, Russian 8.3%, Polish 3.1%, Ukrainian 1.7%, other 2.4%, unspecified 0.9%

**Languages:**
Belarusian (official) 23.4%, Russian (official) 70.2%, other 3.1% (includes small Polish- and Ukrainian-speaking minorities), unspecified 3.3% (2009 est.)

**Religions:**
Eastern Orthodox 80%, other (including Roman Catholic, Protestant, Jewish, and Muslim) 20%

**Population:**
9,608,058
**country comparison to the world:** 93

**Age structure:**
**0-14 years:** 15.4% (male 759,285/female 717,118)
**15-24 years:** 11.7% (male 575,907/female 544,170)
**25-54 years:** 45.5% (male 2,141,419/female 2,227,433)
**55-64 years:** 13.3% (male 562,639/female 716,216)
**65 years and over:** 14.2% (male 430,225/female 933,646)
**population pyramid:**

**Dependency ratios:**
**total dependency ratio:** 41.5 %
**youth dependency ratio:** 22 %
**elderly dependency ratio:** 19.6 %
**potential support ratio:** 5.1 (2014 est.)

**Median age:**
**total:** 39.4 years
**male:** 36.3 years
**female:** 42.4 years (2014 est.)

**Population growth rate:**
-0.19% (2014 est.)
**country comparison to the world:** 213

**Birth rate:**
10.86 births/1,000 population (2014 est.)

**country comparison to the world:** 179

**Death rate:**
13.51 deaths/1,000 population (2014 est.)
**country comparison to the world:** 16

**Net migration rate:**
0.78 migrant(s)/1,000 population (2014 est.)
**country comparison to the world:** 65

**Urbanization:**
**urban population:** 75% of total population (2011)
**rate of urbanization:** 0.21% annual rate of change (2010-15 est.)

**Major urban areas - population:**
MINSK (capital) 1.861 million (2011)

**Sex ratio:**
**at birth:** 1.06 male(s)/female
**0-14 years:** 1.06 male(s)/female
**15-24 years:** 1.06 male(s)/female
**25-54 years:** 0.96 male(s)/female
**55-64 years:** 0.87 male(s)/female
**65 years and over:** 0.46 male(s)/female
**total population:** 0.87 male(s)/female (2014 est.)

**Mother's mean age at first birth:**
25.1 (2011 est.)

**Maternal mortality rate:**
4 deaths/100,000 live births (2010)
**country comparison to the world:** 181

**Infant mortality rate:**
**total:** 3.64 deaths/1,000 live births
**country comparison to the world:** 206
**male:** 4.07 deaths/1,000 live births
**female:** 3.19 deaths/1,000 live births (2014 est.)

**Life expectancy at birth:**
**total population:** 72.15 years
**country comparison to the world:** 138
**male:** 66.53 years
**female:** 78.1 years (2014 est.)

**Total fertility rate:**
1.47 children born/woman (2014 est.)
**country comparison to the world:** 195

**Contraceptive prevalence rate:**
72.6%

**Health expenditures:**
5.3% of GDP (2011)
**country comparison to the world:** 131

**Physicians density:**
3.76 physicians/1,000 population (2011)

**Hospital bed density:**
11.1 beds/1,000 population (2011)

**Drinking water source:**
**improved:**
urban: 99.8% of population
rural: 99% of population
total: 99.6% of population
**unimproved:**
urban: 0.2% of population
rural: 1% of population
total: 0.4% of population (2012 est.)

**Sanitation facility access:**
**improved:**
urban: 94% of population
rural: 95.3% of population
total: 94.3% of population
**unimproved:**
urban: 6% of population
rural: 4.7% of population
total: 5.7% of population

**HIV/AIDS - adult prevalence rate:**
0.4%
**country comparison to the world:** 76

**HIV/AIDS - people living with HIV/AIDS:**
23,200
**country comparison to the world:** 78

**HIV/AIDS - deaths:**
1,200
**country comparison to the world:** 69

**Obesity - adult prevalence rate:**
24.3%
**country comparison to the world:** 65

**Children under the age of 5 years underweight:**
1.3%
**country comparison to the world:** 130

**Education expenditures:**
5.1% of GDP
**country comparison to the world:** 71

**Literacy:**
**definition:** age 15 and over can read and write
**total population:** 99.6%
**male:** 99.8%
**female:** 99.5%

**School life expectancy (primary to tertiary education):**
**total:** 16 years
**male:** 15 years
**female:** 16 years

**Child labor - children ages 5-14:**
**total number:** 54,218
**percentage:** 5 %

**Unemployment, youth ages 15-24:**
**total:** 12.6%
**country comparison to the world:** 96
**male:** 12.4%
**female:** 12.6%

## GOVERNMENT

**Country name:**
**conventional long form:** Republic of Belarus
**conventional short form:** Belarus
**local long form:** Respublika Byelarus'/Respublika Belarus'
**local short form:** Byelarus'/Belarus'
**former:** Belorussian (Byelorussian) Soviet Socialist Republic

**Government type:**
republic in name, although in fact a dictatorship

**Capital:**
**name:** Minsk
**geographic coordinates:** 53 54 N, 27 34 E
**time difference:** UTC+2 (7 hours ahead of Washington, DC, during Standard Time)

**Administrative divisions:**
6 provinces (voblastsi, singular - voblasts') and 1 municipality* (horad); Brest, Homyel' (Gomel), Horad Minsk* (Minsk City), Hrodna (Grodno), Mahilyow (Mogilev), Minsk, Vitsyebsk (Vitebsk)
***note:*** administrative divisions have the same names as their administrative centers; Russian spelling provided for reference when different from Belarusian

**Independence:**
25 August 1991 (from the Soviet Union)

**National holiday:**
Independence Day, 3 July (1944); note - 3 July 1944 was the date Minsk was liberated from German troops, 25 August 1991 was the date of independence from the Soviet Union

**Constitution:**
several previous; latest drafted between late 1991 and early 1994, signed 15 March 1994; amended 1996, 2004 (2013)

**Legal system:**
civil law system; note - nearly all major codes (civil, civil procedure, criminal, criminal procedure, family and labor) have been revised and came into force in 1999 or 2000

**International law organization participation:**
has not submitted an ICJ jurisdiction declaration; non-party state to the ICCt

**Suffrage:**
18 years of age; universal

**Executive branch:**
**chief of state:** president Aleksandr LUKASHENKO (since 20 July 1994)
**head of government:** prime minister Andrey KOBYAKOV (since 27 December 2014); first deputy prime minister Vasily MATYUSHEVSKIY (since 27 December 2014)
**cabinet:** Council of Ministers appointed by the president

**elections/appointments:** president directly elected by absolute majority popular vote in 2 rounds if needed for a 5-year term (no term limits); first election took place on 23 June and 10 July 1994; according to the 1994 constitution, the next election should have been held in 1999; however, Aleksandr LUKASHENKO extended his term to 2001 via a November 1996 referendum; subsequent election held on 9 September 2001; an October 2004 referendum ended presidential term limits and allowed the president to run and win in a third (19 March 2006), fourth (19 December 2010), and fifth election (11 October 2015); next election in 2020; prime minister and deputy prime ministers appointed by the president and approved by the National Assembly
**election results:** Aleksandr LUKASHENKO reelected president; percent of vote - Aleksandr LUKASHENKO (independent) 83.5%, Tatsiana KARATKEVICH (Tell the Truth) 4.4%, Sergey GAYDUKEVICH (LDP) 3.3%, other 8.8%; note - election marred by electoral fraud

**Legislative branch:**

**description:** bicameral National Assembly or Natsionalnoye Sobraniye consists of the Council of the Republic or Sovet Respubliki (64 seats; 56 members indirectly elected by regional and Minsk city councils and 8 members appointed by the president; members serve 4-year terms) and the House of Representatives or Palata Predstaviteley (110 seats; members directly elected in single-seat constituencies by absolute majority vote in 2 rounds if needed; members serve 4-year terms); note - the US does not recognize the legitimacy of the National Assembly

**elections:** House of Representatives - last held on 11 September 2016 (next to be held in 2020); OSCE observers determined that the election was neither free nor impartial and that vote counting was problematic in a number of polling stations; pro-LUKASHENKO candidates won virtually every seat, with only the UCP member and one independent forming alternative representation in the House; international observers determined that the previous elections, on 28 September 2008 and 23 September 2012, also fell short of democratic standards, with pro-LUKASHENKO candidates winning every seat
**election results:** Council of the Republic - percent of vote by party - NA; seats by party - NA; House of Representatives - percent of vote by party - NA; seats by party - KPB 8, Belarusian Patriotic Party 3, Republican Party of Labor and Justice 3, LDP 1, UCP 1, independent 94

**Judicial branch:**
**highest court(s):** Supreme Court (consists of the chairman, deputy chairman, and NA judges); Constitutional Court (consists of 12 judges including a chairman and deputy chairman)
**judge selection and term of office:** Supreme Court judges appointed by the president with the consent of the Council of the Republic; judges initially appointed for 5 years and evaluated for life appointment; Constitutional Court judges - 6 appointed by the president and 6 elected by the Chamber of Representatives; term

of judges is 11 years with an age limit of 70
**subordinate courts:** regional, district, city, town, and military courts

**Political parties and leaders:**
**pro-government parties:**
Belarusian Agrarian Party or AP [Mikhail SHIMANSKY]
Belarusian Patriotic Movement (Belarusian Patriotic Party) or BPR [Nikolay ULAKHOVICH, chairman]
Communist Party of Belarus or KPB [Igor KARPENKO]
Liberal Democratic Party or LDP [Sergey GAYDUKEVICH]
Republican Party of Labor and Justice [Vasiliy ZADNEPRYANYY]
**opposition parties:**
Belarusian Christian Democracy Party [Pavel SEVERINETS] (unregistered)
Belarusian Party of the Left "Fair World" [Sergey KALYAKIN]
Belarusian Popular Front or BPF [Aleksey YANUKEVICH]
Belarusian Social-Democratic Hramada [Stanislav SHUSHKEVICH]
Belarusian Social Democratic Party Hramada ("Assembly") or BSDPH [Irina VESHTARD]
Belarusian Social Democratic Party People's Assembly ("Narodnaya Hramada") [Nikolay STATKEVICH] (unregistered)
Christian Conservative Party or BPF [Zyanon PAZNIAK]
European Belarus Campaign [Andrey SANNIKOV]
Party of Freedom and Progress [Vladimir NOVOSYAD] (unregistered)
"Tell the Truth" Campaign [Vladimir NEKLYAYEV]
United Civic Party or UCP [Anatoliy LEBEDKO]

**Political pressure groups and leaders:**
Assembly of Pro-Democratic NGOs [Sergey MATSKEVICH] (unregistered)
Belarusian Congress of Democratic Trade Unions [Aleksandr YAROSHUK]
Belarusian Association of Journalists [Zhana LITVINA]
Belarusian Helsinki Committee [Aleh HULAK]
Belarusian Independence Bloc (unregistered) and For Freedom movement [Aleksandr MILINKEVICH]
Belarusian Organization of Working Women [Irina ZHIKHAR]
BPF-Youth [Andrus KRECHKA] (unregistered)
Charter 97 [Andrey SANNIKOV] (unregistered)
Perspektiva small business association [Anatol SHUMCHENKO]
Nasha Vyasna ("Our Spring") human rights center [Ales BYALYATSKI] (unregistered)
"Tell the Truth" Movement [Vladimir NEKLYAYEV] (unregistered)
Women's Independent Democratic Movement [Ludmila PETINA]
Young Belarus (Malady Belarus) [Zmitser KASPYAROVICH] (unregistered)
Youth Front (Malady Front) [Zmitser DASHKEVICH] (unregistered)

**International organization participation:**
BSEC (observer), CBSS (observer), CEI, CIS, CSTO, EAEC, EAPC, EBRD, FAO, GCTU, IAEA, IBRD, ICAO, ICC (NGOs), ICRM, IDA, IFC, IFRCS, ILO, IMF, IMSO,

Interpol, IOC, IOM, IPU, ISO, ITU, ITUC (NGOs), MIGA, NAM, NSG, OPCW, OSCE, PCA, PFP, SCO (dialogue member), UN, UNCTAD, UNESCO, UNIDO, UNIFIL, UNWTO, UPU, WCO, WFTU (NGOs), WHO, WIPO, WMO, WTO (observer), ZC

**Diplomatic representation in the US:**
**chief of mission:** Ambassador (vacant; recalled by Belarus in 2008); Charge d'Affaires Pavel SHIDLOVSKIY (since 23 April 2014)
**chancery:** 1619 New Hampshire Avenue NW, Washington, DC 20009
**telephone:** [1] (202) 986-1606
**FAX:** [1] (202) 986-1805
**consulate(s) general:** New York

**Diplomatic representation from the US:**
**chief of mission:** Ambassador (vacant; left in 2008 upon insistence of Belarusian Government); Charge d'Affaires Robert RILEY (since 22 August 2016)
**embassy:** 46 Starovilenskaya Street, Minsk 220002
**mailing address:** Unit 7010 Box 100, DPO AE 09769
**telephone:** [375] (17) 210-1283

**Flag description:**
red horizontal band (top) and green horizontal band one-half the width of the red band; a white vertical stripe on the hoist side bears Belarusian national ornamentation in red; the red band color recalls past struggles from oppression, the green band represents hope and the many forests of the country

**National symbol(s):**
mounted knight known as Pahonia (the Chaser)

**National anthem:**
**name:** "My, Bielarusy" (We Belarusians)

## ECONOMY

As part of the former Soviet Union, Belarus had a relatively well-developed, though aging industrial base; it retained this industrial base - which is now outdated, energy inefficient, and dependent on subsidized Russian energy and preferential access to Russian markets - following the breakup of the USSR. The country also has a broad agricultural base which is largely inefficient and dependent on government subsidies. After an initial burst of capitalist reform between 1991 and 1994, including privatization of smaller state enterprises and some service sector businesses, creation of institutions of private property, and development of entrepreneurship, Belarus' economic development greatly slowed. About 80% of all industry remains in state hands, and foreign investment has been hindered by a reluctance to welcome private investment absent joint ownership or affiliation with the state. A few businesses, which had been privatized after independence, were renationalized. State banks account for 75% of the banking sector.

Economic output declined for several years following the collapse of the Soviet Union, but revived in the mid-2000s due to the boom in oil prices. Belarus has only small reserves of crude oil, though it imports most of its crude oil and natural gas from Russia at prices substantially below world market prices. Belarus then derives export revenue by refining Russian crude and selling it at market prices. In late 2006, Russia began a process of rolling back its subsidies on oil and gas exports to Belarus. Several times since, Russia and Belarus have had serious disagreements over the level and price of Russian energy supplies. At one point in 2010, Russia stopped the export of all subsidized oil to Belarus save for domestic needs before the two countries reached a deal to restart the export of discounted oil to Belarus. Beginning in early 2016, Russia claims Belarus began accumulating debt – reaching $740 million by April 2017 – for paying below an agreed price for Russian natural gas. Russia decided to reduce its export of crude oil as a result of the debt. In April 2017, Belarus agreed to pay its gas debt and Russia restored the flow of crude.

New non-Russian foreign investment has been limited in recent years. In 2011, a financial crisis began, triggered by government-directed salary hikes, compounded by an increased cost in Russian energy inputs and an overvalued Belarusian ruble that lead to a nearly three-fold devaluation of the Belarusian ruble. In November 2011, Belarus agreed to sell to Russia its remaining shares of Beltransgaz, the Belarusian natural gas pipeline operator, in exchange for reduced prices for Russian natural gas. The situation stabilized in 2012, after Belarus received part of a $3 billion loan from the Russian-dominated Eurasian Economic Community Bailout Fund, a $1 billion loan from the Russian state-owned bank Sberbank, and $2.5 billion from the sale of Beltransgaz to Russian state-owned Gazprom; nevertheless, the Belarusian currency lost more than 60% of its value, as inflation reached new highs in 2011 and 2012, before calming in 2013. In December 2013, Russia announced a new loan for Belarus of up to $2 billion for 2014. Notwithstanding foreign assistance, the Belarusian economy continued to struggle under the weight of high external debt servicing payments and trade deficit. In mid-December 2014, structural economic shortcomings were aggravated by the devaluation of the Russian ruble, which triggered a near 40% devaluation of the Belarusian ruble.

Since 2012, Belarus's economy has suffered stagnation, which has led to widening productivity and income gaps between Belarus and neighboring countries. Since 2015, the Belarusian government has tightened its monetary policies (including allowing a more flexible exchange rate regime) and reduced subsidized government lending to state-owned industrial and agricultural enterprises, amid a drop in state budget revenues owing to falling global prices on key Belarusian export commodities - petroleum products and potash fertilizer. Belarus entered 2016 with a contracting economy and minimal hard currency reserves. GDP and foreign trade fell and unemployment rose, while inflation declined and hard currency reserves increased.

**GDP (purchasing power parity):**

$166 billion (2016 est.)
$170.5 billion (2015 est.)
$177.4 billion (2014 est.)
**note:** data are in 2016 dollars
**country comparison to the world:** 73

**GDP (official exchange rate):**
$48.13 billion (2016 est.)

**GDP - real growth rate:**
-2.6% (2016 est.)
-3.9% (2015 est.)
1.7% (2014 est.)
**country comparison to the world:** 212

**GDP - per capita (PPP):**
$17,500 (2016 est.)
$17,900 (2015 est.)
$18,700 (2014 est.)
**note:** data are in 2016 dollars
**country comparison to the world:** 94

**Gross national saving:**
21.9% of GDP (2016 est.)
30.2% of GDP (2015 est.)
28.5% of GDP (2014 est.)
**country comparison to the world:** 72

**GDP - composition, by end use:**
**household consumption:** 54.6%
**government consumption:** 15.8%
**investment in fixed capital:** 30.1%
**investment in inventories:** 2.6%
**exports of goods and services:** 57.2%
**imports of goods and services:** -60.3% (2016 est.)

**GDP - composition, by sector of origin:**
**agriculture:** 9.2%
**industry:** 40.9%
**services:** 49.8% (2016 est.)

**Agriculture - products:**
grain, potatoes, vegetables, sugar beets, flax; beef, milk
**Industries:**
metal-cutting machine tools, tractors, trucks, earthmovers, motorcycles, , synthetic fibers, fertilizer, textiles, , refrigerators, washing machines and other household appliances

**Industrial production growth rate:**
-0.4% (2016 est.)
**country comparison to the world:** 191

**Labor force:**
4.381 million (2016 est.)
**country comparison to the world:** 89

**Labor force - by occupation:**
**agriculture:** 9.7%
**industry:** 23.4%
**services:** 66.8% (2015 est.)

**Unemployment rate:**
0.8% (2016 est.)
1% (2015 est.)
**note:** official registered unemployed; large number of underemployed workers
**country comparison to the world:** 4

**Population below poverty line:**
5.7% (2016 est.)
**Household income or consumption by percentage share:**
**lowest 10%:** 3.8%
**highest 10%:** 21.9% (2008)

**Distribution of family income - Gini index:**
26.5 (2011)
21.7 (1998)
**country comparison to the world:** 140

**Budget:**
**revenues:** $21.21 billion
**expenditures:** $20.92 billion (2016 est.)

**Taxes and other revenues:**
44.1% of GDP (2016 est.)
**country comparison to the world:** 24

**Budget surplus (+) or deficit (-):**
0.6% of GDP (2016 est.)
**country comparison to the world:** 24

**Public debt:**
60.7% of GDP (2016 est.)
48.5% of GDP (2015 est.)
**country comparison to the world:** 67

**Fiscal year:**
calendar year

**Inflation rate (consumer prices):**
14% (2016 est.)
13.6% (2015 est.)
**country comparison to the world:** 213

**Central bank discount rate:**
14% (19 April 2017)
15% (15 March 2017)
**country comparison to the world:** 6

**Commercial bank prime lending rate:**
18% (31 December 2016 est.)
18.08% (31 December 2015 est.)
**country comparison to the world:** 23

**Stock of narrow money:**
$2.232 billion (31 December 2016 est.)
$2.301 billion (31 December 2015 est.)
**country comparison to the world:** 125

**Stock of broad money:**
$5.651 billion (31 December 2015 est.)
$7.608 billion (31 December 2014 est.)
**country comparison to the world:** 128

**Stock of domestic credit:**
$24.09 billion (31 December 2016 est.)
$22.23 billion (31 December 2015 est.)
**country comparison to the world:** 83

**Current account balance:**
-$2.118 billion (2016 est.)
-$2.037 billion (2015 est.)
**country comparison to the world:** 151

**Exports:**
$22.65 billion (2016 est.)
$26.19 billion (2015 est.)
**country comparison to the world:** 64

**Exports - commodities:**
machinery and equipment, mineral products, chemicals, metals, textiles, foodstuffs

**Exports - partners:**
Russia 39.1%, UK 11.1%, Ukraine 9.5%, Netherlands 4.3%, Germany 4.1%

**Imports:**
$25.44 billion (2016 est.)
$28.33 billion (2015 est.)
**country comparison to the world:** 66

**Imports - commodities:**
mineral products, machinery and equipment, chemicals, foodstuffs, metals

**Imports - partners:**
Russia 56.6%, China 7.9%, Germany 4.6%

**Reserves of foreign exchange and gold:**
$4.206 billion (31 December 2016 est.)
$4.176 billion (31 December 2015 est.)
**country comparison to the world:** 96

**Debt - external:**
$34.75 billion (31 December 2016 est.)
$34.85 billion (31 December 2015 est.)
**country comparison to the world:** 74

**Stock of direct foreign investment - at home:**
$6.929 billion (31 December 2016 est.)
$7.241 billion (31 December 2015)
**country comparison to the world:** 97

**Stock of direct foreign investment - abroad:**
$3.547 billion (31 December 2016 est.)
$4.649 billion (31 December 2015)
**country comparison to the world:** 68

**Exchange rates:**
Belarusian rubles (BYB/BYR) per US dollar -
18,500 (2016 est.)
15,926 (2015 est.)
15,926 (2014 est.)
10,224.1 (2013 est.)
8,336.9 (2012 est.)

## ENERGY

**Electricity - production:**
32.82 billion kWh
**country comparison to the world:** 64

**Electricity - consumption:**
31.74 billion kWh

**country comparison to the world:** 61

**Electricity - exports:**
5.067 billion kWh
**country comparison to the world:** 28

**Electricity - imports:**
7.767 billion kWh
**country comparison to the world:** 29

**Electricity - installed generating capacity:**
8.032 million kW
**country comparison to the world:** 65

**Electricity - from fossil fuels:**
99.7% of total installed capacity
**country comparison to the world:** 49

**Electricity - from nuclear fuels:**
0% of total installed capacity
**country comparison to the world:** 54

**Electricity - from hydroelectric plants:**
0.2% of total installed capacity
**country comparison to the world:** 147

**Electricity - from other renewable sources:**
0.1% of total installed capacity
**country comparison to the world:** 104

**Crude oil - production:**
32,070 bbl/day
**country comparison to the world:** 65

**Crude oil - exports:**
0 bbl/day
**country comparison to the world:** 89

**Crude oil - imports:**
294,800 bbl/day
**country comparison to the world:** 26

**Crude oil - proved reserves:**
198 million bbl

**country comparison to the world:** 60

**Refined petroleum products - production:**
346,000 bbl/day
**country comparison to the world:** 39

**Refined petroleum products - consumption:**
188,800 bbl/day
**country comparison to the world:** 61

**Refined petroleum products - exports:**
224,200 bbl/day
**country comparison to the world:** 28

**Refined petroleum products - imports:**
43,240 bbl/day
**country comparison to the world:** 76

**Natural gas - production:**
220 million cu m
**country comparison to the world:** 78

**Natural gas - consumption:**
21.82 billion cu m
**country comparison to the world:** 34

**Natural gas - exports:**
0 cu m
**country comparison to the world:** 69

**Natural gas - imports:**
21.02 billion cu m
**country comparison to the world:** 20

**Natural gas - proved reserves:**
2.832 billion cu m
**country comparison to the world:** 97

**Carbon dioxide emissions from consumption of energy:**
67.16 million Mt

## COMMUNICATIONS

**Telephones - main lines in use:**
4.407 million

**country comparison to the world:** 37

**Telephones - mobile cellular:**
10.675 million
**country comparison to the world:** 75

**Telephone system:**
**general assessment:** Belarus lags behind its neighbors in upgrading telecommunications infrastructure; modernization of the network progressing with roughly two-thirds of switching equipment now digital
**domestic:** state-owned Beltelcom is the sole provider of fixed-line local and long distance service; fixed-line teledensity is improving although rural areas continue to be underserved; multiple GSM mobile-cellular networks are experiencing rapid growth; mobile-cellular teledensity now exceeds 100 telephones per 100 persons
**international:** country code - 375; Belarus is a member of the Trans-European Line (TEL), Trans-Asia-Europe (TAE) fiber-optic line, and has access to the Trans-Siberia Line (TSL); 3 fiber-optic segments provide connectivity to Latvia, Poland, Russia, and Ukraine; worldwide service is available to Belarus through this infrastructure; additional analog lines to Russia; Intelsat, Eutelsat, and Intersputnik earth stations

**Broadcast media:**
4 state-controlled national TV channels; Polish and Russian TV broadcasts are available in some areas; state-run Belarusian Radio operates 3 national networks and an external service; Russian and Polish radio broadcasts are available

**Internet country code:**
.by

**Internet hosts:**
295,217
**country comparison to the world:** 64

**Internet users:**
2.643 million
**country comparison to the world:** 69

## TRANSPORTATION

**Airports:**
65
**country comparison to the world:** 75

**Airports - with paved runways:**
**total:** 33
**over 3,047 m:** 1

**2,438 to 3,047 m:** 20
**1,524 to 2,437 m:** 4
**914 to 1,523 m:** 1
**under 914 m:** 7

**Airports - with unpaved runways:**
**total:** 32
**over 3,047 m:** 1
**1,524 to 2,437 m:** 1
**914 to 1,523 m:** 2
**under 914 m:**
28

**Heliports:**
1

**Pipelines:**
gas 5,386 km; oil 1,589 km; refined products 1,730 km

**Railways:**
**total:** 5,537 km
**country comparison to the world:** 32
**broad gauge:** 5,512 km 1.520-m gauge (874 km electrified)
**standard gauge:** 25 km 1.435-m gauge

**Roadways:**
**total:** 86,392 km
**country comparison to the world:** 54
**paved:** 74,651 km
**unpaved:** 11,741 km

**Waterways:**
2,500 km (major rivers are the west-flowing Western Dvina and Neman rivers and the south-flowing Dnepr River and its tributaries, the Berezina, Sozh, and Pripyat rivers) (2011)
**country comparison to the world:** 36

**Ports and terminals:**
**river port(s):** Mazyr (Prypyats')

## MILITARY

**Military branches:**
Belarus Armed Forces: Land Force, Air and Air Defense Force, Special Operations Force

**Military service age and obligation:**
18-27 years of age for compulsory military service; conscript service obligation is 12-18 months, depending on academic qualifications; 17 year olds are eligible to become cadets at military higher education institutes, where they are classified as military personnel
**Manpower available for military service:**
**males age 16-49:** 2,401,785
**females age 16-49:** 2,429,653
**Manpower fit for military service:**
**males age 16-49:** 1,693,626
**females age 16-49:** 2,012,401
**Manpower reaching militarily significant age annually:**
**male:** 51,855
**female:** 48,760

**Military expenditures:**
1.2% of GDP
**country comparison to the world:** 85
1.27% of GDP
1.2% of GDP

## TRANSNATIONAL ISSUES

**Disputes - international:**
boundary demarcated with Latvia and Lithuania; as a member state that forms part of the EU's external border, Poland has implemented strict Schengen border rules to restrict illegal immigration and trade along its border with Belarus

**Refugees and internally displaced persons:**
**stateless persons:** 6,969 (2012)

**Trafficking in persons:**
**current situation:** Belarus is a source, transit, and destination country for women, men, and children subjected to sex trafficking and forced labor; women and children are trafficked to European and Middle Eastern countries and within Belarus for sexual exploitation; Belarusian men, women, and children are found in forced labor in the construction industry and other sectors in Russia and Belarus; Belarusian men seeking work abroad are increasingly subjected to forced labor
**tier rating:** Tier 2 Watch List - Belarus does not fully comply with the minimum standards for the elimination of trafficking; however, it is making significant efforts to do so; the government demonstrates decreased law enforcement efforts, conducting fewer trafficking investigations and convicting only one trafficking offender; while two new anti-trafficking laws were passed, they have not been fully implemented and government services to victims remain very limited; the government continues its efforts to prevent trafficking through public awareness campaigns and NGO-operated anti-trafficking hotlines

**Illicit drugs:**
limited cultivation of opium poppy and cannabis, mostly for the domestic market; transshipment point for illicit drugs to and via Russia, and to the Baltics and Western Europe; a small and lightly regulated financial center; anti-money-laundering legislation does not meet international standards and was weakened further when know-your-customer requirements were curtailed in 2008; few investigations or prosecutions of money-laundering activities

# IMPORTANT INFORMATION FOR UNDERSTANDING BELARUS

## PROFILE

**OFFICIAL NAME: Republic of Belarus**

### Geography

Area: 207,600 sq. km. (80,100 sq. mi.); slightly smaller than Kansas.
Cities: *Capital*--Minsk.
Terrain: Landlocked, low-lying with thick forests, flat marshes and fields.
Climate: Cold winters, cool and moist summers, transitional between continental and maritime.

### People

Nationality: *Noun*--Belarusian(s). *Adjective*--Belarusian.
Population: 9,648,533 (urban 73%; rural 27%).
Population decline (2009 est.): -0.378%.
Ethnic groups (1999 census): Belarusian (81.2%), Russian (11.4%), Polish (3.9%), Ukrainian (2.4%), Jewish (0.3%), other (0.8%).
Religions (2004 est.): Eastern Orthodox 80%, Catholic 14%, Protestant 2%, other (including Autocephalous Orthodox, Jewish, Muslim, and Krishna) 4%.
Languages: Belarusian and Russian (official).
Education: *Literacy*--99.6%.
Health: *Infant mortality rate* (2009 est.)--6.43/1,000. *Life expectancy* (2009 est.)--70.63 years (men 64.95 years, women 76.67 years).
Work force (4.3 million as of December 31, 2005): *Industry*—34.7%; *agriculture and forestry*--14%; *construction*--7.9%; *transportation, communications*--7.6%; *trade, catering*--12.2%; *education*--10.7%; *other*--24.3%.

### Government

Type: Republic.
Constitution: March 30, 1994; revision by unrecognized national referendum of November 24, 1996, gave presidency greatly expanded powers and became effective November 27, 1996.
Independence: 1991 (from Soviet Union).
Branches: *Executive*--President (head of state), Prime Minister (head of government), Council of Ministers (cabinet). *Legislative*--bicameral: the House of Representatives (110 deputies) and the Council of the Republic (64 deputies). *Judicial*--Supreme Court and the Constitutional Court.
Administrative subdivisions: Six oblasts (regions) and one municipality.
Political parties: Belarus has 15 registered political parties, including: Agrarian Party (AP); Belarusian Communist Party (KPB); Green Party Belarusian Social and Sports Party; Belarusian Patriotic Movement (BPR); Belarusian Popular Front (BNF); Belarusian Social-Democrat Party (BSDP); Social-Democratic Hramada Party; Conservative Christian Party-BNF; United Civic Party (UCP); Liberal Democratic Party of Belarus (LDBP); Party of Communists Belarusian (PKB); Party of Popular Accord; Republican Party of Labor and Justice (RPPS); Social Democratic Party of Popular

Accord (PPA);Several of these parties exist in name only. Other, unregistered parties are also active, such as: Belarusian Christian Democracy, Belarusian Party of Labor, Women's Party Nadezhda, Christian Conservative Party, and Party of Freedom and Progress.
Suffrage: Universal at age 18.

**Economy**
Natural resources: Forest land, peat deposits, potash, small amounts of oil and natural gas.
Agriculture: *Products*--grain, potatoes, vegetables, flax, beef, milk.
Industry: *Types*--machinery and transport equipment, chemical products, fabrics, and consumer goods.
Trade (2008): *Exports*--$31.81 billion (refined petroleum, potash fertilizers, machinery and transport equipment, chemicals, foodstuffs, metals, and textiles). *Major markets*--Russia, Germany, Netherlands, Poland, Great Britain, Ukraine, and Latvia. *Imports*--$36.64 billion (mineral products, machinery and equipment, metals, crude oil and natural gas, chemicals, foodstuffs). *Major suppliers*--Russia, Germany, Ukraine, Poland, Italy, Lithuania.
Exchange rate (June 2009): 2,852 BYR (Belarusian rubles) = U.S. $1.

## HISTORICAL HIGHLIGHTS

While archeological evidence points to settlement in today's Belarus at least 10,000 years ago, recorded history begins with settlement by Baltic and Slavic tribes in the early centuries A.D. With distinctive features by the ninth century, the emerging Belarusian state was then absorbed by Kievan Rus' in the ninth century. Belarus was later an integral part of what was called Litva, which included today's Belarus as well as today's Lithuania. Belarus was the birthplace of the Grand Duchy of Lithuania. Belarusian was the state language of the Grand Duchy until 1697, in part owing to the strong flowering of Belarusian culture during the Renaissance through the works of leading Belarusian humanists such as Frantzisk Skaryna. Belarus was the site of the Union of Brest in 1597, which created the Greek Catholic Church, for long the majority church in Belarus until suppressed by the Russian empire, and the birthplace of Thaddeus Kosciuszko, who played a key role in the American Revolution. Occupied by the Russian empire from the end of the 18th century until 1918, Belarus declared its short-lived National Republic on March 25, 1918, only to be forcibly absorbed by the Bolsheviks into what became the Soviet Union (U.S.S.R.). Suffering devastating population losses under Soviet leader Josif Stalin and the German Nazi occupation, including mass executions of 800,000 Jews, Belarus was retaken by the Soviets in 1944. It declared its sovereignty on July 27, 1990, and independence from the Soviet Union on August 25, 1991. It has been run by authoritarian Alyaksander Lukashenka since 1994.

## GOVERNMENT

The constitution provides for a directly elected president who serves a 5-year term. The bicameral parliament consists of the 64-seat Council of the Republic and the 110-seat House of Representatives. The Council of the Republic is the house of territorial representation. Eight members of the Council are appointed directly by the president of the Republic of Belarus, while local regional councils elect the rest. The deputies to the

House of Representatives are elected directly by the voters. The president appoints the prime minister, who is the head of government.

## POLITICAL CONDITIONS

Since his election in July 1994 as the country's first President, Alyaksander Lukashenka has consolidated power steadily in the executive branch through authoritarian means and has dominated all branches of government. He used a non-democratic referendum in November 1996 to amend the 1994 constitution to broaden his powers and illegally extend his term in office. He began to count his 5-year term in 1996, thereby adding 2 years to his first term in office. Based on the unrecognized 1996 constitution, Lukashenka announced that presidential elections were to be held in 2001. In 2004, he engineered a fraudulent referendum that removed term limits on the presidency. Independent exit polling of the referendum showed results far different from those officially announced. In 2006, Lukashenka "won" another term in an undemocratic election. In January 2007, he further consolidated his rule through local elections that failed to meet international standards.

In October 2000, parliamentary elections occurred for the first time since the disputed referendum of 1996. According to the Organization for Security and Cooperation in Europe's Office for Democratic Institutions and Human Rights (OSCE/ODIHR), these elections failed to meet international democratic standards. International monitors noted sweeping human rights violations and undemocratic practices throughout the election period, including massive vote-counting fraud. These irregularities led the OSCE/ODIHR to find that these elections failed to meet Belarus' OSCE commitments for democratic elections. March 2003 local elections and October 2004 parliamentary elections also failed to meet international standards of freedom and fairness. OSCE/ODIHR observers declared that the parliamentary elections fell far short of international standards, citing abuses in the campaign period and the vote counting.

The March 19, 2006 presidential election marked another low point in the government's treatment of its own citizens. OSCE/ODIHR observers noted that the election failed to meet international standards, was characterized by a disregard for the basic rights of freedom of assembly, association, and expression, and included a highly problematic vote count. Authorities detained many opposition and civic activists during the campaign and used force against demonstrators protesting the fraudulent election. Opposition presidential candidate Alyaksandr Kazulin was beaten and arrested during post-election protests. He was sentenced to a 5-year jail term. The Belarusian authorities released Kazulin on August 16, 2008.

Belarus held parliamentary elections in late September 2008. Despite Belarusian authorities' public assurances that the elections would be "unprecedentedly" democratic and transparent, the OSCE/ODIHR election observation mission determined the elections fell short of OSCE standards. The authorities denied registration for approximately 20% of opposition candidates as well as candidates overall. While candidates were allotted their mandatory campaign airtime on various media outlets, restrictions on this access made it difficult for candidates to adequately present their platforms to the public. OSCE/ODIHR observers noted good access to polling stations during early voting and election day. However, the Belarusian authorities fell short on access for OSCE/ODIHR and other observers to the vote count, a crucial aspect for determining the transparency of the elections. OSCE/ODIHR observers assessed transparency of the vote count to have been bad or very bad in 48% of observed cases. The OSCE recognized minor improvements in the conduct of the elections, but the lack of a transparent vote count made it impossible to determine the validity of the elections. The Department of State issued a statement following OSCE/ODIHR's preliminary assessment, expressing disappointment with the failure of the Belarusian elections to meet international standards.

Although government restrictions on basic freedoms spiked in connection with elections, they continued even in non-election periods. Efforts to further infringe upon press freedoms included the continued use of libel laws, restrictions on foreign funding, pressure on businesses not to advertise with independent media, limitations on access to newsprint and printing presses, prohibiting access to state distribution networks, censorship, restrictions on the import of media-related materials, temporary and permanent suspension of independent and opposition periodicals, confiscation in quantity of printed publications, and detention of those distributing such material. In December 2004, the government adopted new legislation establishing criminal penalties for "discrediting Belarus" and organizing activities of an unregistered non-governmental organization (NGO). The government has continued to make use of its monopoly on television broadcasting to present biased news coverage and to minimize the presentation of opposing points of view. All Internet service providers in Belarus operate through a state-controlled portal. Despite constitutional provisions, a 1998 government decree limited citizens' rights to express their own opinions. A new media law came into force in February 2009. The law prohibits Belarusian media outlets from obtaining technical or monetary support from foreign organizations or individuals unless they are co-founders, requires re-registration of most existing media and accreditation of journalists, and subjects online news media to the same requirements as print and broadcast media. These new restrictions threaten to undermine the last outlets of free speech online in Belarus. However, the Belarusian authorities have publicly stated they will in practice suspend the requirements for online media. In late 2008, the authorities took a number of positive steps, including distributing two leading independent newspapers--*Nasha Niva* and *Narodnaya Volya*--through state networks, registering the "For Freedom" movement, and creating a public council to engage civil society.

The 1994 and 1996 constitutions both provide for freedom of peaceful assembly; however, the regime severely restricts this right in practice. Demonstrations require an application at least 15 days in advance of the event, and the local government must then respond positively or negatively at least 5 days prior to the event. Applications by opposition groups are usually rejected. Following many unsanctioned demonstrations, police and other security officials detain, harass, and beat demonstration participants. Police also often film sanctioned events.

The constitution provides for freedom of religion; however, the authorities restrict this right in practice. Although Article 16 of the 1996 amended constitution reaffirms the equality of religions and denominations before the law, it also contains restrictive language stipulating that cooperation between the state and religious organizations "is regulated with regard for their influence on the formation of spiritual, cultural, and country traditions of the Belarusian people."

The government also restricts religious freedom in accordance with the provisions of a 2002 law on religion and a 2003 concordat with the Belarusian Orthodox Church (BOC), a branch of the Russian Orthodox Church (ROC) and the only officially recognized Orthodox denomination. Although there is no state religion, the concordat grants the BOC privileged status. Protestants in particular have attracted negative attention. Numerous anti-Semitic acts and attacks on religious monuments, buildings, and cemeteries have occurred with little discernable response from the government. Authorities have kept many religious communities waiting as long as several years for decisions about property registration or restitution. Authorities also harassed and fined members of certain religious groups, especially those that the authorities appear to regard as bearers of foreign cultural influence or as having a political agenda. Foreign missionaries, clergy, and humanitarian workers affiliated with churches have faced many government-imposed obstacles, including deportation and visa refusal or cancellation.

On December 17, 2007, President Lukashenka abolished exit stamps in favor of a computerized system that verifies the validity of passports. At the same time, however, he authorized the Interior Ministry to ban travel by individuals who had access to state secrets, who were facing criminal prosecution or civil suits, and who had outstanding financial commitments. The travel ban list allegedly has 100,000 names. Several opposition leaders and activists are subject to this travel ban and have been prevented from temporary travel abroad.

The constitution provides for the right of workers, except for state security and military personnel, to voluntarily form and join independent unions and to carry out actions in defense of workers' rights, including the right to strike. In practice, however, these rights are limited. The Belarusian Free Trade Union (FTUB) was established in 1991 and registered in 1992. Following the 1995 Minsk metro workers strike, the President suspended its activities. In 1996, FTUB leaders formed a new umbrella organization, the Belarusian Congress of Democratic Trade Unions (BCDTU), which encompasses four leading independent trade unions and is reported to have about 15,000 members. In late 2003, the BCDTU became a member of the International Confederation of Free Trade Unions (ICFTU).

In May 2001, a complaint was lodged with the International Labor Organization (ILO) by several trade union organizations alleging the government was attempting to destroy the independent unions. A campaign was carried out to raise international awareness about trade unions and to put pressure on the Belarusian authorities. Late in 2001, the regime attempted to further restrict the unions by refusing to turn over dues paid by members. Once it became clear that the unions and the FTUB were adjusting to this change, the government embarked on a takeover of the FTUB and several of its branch unions in June of 2002. The FTUB subsequently became an arm of the government, and the election of Leonid Kozik to the position of Chairman of the FTUB has been challenged by the ILO.

In November 2003, the ILO approved the establishment of a Commission of Inquiry to investigate alleged serious violations of workers' rights in the country. That same month the Ministry of the Economy informed the ILO that all activities related to its technical assistance project to labor unions must cease because the registration of the project was denied. In 2004, the ILO presented the government with a list of 12 recommendations to improve its treatment of independent unions. A January 2006 ILO mission found that the government had not implemented any of these recommendations. As a result, in June 2007, the European Union (EU) suspended Belarus' trading preferences under the Generalized System of Preferences (GSP). The United States had suspended GSP preferences in 2000 due to Belarus' failure to take steps that would allow the right of association and collective bargaining.

In March 2004 the government began forcing state employees (some 80% of Belarusian workers) to sign short-term work contracts. Although contracts may be concluded for a period of five years, most expire after one year, which essentially grants the government the opportunity to annually fire anyone in its employ. Many members of independent unions, political parties, and civil society groups have lost their jobs when their contracts were not renewed.

The State Department's report on human rights practices in Belarus is located at http://www.state.gov/g/drl/rls/hrrpt/2008/eur/119069.htm.

**Principal Government Officials**

| Portfolio | Name |
|---|---|
| Prime Minister | Andrei Kobyakov |
| First Deputy Prime Minister | Vasily Matyushevsky |
| Deputy Prime Minister | Anatoly Kalinin |
| Vice Prime Minister | Natalia Kochanova |
| Deputy Prime Minister | Mikhail Rusyi |
| Deputy Prime Minister | Vladimir Semashko |
| Ministry of Agriculture and Food | Leonid Zayats |
| Ministry of Architecture and Construction | Anatoly Cherny |
| Ministry of Communication and Informatization | Sergei Popkov |
| Ministry of Culture | Boris Svetlov |
| Ministry of Defence | Andrei Ravkov |
| Ministry of Economy | Vladimir I. Zinovsky |
| Ministry of Education | Mikhail Zhuravkov |
| Ministry of Emergency Situations | Vladimir Vashchenko |
| Ministry of Energy | Vladimir Potupchik |
| Ministry of Finance | Vladimir Amarin |
| Ministry of Foreign Affairs | Vladimir Makey |
| Ministry of Forestry | Mikhail Amelianovich |
| Ministry of Public Health | Vasily Zharko |
| Ministry of Housing and Communal Services | Alexander Terekhov |
| Ministry of Industry | Vitaly Vovk |
| Ministry of Information | Lilia Ananic |

| | |
|---|---|
| Ministry of Internal Affairs | Igor Shunevich |
| Ministry of Justice | Oleg Slizhevsky |
| Ministry of Labour and Social Protection | Marianna Shchetkina |
| Ministry of Natural Resources and Environmental Protection | Vacant |
| Ministry of Tax Collection | Sergey Nalivayko |
| Ministry of Sports and Tourism | Alexander Shamko |
| Ministry of Trade | Valentin Chekanov |
| Ministry of Transport and Communications | Anatoly Sivak |
| Heads of several governmental institutions are members of the Council of Ministers: | |
| State Security Committee | Valery Vakulchik |
| State Military-Industrial Committee | Sergei Gurulev |
| State Committee on Property | Georgy Kuznetsov |
| State Science and Technology Committee | Igor Voitov |
| State Committee on Standardization | Victor Nazarenko |
| State Border Committee | Alexander Boechko |
| State Customs Committee | Aleksandr Shpilevsky |
| State Control Committee | Leonid Anfimov |
| Head of the Presidential Administration | Aleksandr Kosinets |
| Chairman of the Board of the National Bank | Pavel Kallaur |
| Chairman of the Board of the Development Bank | Sergei Rumas |

Belarus' embassy in the U.S. is at 1619 New Hampshire Ave., NW, Washington, DC 20009; tel: 202-986-1606; fax: 202-986-1805; website: http://www.belarusembassy.org

## ECONOMY

| Currency | Belarusian ruble (BYB/BYR) |
|---|---|
| Fiscal year | Calendar year |
| Trade organisations | CIS |
| | Statistics |
| GDP | $63.267 billion<br>$147.565 billion (PPP; 2est.) |
| GDP rank | 57th (2012, PPP) |
| GDP growth | 5.5%<br>1.5%<br>2.1% |
| GDP per capita | $15,592 (PPP; est.) |
| GDP by sector | agriculture (9.1%), industry (47.2%), services (43.7%) |
| GDP by component | household consumption: 46.7% government consumption: 14.6%<br>investment in fixed capital: 32.8% investment in inventories: 1.6%<br>exports of goods and services: 81.6%<br>imports of goods and services: -77.1% |

| | |
|---|---|
| Inflation (CPI) | 21.8%<br>59.2%<br>20.5% |
| Population below poverty line | 27.1%<br>10%<br>7.3% |
| Gini coefficient | 27.7<br>26.5 |
| Labour force | 4.504 million |
| Labour force by occupation | agriculture (9.4%), industry (45.9%), services (44.7%) |
| Unemployment | 1% (2009 est.; only officially registered as unemployed included) |
| Average gross salary | 3,559,600 BYR / 436 $, monthly |
| Main industries | petrochemicals, potash, foodstuffs, timber, metal-cutting machine tools, tractors, trucks, earthmovers, motorcycles, televisions, synthetic fibers, fertilizers, textiles, radios, refrigerators<br>Agriculture prod.: grain, potatoes, vegetables, sugar beets, flax; beef, milk |
| Ease-of-doing-business rank | 63rd |
| | External |
| Exports | $51.861 billion |
| Export goods | machinery and equipment, mineral products, chemicals, metals, textiles, foodstuffs |
| Main export partners | Russia 35.4%<br>Netherlands 16.5%<br>Ukraine 12.1%<br>Latvia 7.1% |
| Imports | $48.852 billion |
| Import goods | mineral products, machinery and equipment, chemicals, foodstuffs, metals |
| Main import partners | Russia 59.3%<br>Germany 5.9%<br>China 5.1%<br>Ukraine 5.0% |
| FDI stock | $10.358 billion |
| Gross external debt | $34.02 billion<br>$34.12 billion |
| | Public finances |
| Public debt | 43.4% of GDP<br>36.9% of GDP<br>35.6% of GDP |
| Revenues | $22.38 billion |
| Expenses | $21.96 billion |
| Credit rating | B+ (Domestic)<br>B (Foreign)<br>B (T&C Assessment)<br>(Standard & Poor's) |

| | |
|---|---|
| | $8,1 billion |
| Foreign reserves | $7,926.93 billion |
| | $6,9 billion |

After the fall of the Soviet Union, all former Soviet republics faced a deep economic crisis. Belarus has however chosen its own way of overcoming this crisis. After the 1994 election of Alexander Lukashenko as the first President, launched the country on the path of "market socialism" as opposed to what Lukashenko considered "wild capitalism" chosen by Russia at that time. In keeping with this policy, administrative controls over prices and currency exchange rates were introduced. Also the state's right to intervene in the management of private enterprise was expanded, but on March 4, 2008, the President issues a decree abolishing the golden share rule in a clear movement to improve its international rating regarding the foreign investment.

As part of the former Soviet Union, Belarus had a relatively well developed industrial base; it retained this industrial base following the break-up of the USSR. The country also has a broad agricultural base and a high education level. Among the former republics of the Soviet Union, it had one of the highest standards of living. But Belarusians now face the difficult challenge of moving from a state-run economy with high priority on military production and heavy industry to a civilian, free-market system.

From 1991–1995, all sectors of the national economy were affected by the profound economic crisis, triggered by the collapse of the Soviet Union. At first, this event triggered the end of traditional economic processes, the sharp drop in the economic capacity of enterprises and of the population of the republics of the former Soviet Union that were key consumers of Belarus products, cessation of financing from the Soviet Union's military sector which accounted for a considerable share of Belarus' industry, shocks of price liberalization, and, above all, outpacing growth in prices for raw materials and energy resources. Moreover, Belarus, like the rest of the former Soviet Union republics, was characterized by a general lack of preparedness of the country's institution and society for the market system of relations. The sharp growth in prices for raw materials and energy resources revealed the technological weakness of the economy with its resource-intensive and low-quality output. At the same time, the weak competitiveness of the local products, legal inter-government restrictions, and absence of marketing and financial management skills prevented the country's economic entities from making up for the drop in effective demand at the traditional markets through the conquer of new export markets.

Peat, the country's most valuable mineral resource, is used for fuel and fertilizer and in the chemical industry. Belarus also has deposits of clay, sand, chalk, dolomite, phosphorite, and rock and potassium salt. Forests cover about a third of the land, and lumbering is an important sector.

The massive nuclear accident (April 26, 1986) at the Chernobyl nuclear power plant, across the border in Ukraine, had a devastating effect on Belarus; as a result of the radiation release, agriculture in a large part of the country was destroyed, and many villages were abandoned. Resettlement and medical costs were substantial and long-term

As part of the former Soviet Union, Belarus had a relatively well-developed industrial base; it retained this industrial base following the breakup of the U.S.S.R. The country also has a broad agricultural base and a high education level. Among the former republics of the Soviet Union, it had one of the highest standards of living. But Belarusians now face the difficult challenge of moving from a state-run economy with a high priority on military production and heavy industry to a civilian, free-market system.

After an initial outburst of capitalist reform from 1991-94, including privatization of state enterprises, creation of institutions of private property, and development of entrepreneurship, Belarus has greatly slowed under Lukashenka, and in many cases, reversed its pace of privatization and other market reforms while emphasizing the need for a "socially oriented market economy." About 80% of all industry remains in state hands, and foreign investment has been hindered by a climate hostile to business. The banks, which had been privatized after independence, were renationalized under Lukashenka. The government has also renationalized companies using the "Golden Share" mechanism, which allows government control in all companies with foreign investment, as well as through other administrative means.

Economic output, which declined for several years, revived in the late 1990s and early 2000s, but the economy has been dependent on heavy discounts in oil and natural gas prices from Russia. Belarus has historically re-exported the oil and oil products at world market prices, using the windfall profits to subsidize state enterprises. In December 2006, Belarus and Russian gas giant Gazprom signed a deal which will eventually end Russia's subsidies of gas for Belarus. Under the deal, Gazprom raised prices for Belarus gas deliveries in 2007 to $100 per 1,000 cubic meters, a significant rise from the subsidized previous price of $46, but still far less than the price paid by EU member states. The price for Russian gas will continue to increase incrementally until 2011, when it will equal the price paid by EU members. However, Belarusian officials stated in late 2008 and early 2009 Belarus' interest in postponing the rise to EU prices until 2014-2015. Under the 2006 agreement, Gazprom will also gradually acquire a 50% stake in Beltransgaz, the Belarusian gas pipeline firm. In January 2007, Russia followed up with a steep duty on oil deliveries, which caused a significant drop in revenue from exports of oil products and Russian-sourced crude oil. The increase in gas prices and simultaneous moves by Moscow to reduce the profitability of refining Russian oil in Belarus for re-export disrupted plans to upgrade industries ranging from oil refining to cement production.

Peat, the country's most valuable mineral resource, is used for fuel, for fertilizer, and in the chemical industry. Belarus also has deposits of clay, sand, chalk, dolomite, phosphorite, and rock and potassium salt. Forests cover about a third of the land, and lumbering is an important occupation. Potatoes, flax, hemp, sugar beets, rye, oats, and wheat are the chief agricultural products. Dairy and beef cattle, pigs, and chickens are raised. Belarus has only small reserves of petroleum and natural gas, and it imports most of its oil and gas from Russia. The main branches of industry produce tractors and trucks, earthmovers for use in construction and mining, metal-cutting machine tools, agricultural equipment, motorcycles, chemicals, fertilizer, textiles, and consumer goods. The chief trading partners are Russia, Germany, Ukraine, and Poland.

The massive April 26, 1986 nuclear accident at the Chernobyl power plant, across the border in Ukraine, had a devastating effect on Belarus. As a result of the radiation released, agriculture in a large part of the country was destroyed and many villages were abandoned. Resettlement and medical costs were substantial and long-term. Many living in Chernobyl afflicted zones have infrequent access to medical treatment due to remoteness, inadequate equipment, and substantial costs. Although the Belarusian authorities claim otherwise, many radiation monitoring stations, especially in rural areas, are either ill-equipped, poorly staffed, and/or no longer in operation. Resettlement of those in affected areas remains incomplete.

Due to the economic and political climate, little new foreign investment has occurred in recent years. In 2002, two major companies, the Swedish furniture firm Ikea and Russian beer producer Baltika, ended operations in Belarus due to unrealized government commitments or unwelcome interference. Ford Motors did the same in 1999. Economic pressures in 2007 may have led to the unexpected and non-transparent sale of a state telecommunications company to an Austrian firm.

Growth continued to be robust in 2007. Consumer price inflation averaged about 8.3% in 2007, but higher energy import prices are expected to drive up inflation for 2008 and subsequent years. Large wage increases, which were typical in the 1990s and early 2000s, fueled some increased consumption but also made Belarusian firms less competitive. Close to 20% of enterprises and a majority of collective farms currently operate at a loss, a percentage that has remained steady since 2002. Beginning in late 2008, Belarus increasingly felt the effects of the global financial crisis, as exports decreased to other severely impacted economies, notably Russia. In light of the crisis, Belarus secured a $2 billion loan from Russia in November 2008 and a $2.5 billion stand-by arrangement from the International Monetary Fund (IMF) in January 2009.

Belarus continues to be heavily dependent on Russia, with the potential for greater economic dependency in a long-proposed EU-style union between the two states. Prospects for an eventual union state remain weak, however, largely due to the apparent lack of interest on the part of the leadership of both countries. However, Russia, Belarus, and Kazakhstan have announced plans to move ahead with the formation of a customs union that they expect to be completed by 2010.

The World Bank announced a new 4-year country assistance strategy for Belarus in December 2007, which focuses on global environment and energy challenges, enhances the competitiveness of the Belarusian economy to assure rising incomes, and protects the welfare of the most vulnerable. As part of the strategy, the World Bank is financing improvements to schools, hospitals, and homes for orphans, the elderly, and the disabled throughout Belarus, with particular emphasis on improving the energy efficiency of those facilities. In 2004, Belarus rejected a World Bank loan to help fight AIDS and tuberculosis. IMF cooperation is currently limited to policy and technical consultations.

**Environmental Issues**

Belarus has established ministries of energy, forestry, land reclamation, and water resources, as well as state committees to deal with ecology and safety procedures in the nuclear power industry. The most serious environmental issue in Belarus results from the 1986 accident at the Chernobyl nuclear power plant. About 70% of the nuclear fallout from the plant landed on Belarusian territory and about 20% of the land remains contaminated. Government restrictions on residence and use of contaminated land are not strictly enforced, and the government even announced plans in 2004 to increase agricultural production in the contaminated regions. The government receives U.S. assistance in its efforts to deal with the consequences of the radiation. Belarus also faces growing air, land, and water pollution levels from potash mining in the south of the country.

## DEFENSE AND MILITARY ISSUES

The United States continues to support Belarus' adherence to arms control agreements and treaties into which it has previously entered, including the Open Skies Treaty, which Belarus ratified in 2001. Cooperation in all such agreements has been exemplary.

Humanitarian aid continues to be the primary engagement between the U.S. military and Belarus. Humanitarian assistance programs have provided a tangible, long-lasting service and have encouraged goodwill toward the U.S. Government and the U.S. military. Humanitarian assistance has two principal elements--the Humanitarian Assistance Program-Excess Property donates non-lethal goods and technical assistance for humanitarian purposes while other assistance focuses on projects such as the refurbishment of medical facilities and the construction of school buildings.

Direct military to military cooperation continues to be minimal. Belarus currently has no International Military Education and Training (IMET) program, and bilateral exercises and cooperation are nonexistent. There is a great desire on the Belarusian side to re-establish such cooperation and contacts, but it has not been possible due to the political situation. The only program that is still functional within this category is the attendance of Belarusian military officers at George C. Marshall Center programs.

Belarus is currently cooperating with the North Atlantic Treaty Organization, through the Partnership for Peace Trust Fund, to destroy a total of 700,000 conventional landmines. Belarus also has a stockpile of over 3 million non-conventional anti-personnel mines, which it pledged to destroy by March 2008. However, the bidding process for the project of destroying the mines is still ongoing. In addition, there are numerous World War II-vintage minefields, which are still in place and kill or injure several Belarusians every year.

The Ministry of Defense is experiencing success in the area of military reform. Planned changes include combining the Air and Air Defense Forces, downsizing the force structure about 30% from 83,000 to 60,000, transitioning from a conscript to a contract force, and modernizing the command and control structure by creating a Ground Forces Command between the Ministry of Defense and the units in the field. Implementation of these reforms will take an unspecified amount of time.

There have been numerous reports of Belarusian sales or delivery of weapons or weapons-related technologies to states of concern, including state sponsors of terrorism. In April and September 2004, the United States imposed sanctions on a Belarusian entity, Belvneshpromservice, pursuant to the Iran Nonproliferation Act of 2000 for the transfer to Iran of items on a multilateral export control list, or items having the potential of making a material contribution to weapons of mass destruction (WMD), or cruise or ballistic missile systems.

## FOREIGN RELATIONS

Under an arrangement with the former U.S.S.R., Belarus was an original member of the United Nations. It also is a member of the Commonwealth of Independent States (CIS - a group of 12 former Soviet republics) and its customs union, the Belarusian and Russian Union State, the Eurasian Economic Community, the Collective Security Treaty Organization (CSTO), the Organization for Security and Cooperation in Europe (OSCE), the North Atlantic Treaty Organization's (NATO) Partnership for Peace, the North Atlantic Cooperation Council, the Non-Aligned Movement, the International Organization for Migration (IOM), the International Monetary Fund, and the World Bank.

Following the recognition of Belarus as an independent state in December 1991 by the European Community, EU-Belarus relations initially experienced a steady progression. The signature of the Partnership and Cooperation Agreement (PCA) in 1995 signaled a commitment to political, economic, and trade cooperation. Significant assistance was provided to Belarus within the framework of the TACIS technical assistance program and also through various aid programs and loans. However, progress in EU-Belarus relations stalled in 1996 after serious setbacks in the development of democracy. The EU did not recognize the 1996 constitution that replaced the 1994 constitution. Neither the PCA nor its trade-related elements were implemented, and Belarus was not invited to join the EU's Neighborhood Policy. Belarusian membership in the Council of Europe was not supported, bilateral relations at the ministerial level were suspended, and EU technical assistance programs were frozen. In 1998, relations were further worsened when President Lukashenka evicted several western ambassadors from their homes in the Drozdy area of Minsk. In 2004, the Council of Europe adopted a report written by special rapporteur Christos Pourgourides calling on Belarusian authorities to suspend various high-level officials after conducting a thorough investigation of the cases of several prominent Belarusian political figures who have disappeared and remain unaccounted for.

In line with the U.S., the EU spoke strongly against the government's conduct of the 2006 election, noting that additional restrictive measures would be imposed against those officials responsible for abuses. After the election, the U.S. and EU imposed travel restrictions and financial sanctions against those responsible for abuses. The EU also launched a two-year, two million Euro project to support Belarusian access to independent information, which complements U.S. assistance programs. In June 2007, the EU announced the withdrawal of GSP trade preferences for Belarus, following an assessment by the International Labor Organization that Belarus had not acted to ensure the protection of labor rights and freedom of association. After the September 2008 parliamentary elections, the EU issued a statement expressing its concern about the conduct of the elections, which despite some progress did not correspond to the OSCE's democratic standards. In October 2008, the EU suspended its visa sanctions for six months on numerous Belarusian officials, including President Lukashenka, in response to Belarus' release of political prisoners in August; this suspension has been extended until December 2009. In May 2009, the EU invited Belarus to take part in the Eastern Partnership Initiative.

Acknowledging the lack of progress in relation to bilateral relations and the internal situation following the position adopted in 1997, the EU adopted a benchmark approach in 1999, whereby relations would be gradually improved upon fulfillment of the four benchmarks set by the OSCE. In 2000, some moderately positive developments toward the implementation of recommendations made by the OSCE Advisory and Monitoring Group (AMG) were observed, but were not sufficient in the realm of access to fair and free elections. The Belarusian authorities, objecting to the OSCE AMG's activities, forced it to shutdown by failing to renew visas or extend accreditation of its professional staff. The Belarusian authorities agreed to a successor OSCE presence after 14 EU member countries and the U.S. imposed visa restrictions on the travel of high-ranking Belarusian officials. The OSCE Office in Minsk formally came into existence on January 1, 2003 with a mandate to "assist the Belarusian authorities in further promoting institution-building, in further consolidating the Rule of Law and in developing relations with civil society, in accordance with OSCE principles and commitments."

Russia is the largest partner for Belarus in the economic and political fields. In terms of trade, over one-third of Belarusian exports go to Russia. Due to the structure of Belarusian industry, Belarus relies heavily on other CIS countries, and Russia in particular, both for export markets and for the supply of raw materials, subsidized energy, and components. The steep increase in the price of natural gas in 2007, as well as higher tariffs on Russian-sourced oil and oil products, has contributed to a crisis in the Belarusian economy, forcing the regime to cut popular subsidies and to borrow from outside sources to finance the budget. Belarus received a $1.5 billion stabilization loan in late 2007 and a $2 billion loan in late 2008 from Russia.

The framework for the Russia-Belarusian Union was set out in the Treaty on the Formation of a Community of Russia and Belarus (1996), the Treaty on Russia-Belarus Union, the Union Charter (1997), and the Treaty of the Formation of a Union State (1999). The integration treaties contain commitments to monetary union, equal rights, single citizenship, and a common foreign and defense policy. They also have established a range of institutions modeled after the EU. After protracted disputes and setbacks, the two countries' customs duties were unified as of March 2001. Belarus has made progress in monetary stabilization in the context of ongoing negotiation with the Russian Central Bank on monetary union. However, Belarus has repeatedly pushed back the date for implementing a monetary union. A dispute with Russia in late 2006 and early 2007 over gas prices and oil import duties raised further doubts about the future of the union, and many of the provisions of the union have yet to be implemented. Most recently, talks in October 2008 focused on plans to move forward with unification of customs rates for the Union State, supposedly to be completed by the end of the year, and the use of the Russian ruble for mutual payments. South Ossetia and Abkhazia have both expressed interest in joining the Union State, and in order for them to do so, their application must first be approved by the Union Parliament, and then the presidents of Belarus and Russia must approve the Parliament's resolution to accept Abkhazia and South Ossetia.

## U.S.-BELARUSIAN RELATIONS

The United States recognized Belarusian independence on December 25, 1991. After the two countries established diplomatic relations, the U.S. Embassy in Minsk was officially opened on January 31, 1992. Ambassador David H. Swartz, the first Ambassador to Belarus, officially assumed post on August 25, 1992, the first anniversary of Belarusian independence, and departed post on completion of his term in late January

1994. On November 7, 1994, Ambassador Kenneth S. Yalowitz assumed post. He was succeeded by Ambassador Daniel V. Speckhard, who served from August 1997 to August 2000, spending one year recalled to Washington because of a dispute between the government and Western embassies over the confiscation of diplomatic residences. Michael G. Kozak served as U.S. Ambassador from October 2000 to August 2003. George A. Krol served as U.S. Ambassador from September 2003 to July 2006. Karen B. Stewart replaced Ambassador Krol as U.S. Ambassador and arrived in Belarus on September 18, 2006. She was recalled on March 12, 2008 following a threat of expulsion by the Belarusian authorities and the recall of Belarus' Ambassador to the U.S. Belarus subsequently voluntarily reduced the staff at its U.S. missions, excluding the mission to the UN, to five persons and demanded the U.S. reciprocate by reducing the U.S. Embassy in Minsk to five diplomats. When the U.S. refused to comply, the Belarusian authorities expelled several U.S. diplomats to reduce U.S. Embassy staffing to five diplomats. The U.S. has imposed no restrictions on Belarus' diplomatic missions to the U.S.

The two countries exchanged top-level official visits in the early years of independence. Stanislau Shushkevich, the Chairman of the Supreme Soviet of the Republic of Belarus, met with President Clinton in Washington in July 1992, and President Clinton visited Belarus in January 1994. After this high point, bilateral relations cooled following the election of President Alyaksander Lukashenka in July 1994.

In September 1995 three hot air balloons participating in the Coupe Gordon Bennett race entered Belarusian air space. Race organizers had informed the Belarusian authorities about the race in May, and flight plans had been filed, nevertheless, the Belarusian air force shot down one balloon, killing two American citizens, and forced the other two to land. The crews of the other two balloons were fined for entering Belarus without a visa and released. Belarus to date has not apologized or offered compensation for these killings.

In November 1996, the Lukashenka regime conducted an internationally unrecognized constitutional referendum, which resulted in the dissolution of Belarus' legitimate parliament and the centralization of power in the executive branch. In that same year, the Belarusian authorities provoked a diplomatic crisis by demanding and, in contravention of international law, eventually confiscating diplomatic residences in the Drozdy housing compound, including the U.S. Ambassador's residence. This action led the United States and other countries to withdraw their ambassadors from Belarus until the Belarusian authorities provided compensation and guarantees of respect for international law. In addition, Lukashenka used his newly centralized power to repress human rights throughout the country, including persecuting members of the illegally disbanded Belarusian Parliament (13th Supreme Soviet) and former members of his own government.

As a result of these events and tendencies, the United States announced in 1997 its decision to pursue a "selective engagement" policy with the Belarusian authorities. This policy included downgrading government-to-government contacts to the level of Assistant Secretary and below, as well as restricting U.S. Government assistance to the Belarusian authorities, with some exceptions including humanitarian assistance and exchange programs with state-run educational institutions. At the same time, the U.S. greatly expanded contacts with Belarusian civil society to promote democratization in Belarus.

Since 1997, despite growing U.S. engagement with Belarusian society, official bilateral relations have remained at a low level. In 2003, the United States, in tandem with the European Union, proposed a step-by-step, gradual approach to improve bilateral relations: the United States would respond positively to genuine efforts by Belarusian authorities to improve Belarus' human rights and electoral practices. Belarusian authorities failed to take the steps that warranted a positive response.

In October 2004, the U.S. Congress passed, and President George W. Bush signed, the Belarus Democracy Act, which was designed to promote democratization. In signing the act, President Bush noted that the authorities were turning Belarus into "a regime of repression in the heart of Europe," and set out the U.S. policy of working "with our allies and partners to assist those seeking to return Belarus to its rightful place among the Euro-Atlantic community of democracies." After a deeply flawed presidential election in March 2006, the U.S., acting with the EU, imposed travel restrictions and targeted financial sanctions against Belarusian officials implicated in human rights abuses and election fraud. The financial sanctions prohibited U.S. persons from engaging in financial transactions with named persons. On January 12, 2007, President Bush signed the Belarus Democracy Reauthorization Act, which repeated the call for targeted sanctions against Belarusian officials and continued assistance for democracy building activities. In August 2007, the U.S. widened application of travel restrictions on Belarusians to include directors and deputy directors of state enterprises. In November 2007, the Treasury Department froze the U.S. assets of Belarus' oil and chemical conglomerate, Belneftekhim, because of Alyaksander Lukashenka's control of the company. After the Belarusian authorities released the last of its political prisoners in August 2008, the U.S. suspended sanctions for 6 months on two Belneftekhim subsidiaries, Lakokraska and Polotsk Steklovolokno; the suspensions were renewed for 3 months in March 2009 and 6 months in June 2009. To underscore U.S. support for the Belarusian people's democratic aspirations, President Bush and Secretary of State Rice frequently met with Belarusian pro-democracy activists, including during a December 2007 visit to Washington, DC by leaders of Belarusian pro-democracy political parties and NGOs.

**U.S.-Belarusian Economic Relations**

The U.S. Government continues to support the development of the private sector in Belarus and its transition to a free market economy. Under the Lukashenka regime, Belarusian authorities have pursued a generally hostile policy toward the private sector and have refused to initiate the basic economic reforms necessary to create a market-based economy. Most of the Belarusian economy remains in government hands. The government, in particular the presidential administration, exercises control over most enterprises in all sectors of the economy. In addition to driving away major foreign investors, largely through establishment of a "Golden Share" requirement which allows government control in all companies with foreign investment, Belarus' centralization and command approach to the economy has left only a trickle of U.S. Government and international assistance programs in this field.

In February 1993, a bilateral trade treaty guaranteeing reciprocal most-favored-nation status entered into force. In January 1994, the U.S. and Belarus signed a bilateral investment treaty, which has been ratified by Belarus but has not been ratified by the U.S. Senate. In addition, due to continuing repression of labor rights in Belarus, the U.S. removed Belarus from the Generalized System of Preferences (GSP) in 2000.

The United States has encouraged Belarus to conclude and adhere to agreements with the International Monetary Fund (IMF) on macroeconomic stabilization and related reform measures, as well as to undertake increased privatization and to create a favorable climate for business and investment. Although there has been some American direct private investment in Belarus, its development has been relatively slow. An Overseas Private Investment Corporation agreement was signed in June 1992 but has been suspended since 1995 because Belarus did not fulfill its obligations under the agreement. Belarus is eligible for Export-Import Bank short-term financing insurance for U.S. investments, but because of the adverse business climate, no projects have been initiated. The IMF granted Belarus standby credit in September 1995, but it fell off the program and did not receive the second tranche of funding, which had been scheduled for regular intervals throughout 1996. Since that time, Belarus has had an ongoing discussion to relaunch IMF-backed reforms, including an IMF Staff-Monitored Program (SMP) in 2001, which ended in September of that year with relatively disappointing results. In early 2004, Belarus halted negotiations on a follow-on stand-by arrangement due to disagreements with the IMF on macroeconomic policy and the claim that it did not require IMF funding.

Because of the unpredictable, and at times hostile, environment for investors, the U.S. Government currently does not encourage U.S. companies to invest in Belarus. Belarus' continuing problems with an opaque, arbitrary legal system, a confiscatory tax regime, cumbersome licensing system, price controls, and lack of an independent judiciary create a business environment not conducive to prosperous, profitable investment. In fact, several U.S. investors have left Belarus, including the Ford Motor Company.

**U.S. Assistance to Belarus**

U.S. Government assistance programs in Belarus support and encourage civil society development, access to independent information, pro-democracy forces, and the emergence of democracy in a very difficult and challenging environment. Most assistance is in the form of training and exchanges, as well as small grants and capacity-building for local non-governmental organizations. The U.S. also supports external radio and television broadcasting into Belarus, and external websites. Because the Belarusian authorities have not embraced market reforms, the U.S. is able to program only modest activities in support of private entrepreneurs. The U.S. provides some health program funding and supports international organizations' efforts in Belarus to combat the growing problem of trafficking in persons. With very limited exceptions, including humanitarian assistance and exchange programs involving state-run educational institutions, bilateral assistance is not channeled through the Government of Belarus.

For FY 2008, the U.S. provided $11 million to Belarus. Assistance is provided to Belarus under the Freedom for Russia and Emerging Eurasian Democracies and Open Markets

(FREEDOM) Support Act (FSA) enacted in October 1992. U.S. Government assistance to Belarus peaked in 1994 at a level of approximately $76 million (consisting of more than $16 million in FREEDOM Support Act funds and some $60 million in funds from various U.S. Government agencies). However, U.S. assistance levels dropped sharply due to the lack of progress in democratic and economic reforms after Alyaksander Lukashenka came to power in mid-1994.

Belarus was previously a recipient of assistance under the U.S. Defense Department's Cooperative Threat Reduction (CTR) Program, whose objective is to reduce the threat posed to the United States by weapons of mass destruction remaining on the territory of the former Soviet Union by promoting denuclearization and demilitarization and preventing weapons proliferation. However, in February 1997, due to the Belarusian authorities' poor record on human rights, President Clinton de-certified Belarus, thus rendering the country ineligible for further CTR assistance and placing restrictions on other security-related assistance as well. The United States and Belarus signed a government-to-government umbrella agreement on CTR assistance in 1992, seven agency-to-agency CTR implementing agreements, and one memorandum of understanding and cooperation. The umbrella agreement was extended for one year in October 1997 but has now expired.

For more detailed information on U.S. Government assistance to Belarus, please see the annual reports to Congress on U.S. Government Assistance to and Cooperative Activities with Eurasia, which are available in the Bureau of European and Eurasian Affairs section on the State Department's website. A fact sheet on Foreign Operations Appropriated Assistance to Belarus for FY 2007 can be found at http://www.state.gov/p/eur/rls/fs/107776.htm. Information is also available on the U.S. Agency for International Development's (USAID) website at the address: http://www.usaid.gov.

**Principal U.S. Embassy Officials**

**chief of mission:** Ambassador (vacant; left in 2008 upon insistence of Belarusian Government); Charge d'Affaires Robert RILEY (since 22 August 2016)

U.S. Embassy in Budapest, Hungary from 2013-2015, and Political-Economic Counselor there from 2012-2013.

Management Officer--Robert Miller
Consul--Robert Reeves
Regional Security Officer--Christine Putz
Information Management Officer—Eric Rose

The U.S. Embassy in Minsk, Belarus is located at Starovilenskaya 46; tel: (375-17) 210-12-83; fax: (375-17) 234-78-53.

# BELARUS LEGAL SYSTEM BASICS

## LEGAL SYSTEM OF THE REPUBLIC OF BELARUS

Legal system of any state reflects objective laws of development of society, its historical, national and cultural peculiarities. The Republic of Belarus like any other state has its own legal system, which has both common features with legal systems of other countries and its special characteristics.

Analysis of origination and development of the legal system of the Republic of Belarus proofs the fact that the content and the dynamics of this system are being affected not only by politics and political culture but also by the entire cultural wealth of society: religion, philosophy, morals, artistic culture, science. It goes without saying that evolution of the legal system of Belarus has tight connection with economical factor - development of productive forces and labour-management relations, with coming into being market economy. **Continuity** of development of legal systems stipulates formation of the legal system of our country as well: traditional legal values interact with new legal values taken over by the legal system of Belarus from the other legal systems. As the result of such the interaction our legal system should progress.

It's generally known that all legal systems can be categorized into the groups ("law families") depending on some common features. The legal system of the Republic of Belarus as well as legal systems of other states of continental Europe belongs to the **Roman-Germanic Law Family**. Roman Law (jurisprudence of Ancient Rome) is the primary source of this law family. The main characteristics of the Roman-Germanic Law Family are: optimal generalization of a rule of law, dividing of law into public law and private one, separating of different branches of law. A **normative legal act** is the main legal source in the countries with legal systems based on Roman-Germanic Law Family unlike those countries with legal systems based on Common Law Family.

Although the first steps of state system formation in the Belarus were made only at the beginning of the 20$^{th}$ century, the legal system of our country has profound historical roots. The sources of Belorussian Feudal Law rank high among the other world famous ancient legal sources (such as the Code of Hammurabi, the Law of the Twelve Tables, the Justinian Code, the Napoleonic Code). The aforesaid statement regards at the first turn to the famous **Statutes of the Grand Duchy Litovskae of 1529, 1566 and 1588 years**. The Statutes of the Grand Duchy Lithuanian of 1588 used to be the Law in force and the entire legal system of Belarus and Lithuania used to base on this Status within 250 years. The **Polish Constitution of 1791** also should be mentioned here as the remarkable legal document signified in the history of development of the legal system of Belarus. This Constitution along with American and French Constitutions can be described as the most progressive document of 18$^{th}$ century.

The legal system of the Republic of Belarus was influenced essentially by those states which influenced our country in particular historical period (Poland - during the 17$^{th}$-18$^{th}$ centuries, Russia - during the 19$^{th}$-20$^{th}$ centuries). During the most part of the 20$^{th}$ century Belarus used to be a part of the Union of Soviet Socialistic Republics (USSR) and this fact surely affected the legal system of today's Belarus (its legal culture, formation of the branches of law, etc.) After the break-up of the USSR, the legal system of the Republic of Belarus segregated from so-called Socialistic Law Family.

The structure of the legal system of the Republic of Belarus contains three groups of legal elements ("legal phenomena"). **Rules of law, legal principles and legal institutes** (normative aspect) form the first group. The second group contains totality of **legal institutions** (organizational aspect). And the third one is formed with totality of **legal views, opinions, and conceptions** being peculiar for Belorussian society, **standard of legal development**.

***The first group of elements*** of the structure of the legal system of Belarus can be described as the system of law of Belarus. The system of law of Belarus is historically formed and objectively existing outer structure of law. Such the structure is defined by the character of social relations regulated and appears in the unity and coherence of interrelated rules of law and their dividing into branches of law (sub-branches of law) and legal institutes.

A branch of law is the basic structural division of the system of law of Belarus. Our republic as well as the other countries of the former USSR inherited that structure of system of law, which had been formed during the soviet era.

The system of law of the Republic of Belarus currently consists of the following branches: constitutional law, civil law, administrative law, criminal law, labour law, family law, land law, financial law, law of criminal procedure, law of civil procedure, law of execution of criminal punishment, etc.

Rules of law, being a content of legal institutes and branches of law, are created while lawmaking activity of competent state bodies of the Republic of Belarus, and thus the rules of law assume some exterior forms. Such the exterior forms are first of all **legal acts** of the Republic of Belarus - fundamental sources of law in the Republic of Belarus. All the legal acts of the Republic of Belarus are divided into two big groups: **legislative acts** and **secondary legislation**. **The Constitution of the Republic of Belarus** is the Fundamental Law of the Republic of Belarus, having supreme legal force. Legislative acts also cover **laws** enacted by the Parliament and **ordinances** of the President which may have the force of laws in accordance with the Constitution. **Decrees of the President**, **Decisions of the Government** as well as legal **acts of ministries and other governmental departments** and **acts of Local Councils of Deputies and Local Executive Committees** are the most important acts of secondary legislation.

Totality of legal institutions constitutes ***the second group of elements*** of the structure of the legal system of Belarus. These are first of all state bodies empowered by the Constitution and by other laws with lawmaking function - **the National Assembly (Parliament), the President, the Council of Ministers (Government), ministries, state committees, Local Councils of Deputies and Local Executive Committees of the Republic of Belarus.** Legal institutions also cover law-enforcement bodies (judicial bodies, prosecution bodies, bodies of internal affairs), public law-protection organizations (Belorussian Community of Consumers, Confederacy of Lowers of Belarus) etc.

***The third group of elements*** composing the structure of the legal system of the Republic of Belarus covers **sense of justice** (as one of forms of public consciousness) and **standard of legal development**. Sense of justice is a system of legal theories, views, ideas, conceptions, notions, estimations, dispositions, and feelings expressing attitude of individual persons, social groups, entire Belorussian society towards existing legislation and desirable one, different legal phenomena, behaviour of people and activities of the state in the field of law. **Standard of legal development** characterizes levels of individual and public sense of justice and reflects a degree of functioning of the whole legal system in Belarus.

In 1990[th] the legal system of the Republic of Belarus achieved an absolutely new phase of its development. Obtaining independence and status of an equal member of the world community by our country, adopting the Constitution which declares an individual, his (her) rights, freedoms and guarantees for their attainment as the supreme goal and value of society and the state, appearing of new possibilities of development of Belorussian economy in accordance with market canons - all these factors allows expecting step-by-step development of the legal system of the Republic of Belarus according to standards of law-abiding state and civic society.

However, process of formation of the legal system of any democratic state requires essential period of time. Great number of economic, political, historical factors hampers to evolve this process. For Belarus these are a long-time domination of anti-democratic regime at its territory, originality of the character of Belorussian society, breach of former economic relations having been formed while soviet period.

Therefor each of the elements composing the structure of the legal system of the Republic of Belarus has essential deficiencies.

First of all theses are low standard of legal development of Belorussian society, legal nihilism of people, their lack of faith in the law and lack of desire to obey the law (non-high level of **sense of justice** of Belorussian society).

Imperfection of the system of **legal institutions** is being revealed, for instance, in the following. Tough the Constitution of the Republic of Belarus determines the principle of separation of legislative, executive and judicial powers, de facto there can be noted some merging of these branches (for instance, legislative and executive) i. e. democratic principle of checks and balances doesn't work in proper way regarding the legal system of the Republic of Belarus yet.

And, finally, the system of law of the Republic of Belarus as totality of **branches of law, legal institutes and rules of law** is far from being perfect: there are imperfection of different rules of law including constitutional ones, lack of clear hierarchy of legal acts and contradiction of legal acts.

There is a verity of legal systems at the contemporary world. At the same time a tendency can be clearly observed, which evidences of closing-in processes between different countries, unifying of their legislation, conforming in practical application of law in different spheres especially in regulation of market economy, protection of environment and others. Such the tendency in the Republic of Belarus is revealing itself in constitutional proclamation of supremacy of the universally acknowledged principles of international law as well as in permanent activity of our country on concluding different international treaties and participating in various international organizations (United Nations, Commonwealth of the Independent States).

Presently the legal system of the Republic of Belarus is closely interacting with the legal system of Russia. Pursuant to Article 2 of the Treaty between Belarus and Russian Federation "On Creation of the Union State" dated 8 December 1999, development of the unified democratic legal system is foreseen as one of the objectives of the Union State being created. Time will show real extent of vitality of this legal system.

## BUSINESS LAWS

- On the Entrepreneurship in the Republic of Belarus - Law of the Republic of Belarus of May 28, 1991

- On Foreign Investments on the Territory of the Republic of Belarus - Law of the Republic of Belarus of November 14, 1991
- On Commodity Exchanges - Law of the Republic of Belarus of March 13, 1992
- On Counteraction of Monopolistic Activities and Promotion of Competition - Law of the Republic of Belarus of December 10, 1992
- On Veterinary - Law of the Republic of Belarus of December 2, 1994
- On Standardization - Law of the Republic of Belarus of September 5, 1995
- On Ensuring the Uniformity of Measurements - Law of the Republic of Belarus of September 5, 1995
- On Certification of Products, Works and Services - Law of the Republic of Belarus of September 5, 1995
- On Advertising - Law of the Republic of Belarus of February 18, 1997
- On State Regulation of Alcoholic Products Output and Turnover - Law of the Republic of Belarus of July 20, 1998
- On Financial and Industrial Groups - Law of the Republic of Belarus of June 4, 1999
- On Tourism - Law of the Republic of Belarus of November 25, 1999

- On the Creation and Activities of the Economic Groups in the Republic - Decree of the President of the Republic of Belarus [1] 482 of November 27, 1995
- On State Support of the Development and Export of the Information Technologies - Decree of the President of the Republic of Belarus [1] 234 of May 3, 2001

- On Legal Treatment of Foreign Investments From Member-States of the Commonwealth of Independent States - Ordinance of the President of the Republic of Belarus [1] 13 of August 5, 1998
- On the Regulation of State Registration and Liquidation (Termination of Activities) of Economic Entities - Ordinance of the President of the Republic of Belarus [1] 11 of March 16, 1999

- On Peculiarities of Establishment of Foreign Enterprises on the Territory of the Republic of Belarus - Decision of the Government of the Republic of Belarus [1] 97 of February 24, 1992
- On the Procedure of Referring the Products (Works, Services) of Foreign Companies and Joint Ventures Existing on the Territory of the Republic of Belarus to the Own Made Production - Decision of the Government of the Republic of Belarus [1] 421 of July 10, 1992
- On Approval of the List of Products of Particular Importance the Council of Ministers of the Republic of Belarus is Entitled to Reduse the Profit Tax Rate by 50 Percent for Any Enterprise with Foreign Investments Manufacturing them for a Period of Three Year - Decision of the Government of the Republic of Belarus [1] 345 of May 26, 1993
- On the List of Lines of Activities Subject to Special Permit (License) and Bodies to Issue Such Permits (Licences) - Decision of the Government of the Republic of Belarus [1] 456 of August 21, 1995
- On Introduction of Mandatory Certification of All Types of Alcoholic and Tobacco Goods in the Republic of Belarus - Decision of the Government of the Republic of Belarus [1] 260 of April 16, 1996
- On the Procedure of Opening and Operation of Representations of Foreign Companies and Organizations in the Republic of Belarus - Decision of the Government of the Republic of Belarus [1] 929 of July 22, 1997

# IMMIGRATION SYSTEM AND POLICY - STRATEGIC INFORMATION AND DEVELOPMENTS

## BASIC INFORMATION ON IMMIGRATION TO BELARUS[1]

Every year Belarus becomes more and more attractive country for foreign businessmen. Development of foreign economic relations led to that for the last years the most frequent reason of immigration to Belarus is business opening here, or investments in already existing.

Ordinary foreign citizens as well as businessmen, too with pleasure move to our country. After all in Belarus not only fine ecology and the beautiful nature, but also a worthy standard of living which constantly raises. Besides, all new workplaces not only for citizens of our country, but also for foreigners are annually created.

However it is necessary to take into consideration that in Belarus rather strict laws which concern questions of immigration of foreign citizens. Strong reasons, such as are for this purpose necessary:

- Investments into economy of Republic of Belarus of not less than 150 000 euros;
- The foreign citizen is the ethnic Belarusian;
- Official marriage with the citizen of Republic of Belarus;
- Official employment as the expert whom our country;
- The other bases provided by the Legislation.

So needs, one of ways to immigrate to Belarus on the lawful bases is to have the Belarusian nationality. In this case the foreigner who wants to receive residence permit, should be born in the territory of Republic of Belarus till 1991 (then still the Belarusian Soviet Socialist Republic) and to provide the birth certificate.

One more simple and most widespread way of immigration is the family option. So, if the foreign citizen has the relatives constantly living in the territory of Republic of Belarus and being citizens of Belarus, it has the right to apply for receiving residence permit in our country. Marriage with the citizen of ours coentry also is a strong reason to immigrate in Belarus.

If the foreigner is an expert (the athlete, the scientist) which our country needs, it too can obtain without problems permit to continuous accommodation (especially experts in the agricultural sphere).

Immigration to Belarus on the basis of investments. In recent years this way of immigration becomes more and more popular. Any investments in economy of Republic of Belarus at the rate from 150 000 thousand euros, give a guarantee to the investor on receiving residence permit in Republic of Belarus.

[1] Belarus Governmetn Materials

By number of immigrants Belarus takes leading positions among CIS countries. And it isn't surprising, after all despite the strict legislation, our country is that where it is possible to provide bright future to itself and the children.

### PRINCIPAL LAWS ON IMMIGRATION

2010 Law On the Legal Status of Foreign Nationals and Stateless Persons

2010 Law On External Labour Migration

2010 Law On the Legal Status of Foreign Nationals and Stateless Persons

2009 Law On the Procedure of Entry and Exit for the Citizens of the Republic of Belarus

2008 Law On Refugee Status, Subsidiary and Temporary Protection to Foreign Nationals and Stateless Persons

2006 Law On the Legal Status of Foreign Nationals and Stateless Persons in the Republic of Belarus

2002 Law On Citizenship of the Republic of Belarus

1994 Constitution

## CHANGES TO IMMIGRATION LAW

On 15th July a new immigration law will affect the hiring of foreign nationals in Belarus. The laws have been bought in to reduce high levels of local unemployment and will affect Work Permits (Special Work Permits).

Currently foreign employees in Belarus should obtain a Special Work Permit; all companies that employ more than 10 foreign workers must obtain a separate permit in order to hire foreign employees. The changes set out stricter criteria and procedures, this also includes the definition of "highly qualified employees", all other amendments to the immigration laws are detailed below:

- If you started up the company or are the company"s director, you will not be counted in the 10 foreign workers calculation; you will also be exempt from obtaining labour-market testing approval by the employment office. Students at Belarus universities are also exempt from work permits during their studies and up to a year after their graduation if they gain employment in the field of their degree.
- To be considered as a "highly qualified employee" you must earn 15 times the national average; have a university degree and at least five years" professional experience.
- Special Work Permits which are initially valid for one year can now be renewed for an additional year for one time only, after this the foreign worker must apply for a new Special Work Permit. These limits are also applied to an employer"s permit to include foreign workers.
- All foreign nationals who are not permanent residents and who register employment contracts must ensure they register for a Special Work Permit within one month of their completion. All cancelled, unsigned or expired permits must be returned within five working days. It has also been announced that foreign employees must now contribute to

the Belarus social insurance system, and also if you are working for several employers you must obtain a permit for each of these.

- The cancellation of Special Work Permits may occur on new grounds which includes five plus administration violations in one year or in the situation where the employer fails to comply with the rules on external labour migration.

# BASIC LAWS AND REGULATIONS AGGECTING IMMIGRATION AND MIGRATION

## LAW ON IMMIGRATION

This Law provides a legal framework for immigration in the Republic of Belarus, establishes the procedure for foreign nationals and stateless persons (hereinafter aliens) to obtain permission to reside permanently in the Republic of Belarus, sets rules for the departure of illegal migrants from the Republic of Belarus, and regulates other legal relations that arise in connection with immigration.

### CHAPTER 1. GENERAL PROVISIONS

**Article 1. Legislation of the Republic of Belarus on Immigration**

Immigration in the Republic of Belarus is regulated by the Consitution of the Republic of Belarus, this Law, the Law of the Republic of Belarus "On the Legal Status of Foreign Nationals and Stateless Persons in the Republic of Belarus", by other acts of legislation of the Republic of Belarus, and by international agreements of the Republic of Belarus.

**Article 2. International Agreements**

If rules other than the ones prescribed by this Law, are established by an international agreement of the Republic of Belarus that has been ratified and has come into force, then the rules of the international agreement shall apply.

**Article 3. Basic Concepts Used in the Present Law**

The following basic concepts are used for the purposes of the present Law:

"residence permit": a document identifying the personality of an alien who, in accordance with the legislation of the Republic of Belarus, has been granted permission to reside permanently in the Republic of Belarus;

"reunification of the family": entry into the Republic of Belarus for permanent residence beyond the established immigration quota, of a spouse, minor children, or other children who have not been married, at the invitation, respectively, of the spouse, parents who are citizens of the Republic of Belarus or immigrants;

"deportation": forcible removal of an alien from the Republic of Belarus in accordance with the legislation of the Republic of Belarus;

"immigrant": an alien who resides permanently in the Republic of Belarus;

"immigration visa": leave to enter the Republic of Belarus for permanent residence;

"immigration quota": an annual limit for the admission of immigrants to the Republic of Belarus;

"immigration control": implementation by designated government authorities of a complex of measures aimed at enforcing the immigration legislation of the Republic of Belarus;

"immigration": entry of an alien into the Republic of Belarus for permanent residence;

"foreign national": a person who is not a citizen of the Republic of Belarus and who has proofs of his citizenship of another state;

"stateless person": a person who is not a citizen of the Republic of Belarus and who has no proofs of his citizenship of another state;

"illegal immigration": entry into and/or presence of aliens in the territory of the Republic of Belarus in violation of the legislation of the Republic of Belarus that regulates the procedure for entry into the Republic of Belarus and presence in its territory;

"invitation (call)": a document on the basis of which an alien is issued an immigration visa and which contains undertakings by the inviting party to provide financial support and housing to the alien invited thereby;

"travel document": a document confirming the right of certain categories of aliens permanently residing in the Republic of Belarus, to leave the Republic of Belarus and to enter the Republic of Belarus.

**Article 4. Refugees**

The legal framework for entry into and presence in the Republic of Belarus of aliens who have applied for refugee status, and of refugees shall be defined by the legislation of the Republic of Belarus on refugees.

## CHAPTER 2. TERMS OF REFERENCE OF GOVERNMENT AUTHORITIES IN CONTROLLING IMMIGRATION PROCESSES

**Article 5. The Republican Government Authority for Migration**

The republican government authority for migration shall:

develop proposals concerning the principal areas of the national migration policy and, within its terms of reference, co-ordinate the activities of other government authorities aimed at its implementation;

develop proposals concerning the establishment of immigration quotas, with due regard for the socio-economic possibilities of the republic;

provide for collection, storage, processing and dissemination of information on migration processes throughout the world, and carry out exchange of this information.

**Article 6. The Ministry of Foreign Affairs of the Republic of Belarus**

The Ministry of Foreign Affairs of the Republic of Belarus, diplomatic missions and consular institutions of the Republic of Belarus shall:

identify aliens as belonging to the category of persons who are entitled to an immigration visa;

carry out, within their terms of reference, execution and checking of documents relating to aliens who wish to immigrate in the Republic of Belarus;

issue and register immigration visas in accordance with the established procedure.

**Article 7. The Border Troops of the Republic of Belarus**

The border troops of the Republic of Belarus shall:

perform immigration control by carrying out initial examination of persons entering the Republic of Belarus;

together with other agencies concerned, participate, within their terms of reference, in activities aimed at combating illegal immigration.

**Article 8. The Authorities of the Interior of the Republic of Belarus**

The authorities of the interior of the Republic of Belarus shall:

consider aliens' applications for permission to reside permanently in the Republic of Belarus;

take decisions on the alien's obtaining of permission to reside permanently in the Republic of Belarus, and issue immigrants with the appropriate documents certifying their right to reside permanently in the Republic of Belarus;

detain aliens who stay illegally in the Republic of Belarus;

find out, detain and deport aliens mentioned in Article 28 of this Law;

perform immigration control inside the territory of the Republic of Belarus by checking the legality of the aliens' presence in the Republic of Belarus;

participate, within their terms of reference, together with other agencies concerned, in activities aimed at combating illegal immigration.

### Article 9. The Authorities of State Security of the Republic of Belarus

The authorities of state security of the Republic of Belarus shall:

within their terms of reference, check the persons who wish to immigrate in the Republic of Belarus;

find out persons involved in international terrorist organisations, and take measures to prevent them from entering the Republic of Belarus;

participate, within their terms of reference, together with other agencies concerned, in activities aimed at combating illegal immigration.

### Article 10. Republican Government Authorities, Local Executive and Managing Authorities

Republican government authorities, local executive and managing authorities:

shall perform their functions in matters relating to immigration policy, interacting with the republican government authority for migration, in accordance with the legislation of the Republic of Belarus and taking into account the international practice of regulating migration processes, and

co-operate with international organisations.

## CHAPTER 3. OBTAINING PERMISSION TO RESIDE PERMANENTLY IN THE REPUBLIC OF BELARUS

### Article 11. Determining an Immigration Quota

To secure government regulation of the process of immigration in the Republic of Belarus, the Council of Ministers of the Republic of Belarus, at the representation of the republican government authority for migration, may determine an immigration quota. The immigration quota shall be determined separately for each state.

The President of the Republic of Belarus shall have the right to decide on admitting more immigrants to the Republic of Belarus above the set immigration quota.

**Article 12. The Procedure for Obtaining Permission to Reside Permanently in the Republic of Belarus**

An alien who resides outside of the Republic of Belarus and who wishes to obtain permission to reside permanently in the Republic of Belarus, shall file documents as mentioned in part four of this article, with a diplomatic mission or a consular institution of the Republic of Belarus.

The diplomatic mission or consular institution of the Republic of Belarus shall accept the application and documents presented by the alien applying for permission to reside permanently in the Republic of Belarus, and refer them, in accordance with the established order, to an appropriate authority of the interior of the Republic of Belarus.

An alien who resides temporarily in the Republic of Belarus and wishes to obtain permission to reside in the Republic of Belarus permanently, shall file documents as mentioned in part four of this article, with the authority of the interior of the Republic of Belarus at the place of his intended residence.

To obtain permission to reside permanently in the Republic of Belarus, an alien shall present:

> an application containing detailed information on the activity he intends to engage in in the Republic of Belarus, availability of funds to enter and live in the Republic of Belarus before he finds an employment, and the possibility of remitting these funds to the Republic of Belarus;
>
> a valid passport issued by the state of his nationality or by the state of his permanent residence, or other documents that are accepted in accordance with the legislation of the Republic of Belarus as the ones that identify the personality of the applicant;
>
> a health certificate;
>
> other documents, the list of which is to be determined by the Council of Ministers of the Republic of Belarus.

An application for permission to reside permanently in the Republic of Belarus shall only be accepted after a state duty or consular fee has been paid, the procedure for payment and the size of which are to be established by the Council of Ministers of the Republic of Belarus.

A decision concerning the application for permission to reside permanently in the Republic of Belarus shall be taken by an appropriate authority of the interior of the Republic of Belarus within three months of receipt of the application along with all the necessary materials.

**Article 13. The Right to Obtain Permission to Reside Permanently in the Republic of Belarus Granted to Certain Categories of Aliens**

The right to obtain permission to reside permanently in the Republic of Belarus shall be granted to aliens who have lived in the Republic of Belarus for at least seven years, provided they are:

members of the staff of diplomatic, consular, trade and other missions and institutions of foreign states, or members of their families;

entrepreneurs or members of their families;

members of the staff of international organisations or members of their families;

employees of mass media accredited in the Republic of Belarus, or members of their families.

The right to obtain permission to reside permanently in the Republic of Belarus regardless of the residence in the Republic of Belarus shall be granted to such aliens as:

are highly skilled workers needed by the Republic of Belarus;

possess exceptional abilities or talent;

guarantee an investment of at least 150 thousand US dollars in the economy of the Republic of Belarus, or the implementation of concrete government programmes of the Republic of Belarus;

have been in the service of the Republic of Belarus outside its territory for at least ten years.

A decision concerning the obtaining by the aliens listed in this article of permission to reside permanently in the Republic of Belarus shall be taken by the Ministry of the Interior of the Republic of Belarus at the representation of relevant government authorities, with due regard for immigration quotas.

**Article 14. Grounds for Denying Permission to Reside Permanently in the Republic of Belarus**

An alien may be denied permission to reside permanently in the Republic of Belarus, if:

it is necessitated by the interests of national security, protection of public order, public health, protection of rights and lawful interests of the citizens of the Republic of Belarus and other persons;

facts have been found out of a violation of the legislation of the Republic of Belarus by him during his previous stay in the Republic of Belarus;

upon filing his application for permission to reside permanently in the Republic of Belarus, he gave false information about himself, or failed to present the required documents;

there is evidence that he is involved in smuggling operations, illegal trade in arms, drugs trafficking and smuggling of illegal migrants;

he is or was a member of terrorist of fascist organisations, or a person advocating war, social, ethnic, religious, or racial hostility;

he has been released from custody in the territory of another state and/or has an uncancelled or unquashed conviction;

he has a disease which is on the list of diseases that preclude entry into the territory of the Republic of Belarus.

The list of diseases that preclude entry into the territory of the Republic of Belarus shall be determined by the Ministry of Health of the Republic of Belarus and approved by the Council of Ministers of the Republic of Belarus.

**Article 15. Cancellation of Permission to Reside Permanently in the Republic of Belarus**

Permission to reside permanently in the Republic of Belarus may be cancelled if:

the alien has deliberately given false information about himself, or has concealed circumstances that essentially affected the decision to grant him permission to reside permanently in the Republic of Belarus;

it is necessitated by the interests of national security, protection of public order, public health, protection of rights and lawful interests of the citizens of the Republic of Belarus and other persons;

the alien has left, or received permission to reside permanently in another state;

the marriage contracted with a citizen of the Republic of Belarus or an alien has been nullified by a court of law;

the grounds on which the decision had been taken to grant the alien permission to reside permanently in the Republic of Belarus have been lost.

The decision to cancel permission to reside permanently in the Republic of Belarus in the instances mentioned in paragraphs two, three and four of part one of this article, shall be taken by the authority of the interior that has taken the decision to grant the alien permission to reside permanently in the Republic of Belarus, either on its own initiative or at the representation by competent government authorities.

The decision to cancel permission to reside permanently in the Republic of Belarus in instances mentioned in paragraphs five and six of part one of this article shall be taken through a court procedure.

The decision to cancel permission to reside permanently in the Republic of Belarus, within five days of taking it, shall be dispatched to the immigrant, as well as to the Ministry of Foreign Affairs of the Republic of Belarus.

The immigrant in respect of whom a decision has been taken to cancel permission to reside permanently in the Republic of Belarus, shall have the right to appeal against this decision through a court procedure within one month of being familiarised with the decision.

## CHAPTER 4. THE PROCEDURE FOR ENTRY INTO THE REPUBLIC OF BELARUS

### Article 16. Entry into the Republic of Belarus

Aliens shall only enter the Republic of Belarus for permanent residence under valid passports or papers that are passport substitutes, provided they have an immigration visa issued in accordance with the established procedure.

### Article 17. Immigration Visa

An alien who has been granted permission to reside permanently in the Republic of Belarus, shall be issued with an immigration visa by a diplomatic mission or consular institution of the Republic of Belarus.

The immigration visa shall be valid for entry into the Republic of Belarus within one year of its issue. If the alien, after receiving an immigration visa, failed to enter the Republic of Belarus within a year, and retains his right to an immigration visa, a new immigration visa may be issued to him in accordance with the established procedure.

### Article 18. Unused Immigration Visas

The immigration visa of an alien who has been denied entry into the Republic of Belarus, or an immigration visa whose period of validity has expired whereas the alien failed to apply for its extension within the established period of time, shall be deemed unused.

### Article 19. Registration of Aliens Who Arrive in the Republic of Belarus for Permanent Residence

An alien who arrives in the Republic of Belarus for permanent residence must, within three days, register himself with the authorised registration authority at the place of his actual residence. The alien must inform the authorities of the interior of the Republic of Belarus, within ten days, of all changes in his place of residence

### Article 20. Medical Examination of Aliens

Aliens may be subjected to forced medical examination if there are sufficient grounds to believe that they have diseases that are on the list of dangerous diseases, or if it has been established that they have arrived in the Republic of Belarus from an area of massive epidemics of dangerous human or animal diseases.

A medical examination of aliens in the instances provided for in part one of this article, shall be performed by doctors who are staff members of regional health institutions, following a decision of health institutions with the approval by the prosecutor.

The periods of examination (check-up) of aliens shall be determined by medical indications.

**Article 21. Residence Permit**

Aliens who have been granted permission to reside permanently in the Republic of Belarus shall be issued with an appropriate residence permit of the Republic of Belarus.

The procedure for the issue of the residence permit of the Republic of Belarus shall be established by the Council of Ministers of the Republic of Belarus.

**Article 22. Travel Document**

The travel document shall be issued to certain categories of aliens permanently residing in the Republic of Belarus, for exit from and entry into the Republic of Belarus, for a period that shall not exceed the validity of the residence permit.

The procedure for the issue of the travel document shall be established by the Council of Ministers of the Republic of Belarus.

## CHAPTER 5. REUNIFICATION OF FAMILY

**Article 23. The Right to Reunification of Family**

The right to reunification of the family shall be enjoyed by the spouse, minor children and other children who have not been married, having an invitation, respectively, from the spouse or parents who are citizens of the Republic of Belarus or immigrants.

**Article 24. Special Cases of Reunification of Family**

In some instances the right to reunification of the family may be granted to other close relatives of citizens of the Republic of Belarus or immigrants, provided the inviting person has adequate housing conditions and a lawful source of income to secure a minimum of subsistence for himself and members of his family.

A decision concerning special cases of reunification of the family shall be taken by the Ministry of the Interior of the Republic of Belarus in accordance with the procedure to be established by the Council of Ministers of the Republic of Belarus.

### Article 22. Burden of Proof of the Right to Reunification of Family

In all instances of entry for the purpose of reunification of the family, the alien who wishes to enter the Republic of Belarus or the persons receiving him shall present documentary proof of the right to reunification of the family.

## CHAPTER 6. LIABILITY FOR VIOLATING LEGISLATION OF THE REPUBLIC OF BELARUS ON IMMIGRATION

### Article 26. Liability for Violating Legislation of the Republic of Belarus on Immigration

Violation of the legislation of the Republic of Belarus on immigration shall entail liability in accordance with the legislation of the Republic of Belarus in the event of:

aiding in the illegal entry of an alien into the Republic of Belarus, or illegal delivery of an alien to the Republic of Belarus;

harbouring an alien during his illegal presence in the Republic of Belarus;

bringing in an alien with a view to engaging in an activity that is prohibited in the Republic of Belarus or that is incompatible with the purpose of the alien's entry;

aiding or involvement in illegal transit of an alien through the territory of the Republic of Belarus;

concealment by an official of established facts of an alien's illegal entry into the Republic of Belarus and his illegal presence in its territory;

an alien's entry into the Republic of Belarus in violation of the legislation of the Republic of Belarus;

illegal employment of an alien or aiding in such employment;

other violations of the legislation of the Republic of Belarus on immigration.

### Article 27. Collection of Fines and Reimbursement of Expenses

Fines exacted for violating the legislation of the Republic of Belarus on immigration shall be transferred to the republican budget.

Fines may be paid in freely convertible currency at an exchange rate to be set by the National Bank of the Republic of Belarus as at the date of payment of the fine.

The procedure for the payment of fines and reimbursement of expenses related to the consideration of cases of infringement of the legislation of the Republic of Belarus on immigration shall be determined by the Council of Ministers of the Republic of Belarus.

## CHAPTER 7. DEPORTATION

### Article 28. Aliens to Be Deported

The following aliens are to be deported:

> those who have arrived in the Republic of Belarus and stay in it illegally, unless criminal proceedings have been instituted against them in accordance with the legislation of the Republic of Belarus;
>
> those whose permission to reside permanently in the Republic of Belarus has been canceled;
>
> those who have committed serious crimes outside the Republic of Belarus.

### Article 29. Deportation Procedure

Decisions to deport aliens mentioned in article 28 of this Law shall be taken by the appropriate authorities of the interior or state security of the Republic of Belarus.

Before the decision to deport is taken, the appropriate authorities of the interior or state security of the Republic of Belarus shall send a notice to the alien in question, indicating the reasons for deportation, the place and time of the examination of the matter, and explaining the right of the alien to be present in person at the hearings. Should the alien fail to appear at the hearings, the issue of deportation can be considered in his absence.

The decision of deportation can be appealed against in court in accordance with the established procedure.

A note of the alien's deportation shall be made in the alien's passport or in the document which is a substitute for the passport.

Ten years after the date of deportation, aliens deported from the Republic of Belarus can apply to appropriate authorities for permission to enter the Republic of Belarus.

### Article 30. Detention of Aliens

After the decision to deport an alien has been taken, appropriate authorities of the interior or state security of the Republic of Belarus shall take measures to detain him, with the prosecutor's approval, for the period of time necessary to deport him, if there are reasons to believe that the alien in question may evade fulfilling the deportation decision.

The procedure for setting up temporary detention centres for aliens to be deported from the Republic of Belarus shall be established by the Council of Ministers of the Republic of Belarus.

If the alien has lodged a complaint with a court of law requesting review of the deportation decision, he may be remanded on bail in accordance with the procedure established by the legislation of the Republic of Belarus.

**Article 31. Suspension of Deportation**

The procedure of deportation may be suspended, if:

new circumstances have come to light, as a result of which the alien or members of his family may be granted asylum or refugee status in the Republic of Belarus;

the court of law is considering the alien's appeal for a review of the deportation decision.

**Article 32. Voluntary Departure of Alien**

An alien with respect to whom the procedure of deportation has been started, can declare his willingness to leave the Republic of Belarus voluntarily and at his own expense. The issue of the alien's voluntary departure shall be decided upon by the authorities of the interior of the Republic of Belarus.

An alien leaving the Republic of Belarus voluntarily shall be entitled to choose the country to which he would like to go.

Voluntary departure of the alien shall not be allowed, if the issue of his deportation has been raised because of his illegal activities or activities aimed at subverting national security of the Republic of Belarus, or because of other activities constituting public menace for the Republic of Belarus.

An alien who has left the Republic of Belarus voluntarily, may in five-years' time after departure apply to the relevant authorities for permission to enter the Republic of Belarus.

**Article 33. The State to which an Alien Is Deported**

An alien in respect of whom a decision of deportation has been taken, shall be deported to the state of his nationality or to the state from which he had arrived in the Republic of Belarus.

If the alien is threatened with persecution unrelated to measures of criminal law in the state from which he has arrived in the Republic of Belarus, or if there is a fear that he may be expelled from that state to another state where he might be threatened with such persecution, a decision may be taken to deport this alien to a third state which will express its agreement to receive him.

Escorting of the alien being deported shall be carried out by the authorities of the interior of the Republic of Belarus up to the border crossing point, and it shall be terminated after the alien has crossed the State Border of the Republic of Belarus.

**Article 34. Costs of the Deportation Procedure**

All the costs of the deportation procedure, including investigation and trial in court, shall be covered by the alien in question or by the legal entities or natural persons of the Republic of Belarus that have solicited for his entry.

In certain instances, if it is impossible to have the costs covered by the alien, the deportation procedure shall be carried out at the expense of the budget of the Republic of Belarus, or at the expense of the budget of the state seeking extradition of the alien.

**SECTION V. Concluding Provisions**

**Article 35. Entry into Force of the Present Law**

This Law shall enter into force six months after the date of its publication.

**Article 36. Bringing Acts of Legislation in Agreement with the Present Law**

The Council of Ministers of the Republic of Belarus, within three months of the entry into force of the present Law, shall take measures to bring the legislation of the Republic of Belarus in agreement with the present Law.

# ON CITIZENSHIP OF THE REPUBLIC OF BELARUS

Adopted by the Chamber of Representatives on 18 June 2002 Approved by the Council of Republic on 28 June 2002

*(in edition of the Law of the Republic of Belarus of 22.06.2006 No. 129-Z and of 04.01.2010 No. 105-Z)*

This Law shall stipulate the legal basis for government control in the area of citizenship and it shall regulate the foundations and procedures of acquisition, retention and termination of citizenship of the Republic of Belarus; the order of adoption, execution and appeal of decisions on the issues of citizenship; it shall provide for special cases of citizenship alteration and retention; it shall establish the competency of public agencies, as well as the rights and duties of citizens of the Republic of Belarus in that sphere.

**CHAPTER 1 GENERAL PROVISIONS**

Article 1. Citizenship of the Republic of Belarus

Citizenship of the Republic of Belarus is a firm legal bond of a person with the Republic of Belarus manifested in the aggregate of their mutual rights, duties and accountability and based on acknowledgement and respect of the dignity and basic human rights and freedoms.

Citizenship of the Republic of Belarus is an integral attribute of the national sovereignty of the Republic of Belarus .

Article 2. Legal Regulation of the Issues of Citizenship of the Republic of Belarus

The issues of citizenship in the Republic of Belarus shall be regulated by the Constitution of the Republic of Belarus, this Law, other legislative acts and international treaties of the Republic of Belarus.

If an international treaty of the Republic of Belarus provides for regulations other than those provided in this Law, the regulations of international treaty shall apply.

Article 3. The Principles of Citizenship of the Republic of Belarus

Citizenship of the Republic of Belarus is based on the following principles:

every person is entitled to citizenship;

citizenship of the Republic of Belarus is equal for all citizens of the Republic of Belarus regardless of the grounds for its acquisition;

citizenship of the Republic of Belarus may not be conferred against will of that person;

no one may be deprived of the citizenship of the Republic of Belarus or of his/her right to change his/her citizenship.

The Republic of Belarus strives to avoid cases of statelessness.

Article 4. Protection and Patronage of Citizens of the Republic of Belarus by the State

The State shall guarantee its protection to the citizens of the Republic of Belarus both in the Republic of Belarus and outside of its limits.

If in the country of stay of citizens of the Republic of Belarus there are no diplomatic representations and consular establishments of the Republic of Belarus, the protection of rights and legal interests of citizens of the Republic of Belarus shall be conducted in accordance with international treaties of the Republic of Belarus by appropriate agencies of other countries.

Article 5. Impossibility of Extradition of a Citizen of the Republic of Belarus to a Foreign Country

A citizen of the Republic of Belarus may not be extradited to a foreign country unless international treaties of the Republic of Belarus provide otherwise.

Article 6. Retention of Citizenship of the Republic of Belarus

Residence of a citizen of the Republic of Belarus in a foreign country shall not by itself be the cause of loss of the citizenship of the Republic of Belarus.

Article 7. Citizenship of the Republic of Belarus at Marriage and Divorce

Marriage or divorce of a citizen of the Republic of Belarus with a citizen of another country or with a stateless person shall not by itself constitute acquisition or cessation of citizenship of the Republic of Belarus by either spouse.

A person married to a citizen of the Republic of Belarus shall acquire citizenship of the Republic of Belarus in the presence of his/her will and compliance with the conditions stipulated by this Law.

Article 8. Citizens of the Republic of Belarus

Citizens of the Republic of Belarus are:

persons who are citizens of the Republic of Belarus by the effective date of this Law;

persons who have acquired citizenship of the Republic of Belarus in accordance with this Law.

Citizens of the Republic of Belarus by birth are persons who were born within the current territory of the Republic of Belarus and who were citizens of the former USSR by birth and who acquired citizenship of the Republic of Belarus prior to the effective date of this Law.

Article 9. Foreign Citizens and Stateless Persons

Foreign citizens in the Republic of Belarus are persons who are not citizens of the Republic of Belarus and who possess proof of their affiliation to citizenship (nationality[1]) (hereinafter, if the other is not specified, – citizenship) of another country.

Stateless persons in the Republic of Belarus are persons who are not citizens of the Republic of Belarus and who do not posses a proof of their affiliation to citizenship of another country.

Legal position of foreign citizens and stateless persons in the Republic of Belarus shall be regulated by the legislation of the Republic of Belarus.

Article 10. Documentary Proof of Citizenship of the Republic of Belarus

Documentary proof of citizenship of the Republic of Belarus shall be the passport of a citizen of the Republic of Belarus or another document indicating citizenship of the Republic of Belarus.

Article 11. Non-recognition of Foreign Citizenship as related to a Citizen of the Republic of Belarus

Foreign citizenship of a citizen of the Republic of Belarus shall not be recognized unless international treaties provide otherwise.

Citizens of the Republic of Belarus who also have other citizenships, may not for that reason be limited in rights or evade duties or be exempt from liability ensuing from the citizenship of the Republic of Belarus.

## CHAPTER 2 ACQUISITION OF CITIZENSHIP OF THE REPUBLIC OF BELARUS

Article 12. Foundations for acquisition of citizenship of the Republic of Belarus

Citizenship of the Republic of Belarus may be acquired:

by birth;

as a result of admittance to citizenship of the Republic of Belarus ;

in course of registration;

by other reason provided in this Law or in international treaties of the Republic of Belarus *(in edition of the Law of the Republic of Belarus of 22.06.2006 No. 129-Z)*

Article 13. Acquisition of the Citizenship of the Republic of Belarus by Birth

A child shall obtain the citizenship of the Republic of Belarus by birth provided that on the date of the child's birth:

at least one of the child's parents is a citizen of the Republic of Belarus regardless of the child's place of birth;

the child's parents (single parent) permanently residing in the Republic of Belarus

[1] Here nationality equals citizenship in its sense and meaning. In Russian there are terms "подданство" and "подданные" (for identification of those people). It describes people who are citizens, but citizens of the country where (in the majority of instances) the head of state (even formally) is a sovereign (king, queen, sultan and etc.), like in the United Kingdom. English synonym for this meaning of nationality is "homager".

are stateless persons, provided that the child was born in the Republic of Belarus;

the child's parents (single parent) permanently residing in the Republic of Belarus are foreign citizens provided that the child was born in the Republic of Belarus and the countries of its parents' citizenship(s) (nationality(-ies)) do not confer their citizenship to the child.

A child in the Republic of Belarus, whose parents are unknown, shall become citizen of the Republic of Belarus.

Article 14. Admission to Citizenship of the Republic of Belarus

Any person who has reached 18 years of age may apply for admission to citizenship of the Republic of Belarus, provided that he/she:

observes and respects Constitution of the Republic of Belarus, the other legislative acts of the Republic of Belarus, undertakes the responsibility to follow and respect the Constitution of the Republic of Belarus and other legislative acts of the Republic of Belarus;

knows at least one official language of the Republic of Belarus within communication limits;

resides in the Republic of Belarus after being granted permanent residence permit for the duration of the seven years uninterruptedly, except the cases provided in the Part 3 of this article. The period of the residence on the territory of the Republic of Belarus is considered to be uninterrupted if a person was leaving the territory of the Republic of Belarus for the total period of time of no more than three months during each year;

has legal source of income which provides him/her and incapacitated members of the family who depend on him/her minimum wage of living stipulated in the Republic of Belarus;

does not have citizenship or will be losing foreign citizenship in case of acquisition of citizenship of the Republic of Belarus or has submitted to a competent agency of a foreign country an application on renunciation of nationality that he/she has, except for cases when renunciation of citizenship is impossible for reasons outside of person's control.

Persons who were granted refugee statue in the Republic of Belarus may be admitted to citizenship of the Republic of Belarus after seven years of their recognition as refugees and provided they have followed the conditions of Paragraphs Two, Three, Five and Six of Part One of this Article.

The length of residence established in Paragraph Four of Part One of this Article may be shortened or never applied for:

Belarusians and for persons who identify themselves as Belarusians, their descendants (direct blood relatives: children, grandchildren, great grandchildren) born outside the contemporary territory of the Republic of Belarus;

persons who have outstanding merits to the Republic of Belarus for high achievements in the areas of science, technology, culture or sport, or those who possess a profession or qualification of public interest to the Republic of Belarus;

foreign citizens or stateless persons who have previously been citizens of the Republic of Belarus.

Admission to the citizenship of the Republic of Belarus is being organized taking into consideration the interests of the Republic of Belarus.

Article 15. Acquisition of citizenship of the Republic of Belarus in the Course of Registration.

Any person above 18 years of age who has been residing permanently on the territory of the Republic of Belarus or who was a citizen of the former USSR and did not possess the citizenship of the Republic of Belarus, may apply for acquisition of citizenship of the Republic of Belarus in the course of registration provide d that he/she meets the requirements of the Paragraphs 2, 3 and 6 of the Part Two of this article and if he/she:

was born or resided permanently in the Republic of Belarus before 12 November 1991;

is a husband (wife) of the person who is acquiring the citizenship of the Republic of Belarus in the course of registration on the ground provided in the Paragraph 2 of this Part;

is a descendant of the person who is acquiring, acquired or could have acquired the citizenship of the Republic of Belarus in the course of registration on the ground provided in the Paragraph 2 of this Part.

The citizenship of the Republic of Belarus may be acquired in the course of registration by a person even if he/she does not meet the requirements provided in the Part 1 of this article, if he/she:

is a child permanently residing in the Republic of Belarus – by a joint application of the parents, of whom at least one is the citizen of the Republic of Belarus, or by application of one parent who is a citizen of the Republic of Belarus if the whereabouts of the other parent are unknown, or by an application of a single parent who is a citizen of the Republic of Belarus;

is a child staying in the Republic of Belarus whose only known parent or both parents have died, have been deprived of parental rights, have refused from upbringing the child or have given their consent to his adoption, who have been judicially acknowledged incapable, missing or dead, as well as incapable persons under custody or guardianship

– by application of a guardian (trustee) coordinated with a guardianship and trusteeship agency.

Article 16. Bases for Rejecting Application for Citizenship of the Republic of Belarus

An application for citizenship of the Republic of Belarus shall not be examined if the applicant:

has been convicted of a crime against peace and security of the humanity, for a war crime, a crime against state;

has been convicted for a crime in the Republic of Belarus or outside of it that is recognized as such by the legislation of the Republic of Belarus;

is suspected or accused and subject of criminal prosecution in the Republic of Belarus or in a foreign country for crimes recognized as such by the legislation of the Republic of Belarus – until the sentence or final decision is issued;

has been sentenced and is currently serving a sentence in custody until the end of the term of the sentence;

has been deported or expelled from the Republic of Belarus – until the end of the entrance ban period;

repeatedly (three and more times) were brought to administrative account within the territory of the Republic of Belarus, -until expiry of the term during a person is considered as brought to administrative account;

have provided false information or fake documents;

is serving in the military, police, security, justice or other public agencies of a foreign country.

If instances provided in the Part One of this Article exist, application for acquisition of citizenship of the Republic of Belarus is returned back to the applicant together with all provided materials without any examination of the application.

## CHAPTER 3 TERMINATION OF CITIZENSHIOP OF THE REPUBLIC OF BELARUS

Article 17. Foundations for termination of citizenship of the Republic of Belarus

Citizenship of the Republic of Belarus shall be terminated for the reasons of:

renunciation of citizenship of the Republic of Belarus;

loss of citizenship of the Republic of Belarus.

Article 18. Renunciation of Citizenship of the Republic of Belarus

Citizen of the Republic of Belarus who reached the age of 18 years, has the right to submit an application for renunciation of citizenship of the Republic of Belarus.

Renunciation of citizenship of the Republic of Belarus for a citizen of the Republic of Belarus who did not reach the age of 18 years may be allowed upon application of his/her parents (single parent).

Renunciation of citizenship of the Republic of Belarus is executed in accordance with procedures stipulated by the President of the Republic of Belarus, and if there are no grounds provided in the Article 20 of this Law.

Article 19. Loss of the Citizenship of the Republic of Belarus

Citizenship of the Republic of Belarus is lost in the following cases:

in case of the enlistment of the person to military or police service, services with security, justice or other public agencies of a foreign country in absence of conditions listed in Article 20 of this Law;

on a written application of the parents (of a single parent) concerning their child who obtained by birth the citizenship of the Republic of Belarus along with the citizenship of a foreign State. The loss of the citizenship of a child aged 14-18 years is allowed only if the child gave his/her written consent and if this consent was notarized;

on the grounds listed in the international treaties, ratified by the Republic of Belarus.

Article 20. Reasons to Reject Termination of Citizenship of the Republic of Belarus

Termination of citizenship of the Republic of Belarus shall not be allowed when a citizen of the Republic of Belarus:

is accused or when in his/her regard there is a valid court sentence;

has tax indebtedness or other outstanding debts and liabilities to the Republic of Belarus, its administrative and territorial subdivisions and its legal or physical persons; does not have any other citizenship or a guarantee to acquire such.

## CHAPTER 4 CANCELLATION OF DECISIONS ON ISSUES OF CITIZENSHIP OF THE REPUBLIC OF BELARUS

Article 21. Cancellation of decision on acquisition or termination of citizenship of the Republic of Belarus

The decision on acquisition or revocation of citizenship of the Republic of Belarus may be cancelled if it was taken based on admittedly false data or fake documents.

Article 22. The procedure of Cancellation of a Decision on Acquisition or Termination of Citizenship of the Republic of Belarus

Cancellation of a decision on acquisition or termination of citizenship of the Republic of Belarus may be made by the President of the Republic of Belarus or an appointed agency that has made that decision.

The decision on acquisition or termination of citizenship of the Republic of Belarus in case of cancellation shall be considered invalid from the date of its adoption.

## CHAPTER 5 CITIZENSHIP OF CHILDREN WHEN PARENTS CHANGE THEIR CITIZENSHIP AND AT ADOPTION

Article 23. Citizenship of a child in case of the parents' or foster parents' change of citizenship.

If the parents (single parent) change citizenship, the child's citizenship shall be changed accordingly unless he/she is 14 years old.

Citizenship of children from 14 to 18 years of age shall be changed in case of their parents' change of citizenship, and the citizenship of adopted children, shall be made only upon written consent of children that is certified by a notary public.

By wish of the parents (single parent) of a child in case of their termination of citizenship of the Republic of Belarus, the citizenship of the Republic of Belarus may retain with a child.

Article 24. Retention of citizenship of the Republic of Belarus by child under the custody or guardianship

If both parents or either parent of the child residing in the Republic of Belarus and who is under the custody or guardianship of citizens of the Republic of Belarus, renounce citizenship of the Republic of Belarus or lose it and with that they fail to take part in upbringing the child, the child shall retain citizenship of the Republic of Belarus.

Article 25. Acquisition of citizenship of the Republic of Belarus when either parent acquires citizenship of the Republic of Belarus

If either parent acquires citizenship of the Republic of Belarus while the other remains foreign citizen or stateless, the child may acquire citizenship of the Republic of Belarus upon a joint request of the parents or the parent who acquires citizenship of the Republic of Belarus if the location of the other parent is unknown.

If either of the parents acquires citizenship of the Republic of Belarus while the other remains stateless, the child residing in the Republic of Belarus shall become citizen of the Republic of Belarus if otherwise he will become stateless.

Article 26. Retention of citizenship of the Republic of Belarus by a child when one of the parents renounces or Loses Citizenship of the Republic of Belarus.

If one of the parents renounces or loses citizenship of the Republic of Belarus while the other remains citizen of the Republic of Belarus, the child shall retain citizenship of the Republic of Belarus.

Article 27. Citizenship of a child in case of adoption.

A child who is a foreign citizen or who is stateless, shall become citizen of the Republic of Belarus from the date of adoption, if adopted by a citizen of the Republic of Belarus or a married couple who are citizens of the Republic of Belarus or by a married couple when one spouse is a citizen of the Republic of Belarus and the other is stateless.

A child who is a foreign citizen or a stateless person may acquire citizenship of the Republic of Belarus at joint request of the foster parents, if adopted by a married couple where one spouse is a citizen of the Republic of Belarus and the other is a foreign citizen.

A child who is a citizen of the Republic of Belarus shall retain citizenship of the Republic of Belarus at adoption by:

married couple who are foreign citizens or by a foreign citizen;

married couple who are stateless persons or by a stateless person;

married couple when one spouse is a citizen of the Republic of Belarus and the other is a foreign citizen or a stateless person.

The citizenship of a child adopted by spouses who are foreign citizens or by a foreign citizen may be terminated in the course of the renunciation of the citizenship after the child have reached the age of 18 years.

## CHAPTER 6 COMPETENCE OF AUTHORITIES TAKING DECISIONS AND PROCESSING DOCUMENTS ON ISSUES OF CITIZENSHIP OF THE REPUBLIC OF BELARUS

Article 28. Taking decisions on issues of citizenship of the Republic of Belarus

Decisions on admittance to citizenship of the Republic of Belarus and its termination shall be made by the President of the Republic of Belarus or in order established by him.

Article 29. State authorities involved in taking decisions on citizenship of the Republic of Belarus

The following state authorities are involved in taking decisions on citizenship of the Republic of Belarus:

the President of the Republic of Belarus;

the interior authorities;

agencies of the Diplomatic Service of the Republic of Belarus abroad.

Article 30. Competency of the President of the Republic of Belarus

The President of the Republic of Belarus shall:

establish the procedure of acquisition of citizenship of the Republic of Belarus and its termination;

issue decrees on admittance to citizenship and renunciation of citizenship of the Republic of Belarus;

issue orders in cases of rejection of applications for admittance to citizenship and renunciation of citizenship of the Republic of Belarus.

Article 31. Competence of the Interior Authorities of the Republic of Belarus

The Interior Authorities of the Republic of Belarus shall:

receive from permanent residents of the Republic of Belarus applications on issues of citizenship of the Republic of Belarus; verify their factual and documentary substantiation;

submit materials on citizenship applications and on renunciation of citizenship of the Republic of Belarus for review by the President of the Republic of Belarus;

determine whether persons staying in the Republic of Belarus possess citizenship of the Republic of Belarus;

resolve issues of acquisition of citizenship of the Republic of Belarus in the course of registration procedure by permanent residents of the Republic of Belarus;

register the loss of the citizenship of the Republic of Belarus by the persons permanently residing in the Republic of Belarus;

resolve the issues regarding the change of a citizenship in accordance with grounds provided in the international agreements of the Republic of Belarus;

control the issue of the termination of the foreign citizenship with regard to the persons who had been admitted to the citizenship of the Republic of Belarus;

resolve in accordance with the legislation of the Republic of Belarus other issues related to citizenship of the Republic of Belarus;

Article 32. Competence of Agencies of the Diplomatic Service of the Republic of Belarus

Agencies of the diplomatic service of the Republic of Belarus shall:

receive from persons permanently residing abroad applications on issues of citizenship of the Republic of Belarus, verify their factual and documentary substantiation;

submit materials on citizenship applications and on denunciation of citizenship of the Republic of Belarus for review by the President of the Republic of Belarus; determine whether persons permanently staying abroad possess citizenship of the Republic of Belarus;

register the loss of the citizenship of the Republic of Belarus by the persons permanently residing abroad;

resolve the issues regarding the change of a citizenship in accordance with the grounds provided in the international agreements of the Republic of Belarus;

control the issue of the termination of the foreign citizenship with regard to the persons who had been admitted to the citizenship of the Republic of Belarus;

resolve issues of acquisition of citizenship of the Republic of Belarus by persons permanently residing abroad in the course of the procedure of registration;

resolve in accordance with the legislation of the Republic of Belarus other issues related to citizenship of the Republic of Belarus.

## CHAPTER 7 PROCEDURE OF SUBMITTAL AND REVIEW OF APPLICATIONS ON ISSUES OF CITIZENSHIP OF THE REPUBLIC OF BELARUS

Article 33. Submittal and drawing up of applications on issues related to citizenship of the Republic of Belarus

Applications on issues of citizenship of the Republic of Belarus shall be submitted to the interior authorities of the Republic of Belarus at the applicant's place of residence, and by persons permanently residing abroad – to an appropriate agency of the diplomatic service of the Republic of Belarus.

Applications on issues of citizenship of the Republic of Belarus shall be submitted by the applicant in person and in writing. Requirements to the form of application and the list of attachments related to the concrete substantiation of acquisition or termination of citizenship of the Republic of Belarus shall be determined by the President of the Republic of Belarus.

Applications on issues of citizenship of the Republic of Belarus of children and incapable persons shall be submitted by their parents or other legal representatives.

If an applicant can not apply personally, the application and attachments may be submitted via another person or by mail.

Article 34. Terms of review of applications on issues related to citizenship of the Republic of Belarus

The period of review of applications on admission to citizenship of the Republic of Belarus shall not exceed one year.

The period of review of applications on denunciation of citizenship of the Republic of Belarus shall not exceed six months.

The period of review of applications on acquisition of citizenship of the Republic of Belarus in the course of the procedure of registration shall not exceed two months.

Article 35. Date of acquisition or denunciation of citizenship of the Republic of Belarus

A person shall acquire citizenship of the Republic of Belarus:

in accordance with Article 13 of this Law – from the child's date of birth;

in accordance with Part One of Article 27 of this Law – from the date of adoption of the child;

in other cases – from the effective date of the Decree of the President of the Republic of Belarus or from the date of decision of its appointed agency.

Citizenship of the Republic of Belarus shall be terminated on the effective date of the Decree of the President of the Republic of Belarus or the date of decision of its appointed agency

Article 36. Repeated review of applications on issues of citizenship of the Republic of Belarus.

Repeated applications for admission to citizenship of the Republic of Belarus or for renunciation of citizenship of the Republic of Belarus shall be accepted no earlier than one year after the previous decision was made. In case of newly accrued significant circumstances that have not been and could not have been known to the applicant, the repeated application may be reviewed in earlier terms.

## CHAPTER 8 EXECUTION OF DECISIONS ON ISSUES OF CITIZENSHIP OF THE REPUBLIC OF BELARUS, APPPEALS OF DECISIONS OF STATE AUTHORITIES AND ACTIONS OF OFFICIALS ON ISSUES RELATED TO CITIZENSHIP OF THE REPUBLIC OF BELARUS

Article 37. State authorities fulfilling decisions on issues related to citizenship of the Republic of Belarus

Decisions on citizenship issues in relation to residents of the Republic of Belarus shall be fulfilled by the interior authorities of the Republic of Belarus and in relation to persons residing abroad – by agencies of the diplomatic service of the Republic of Belarus.

Article 38. Appeal of decisions of state authorities and actions of officials on issues on issues related to citizenship of the Republic of Belarus

Decisions of the President of the Republic of Belarus on issues related to citizenship of the Republic of Belarus may be appealed in the Supreme Court of the Republic of Belarus that shall review such cases as a court of first instance.

Decisions of state authorities appointed by the President of the Republic of Belarus on issues of citizenship may be appealed in Oblasts and Minsk City Courts.

Unsubstantiated rejection of applications for the issues related to citizenship of the Republic of Belarus, violation of terms of application review as well as other illegitimate actions of officials on citizenship issues may be appealed in court.

## CHAPTER 9 FINAL PROVISIONS

Article 39. Validity of documents issued in accordance with the former citizenship legislation of the Republic of Belarus

Documents issued in accordance with the former citizenship legislation of the Republic of Belarus shall remain legally valid provided that they are properly drawn up and that they shall be considered valid on the effective date of this Law.

Article 40. Execution of this Law

This Law shall come into effect ten days after its official publication.

This Law shall apply to legal relationships accrued after it came into effect.

Until the legislation of the Republic of Belarus is brought in line with this Law, it shall apply in part that does not contradict this Law.

Until 1 January 2004, for the purposes of determination of affiliation to citizenship of the Republic of Belarus within legal relationships accrued prior to execution of this Law, the provisions of the Law of the Republic of Belarus of 18 October 1991 "On Citizenship of the Republic of Belarus" (Vedamastsi Vyarhounaga Saveta Respubliki Belarus , 1991, No. 32, Art. 581) and Resolution of the Supreme Soviet of the Republic of Belarus of 18 October 1991 "On Implementation of the Law of the Republic of Belarus "On Citizenship of the Republic of Belarus"(Vedamastsi Vyarhounaga Saveta Respubliki Belarus , 1991, No. 32, Art. 582) shall apply.

Article 41. Bringing legal acts of the Republic of Belarus in line with this Law

The Council of Ministers of the Republic of Belarus shall within six months after this Law comes into effect:

develop and introduce in established order proposals on bringing legal acts of the Republic of Belarus in line with this Law;

bring acts of the Government of the Republic of Belarus in line with this Law;

ensure that the republican authorities subordinate to the Council of Ministers of the Republic of Belarus review and cancel their legal acts that contradict this Law;

take other measures required for implementation of provisions of this Law.

Article 42. Loss of validity of certain legislation acts

In relation with adoption of this Law, the following shall be considered invalid:

Law of the Republic of Belarus of 18 October 1991 "On Citizenship of the Republic of Belarus" (Vedamastsi Vyarhounaga Saveta Respubliki Belarus, 1991, No. 32, Art. 581);

Law of the Republic of Belarus of 15 June 1993 "On Introduction of Addenda and Amendments into the Existing Citizenship Legislation Acts" (Vedamastsi Vyarhounaga Saveta Respubliki Belarus , 1993, No. 26, Art. 320);

Law of the Republic of Belarus of 8 September 1995 "On Introduction of Addenda and Amendments into the Existing Legislation Acts on Citizenship of the Republic of Belarus" (Vedamastsi Vyarhounaga Saveta Respubliki Belarus, 1995, No. 32, Art. 421);

Law of the Republic of Belarus of 3 March 1997 "On Introduction of Addendum into the Law of the Republic of Belarus "On Citizenship of the Republic of Belarus" (Vedamastsi Natsiyanalnaha S'hodu Respubliki Belarus , 1997, No. 9, Art. 194);

Law of the Republic of Belarus of 13 November 1997 "On Introduction of an Amendment into the Resolution of the Supreme Soviet of the Republic of Belarus "On Execution of the Law of the Republic of Belarus " On Citizenship of the Republic of Belarus" (Vedamastsi Natsiyanalnaha S'hodu Respubliki Belarus , 1997, No. 34, Art. 694);

Law of the Republic of Belarus of 22 June 1998 "On Introduction of Amendments and on Addendum into the Law of the Republic of "On Citizenship of the Republic of Belarus" (Vedamastsi Natsiyanalnaha S'hodu Respubliki Belarus, 1998, No. 25-26, Art. 432);

Article 1 of the Law of the Republic of Belarus of 9 November 1999 "On Introduction of Amendments into Certain Legislative Acts of the Republic of Belarus" (National Register of Legal Acts of the Republic of Belarus, 1999, No. 89, 2/82);

Law of the Republic of Belarus of 30 December 1999 "On Introduction of Addenda into the Law of the Republic of Belarus "On Citizenship of the Republic of Belarus" and an Amendment into the Resolution of the Supreme Soviet of the Republic of Belarus "On Execution of the Law of the Republic of Belarus "On Citizenship of the Republic of Belarus" (National Register of Legal Acts of the Republic of Belarus, 2000, No. 4, 2/121);

Law of the Republic of Belarus of 18 June 2001 "On Introduction of Amendments and Addenda into Certain Legislative Acts of the Republic of Belarus on Citizenship of the Republic of Belarus" (National Register of Legal Acts of the Republic of Belarus , 2001, No. 61, 2/776);

Resolution of the Supreme Soviet of the Republic of Belarus of 18 October 1991 "On Execution of the Law of the Republic of Belarus "On Citizenship of the Republic of Belarus" (Vedamastsi Vyarhounaga Saveta Respubliki Belarus, 1991, No. 32, Art. 582);

Decree of the Presidium of the Supreme Soviet of the Republic of Belarus of 19 June 1992 "On Approval of the Resolution on the Procedure of Reviewing Issues Related to Citizenship of the Republic of Belarus" (Vedamastsi Vyarhounaga Saveta Respubliki Belarus, 1992, No 21, Art. 377).

President of the Republic of Belarus A.LUKASHENKO

# ON THE LEGAL STATUS OF FOREIGN CITIZENS AND STATELESS PERSONS IN THE REPUBLIC OF BELARUS

**THE LAW OF THE REPUBLIC OF BELARUS OF JANUARY 4, 2010 NO. 105-Z**
Adopted by the House of Representatives on December 11, 2009

Approved by the Council of the Republic on December 17, 2009

The present law is intended for defining the legal status of foreign citizens and stateless persons in the Republic of Belarus, including the establishment of the procedure of their entry into the Republic of Belarus, stay in the Republic of Belarus and the departure from the Republic of Belarus, as well as for regulating other relations connected with the presence of these persons in the Republic of Belarus.

## CHAPTER 1 GENERAL PROVISIONS

**Article 1.** Key terms used in this Law and their definitions

For the purposes of this Law the following key terms and their definitions are used:

close relatives - parents, adoptive parents, children, adopted as sons (adopted as daughters), full brothers and sisters, grandmother, grandfather, grandchildren;

permit for residence in the Republic of Belarus (hereinafter - the residence permit) - an identity document of a foreign citizen, or stateless person (hereinafter, unless otherwise specified in this Law - the foreigner) on the territory of the Republic of Belarus and certifying the receipt by the foreigner of the permission for permanent residence in the Republic of Belarus (hereinafter - the permanent residence permit);

the visa of the Republic of Belarus (hereinafter - the visa) - permit, which gives a foreigner the right to cross the State border of the Republic of Belarus (hereinafter - the State border) for the purpose of entering the Republic of Belarus and (or) departure from the Republic of Belarus, stay in the Republic of Belarus or transit passage (transit) through the territory of the Republic of Belarus within the period specified in the permit, and which has been issued in accordance with order established by the legislation of the Republic of Belarus;

foreigner temporarily staying in Belarus - a person, who arrived in the Republic of Belarus for a period not exceeding ninety days in a calendar year as from the date of first entry into the Republic of Belarus on the basis of a visa or in the manner not requiring receiving the visa, and not having the permit for temporary residence in the Republic Belarus (hereinafter - the temporary residence permit) or the permanent residence permit, unless otherwise specified in this Law and international treaties of the Republic of Belarus;

foreigner temporarily residing in the Republic of Belarus - a person who has received a temporary residence permit in the manner prescribed by legislative acts of the Republic of Belarus;

deportation from the Republic of Belarus (hereinafter - the deportation) - expulsion of a foreigner out of the Republic of Belarus in accordance with this Law;

document for travel abroad - a valid passport or other document substituting it, intended for travelling abroad and issued by the relevant authority of the State of citizenship or habitual residence of the foreigner or by an international organization;

immigration quota - the maximum annual limit of admission of foreigners for permanent residence into the Republic of Belarus;

foreign citizen - a person who is not a citizen of the Republic of Belarus and has the evidence of his belonging to a citizenship (nationality) (hereinafter, unless otherwise specified in this Law - the citizenship) of another State;

stateless person - a person, who are not a citizen of the Republic of Belarus and has no proof of his belonging to the citizenship of another State;

migration card - a document containing information about the foreigner entering the Republic of Belarus and leaving the Republic of Belarus, and serving the purpose of exercising control over his temporary stay or temporary residence in the Republic of Belarus;

authorities registering foreigners temporarily staying in the Republic of Belarus (hereinafter - the registration authorities) - the Ministry for Foreign Affairs of the Republic of Belarus (hereinafter - the Ministry for Foreign Affairs), internal affairs organs of the Republic of Belarus (further - the internal affairs organs), a hotel, sanatorium, health resort or wellness organization;

foreigner permanently residing in the Republic of Belarus - a person, who has received the permanent residence permit and the residence permit in the manner prescribed by legislative acts of the Republic of Belarus and resolutions of the Council of Ministers of the Republic of Belarus;

temporary residence permit - a document which gives foreigners the right to reside in the Republic of Belarus during the period of its validity and issued in the manner prescribed by the legislation of the Republic of Belarus;

permanent residence permit - a decision of the Ministry for Internal Affairs of the Republic of Belarus (hereinafter - the Ministry for Internal Affairs) and other internal affairs organs, which entitles foreigners to the right of permanent residence in the Republic of Belarus;

Registration of a foreigner temporarily staying in the Republic of Belarus - fixing in the prescribed manner by the registration authorities of the information about the place and time of temporary stay of a foreigner in the Republic of Belarus;

transit passage (transit) of a foreigner through the territory of the Republic of Belarus - the entry of the foreigner into the Republic of Belarus from one State to follow a fixed route through the territory of the Republic of Belarus and exit of the foreigner from the Republic of Belarus to another State.

**Article 2.** Citizenship of foreign citizens, who have multiple nationality

Foreign nationals, who possess the nationality of two or more States, are considered in the Republic of Belarus citizens of the State, using the documents for travel abroad of which they entered into the Republic of Belarus.

**Article 3.** The Legislation of the Republic of Belarus on the legal status of foreigners in the Republic of Belarus

The legislation of the Republic of Belarus on the legal status of foreigners in the Republic of Belarus is based on the Constitution of the Republic of Belarus and consists of this Law and other legislative acts of the Republic of Belarus, including international treaties of the Republic of Belarus.

If an international treaty of the Republic of Belarus establishes other rules than those provided for in this Law, the rules of the international treaty shall be applied.

**Article 4.** Basic principles of the legal status of foreigners in the Republic of Belarus

Foreigners in the Republic of Belarus shall enjoy rights and liberties and fulfil duties on a par with citizens of the Republic of Belarus, unless otherwise specified in the Constitution of the Republic of Belarus, this Law and other legislative acts and international treaties of the Republic of Belarus.

Peculiarities of the legal status of foreigners applying for a refugee status, or additional protection or asylum in the Republic of Belarus, as well as foreigners, who are granted the refugee status, or additional or temporary protection or asylum in the Republic of Belarus, are governed by the specific legislative acts of the Republic of Belarus.

If another State restricts or violates universally accepted rules of the legal status of foreign citizens in respect of citizens of the Republic of Belarus, the Republic of Belarus may impose retaliatory restrictions on the rights and freedoms of citizens (nationals) of that State. Such restrictions, if they are introduced, shall not apply to foreigners listed in the second part of this article.

**Article 5.** Responsibility for violation of this Law

Persons guilty of violation of this Law shall be held liable in accordance with the legislative acts of the Republic of Belarus.

**Article 6.** Funding and material and technical support of activities provided for in this Law

Funding and material and technical support of activities provided for in this Law shall be performed at the expense of the funds of the Republican budget allocated for the upkeep of the relevant Republican organs of the State administration of the Republic of Belarus, and other sources in accordance with the legislation of the Republic of Belarus.

## CHAPTER 2 RIGHTS, FREEDOMS, DUTIES AND RESPONSIBILITY OF FOREIGNERS IN THE REPUBLIC OF BELARUS

**Article 7.** Individual rights and freedoms

Foreigners in the Republic of Belarus in accordance with the Constitution of the Republic of Belarus and other legislative acts of the Republic of Belarus shall enjoy guaranteed inviolability of person and residence and other personal rights and freedoms.

**Article 8.** Movement and choice of the place of stay (residence) within the territory of the Republic of Belarus

Foreigners shall have the right to move freely and choose freely their place of stay (residence) within the territory of the Republic of Belarus in accordance with this Law and other legislative acts of the Republic of Belarus.

The order of movement of foreigners and choice by them of the place of stay (residence) within the territory of the Republic of Belarus is determined by this Law and the Rules of

Stay of Foreign Citizens and Stateless Persons in the Republic of Belarus that are approved by the Council of Ministers of the Republic of Belarus (hereinafter - the Rules of the Stay).

Foreigners are entitled to travel freely within the territory of the Republic of Belarus except for places, visit to which require a special permit issued by authorized State organs or other organizations of the Republic of Belarus, and facilities, entering the territory of which and stay on it requires a special permit issued by administrations of these facilities.

A list of the places, for visiting which foreigners will need the special permit, and the facilities, for entry into the territory of which and stay on it foreigners need the special permit, as well as the list

of State organs and other organizations of the Republic of Belarus authorized to issue such permits is determined by the Council of Ministers of the Republic of Belarus.

**Article 9**. Participation in political parties and other public associations

Foreigners may join trade unions and other public associations created and operating on the territory of the Republic of Belarus, if such possibility is provided for in their charters.

Foreigners cannot be members of political parties and other public associations, established and operating on the territory of the Republic of Belarus and having political objectives.

**Article 10.** Socio-economic rights

Foreigners residing in the Republic of Belarus have all socio-economic rights enjoyed by citizens of the Republic of Belarus, including the right to social security.

Socio-economic rights of foreigners temporarily staying or temporarily residing in the Republic of Belarus are determined by legislative acts and international treaties of the Republic of Belarus.

**Article 11.** Performance of labour, business and other activities in the Republic of Belarus

Foreigners permanently residing in the Republic of Belarus are entitled to conduct labour and entrepreneurial activities on a par with citizens of the Republic of Belarus in the manner prescribed by legislative acts of the Republic of Belarus, subject to the limitations provided for in articles 19 and 20 of this Law.

The order of performance of labour activities by foreigners temporarily staying or temporarily residing in the Republic of Belarus shall be determined by special legislative acts of the Republic of Belarus.

Foreigners temporarily staying or temporarily residing in the Republic of Belarus are not entitled to conduct in the Republic of Belarus entrepreneurial activities without establishment of a legal entity, unless otherwise specified in legislative acts and international treaties of the Republic of Belarus.

Other activities shall be performed by foreigners in the manner prescribed by the legislation of the Republic of Belarus.

**Article 12.** Property and personal non-property rights

Foreigners in the Republic of Belarus are entitled to own property, inherit it or leave it by will, enjoy other property and personal rights in the manner prescribed by the legislation of the Republic of Belarus, including international treaties of the Republic of Belarus.

**Article 13.** Right to health care

Foreigners permanently residing in the Republic of Belarus have the right to access publicly available health care on a par with citizens of the Republic of Belarus, unless otherwise specified in legislative acts and international treaties of the Republic of Belarus.

Foreigners temporarily staying or temporarily residing in the Republic of Belarus are entitled to access publicly available health care at their own expense, expense of legal entities or other sources of funding, unless otherwise specified in legislative acts and international treaties of the Republic of Belarus.

The procedure and conditions for compulsory health insurance of foreigners entering the Republic of Belarus for a temporary stay or temporary residence are determined by legislative acts of the Republic of Belarus.

**Article 14.** Right to education

Foreigners permanently residing in the Republic of Belarus have the equal right to eduction on a par with citizens of the Republic of Belarus, unless otherwise provided for in legislative acts and international treaties of the Republic of Belarus.

Foreigners temporarily staying or temporarily residing in the Republic of Belarus have the right to receive education in the Republic of Belarus in accordance with international treaties of the Republic of Belarus or on the basis of agreements on education, concluded with educational institutions or scientific organizations of the Republic of Belarus, in the manner prescribed by the legislation of the Republic of Belarus, including international treaties of the Republic of Belarus.

Minor foreigners temporarily residing in the Republic of Belarus foreign minors are eligible for receiving preschool and general secondary education on a par with a minor citizens of the Republic of Belarus.

**Article 15.** The right to preserve national culture and respect the national dignity

Foreigners in the Republic of Belarus shall have the right to maintain and develop its national language and culture, follow national traditions and customs in accordance with the laws of the Republic of Belarus.

An insult to ethnic dignity of foreigners entails responsibility in accordance with the legislative acts of the Republic of Belarus.

**Article 16.** Protecting the rights and freedoms

Foreigners in the Republic of Belarus shall enjoy all the legal remedies for protection of the rights and freedoms of the person provided by the legislation of the Republic of Belarus.

**Article 17.** Notification about detention, the use of a measure of restraint in the form taking into custody, putting under house arrest

Foreigners, who are detained, taken in custody or put under house arrest, shall be notified without delay by the organ, that detained them or used a measure of restraint in the form of taking into custody or putting under house arrest, in a language that they understand about the reasons for their detention or using in respect of them the measure of restraint in the form of taking into custody or putting under house arrest and about the rights that they have according to the legislation of the Republic of Belarus.

The organ that detained a foreigner or used in respect of him the measure of restraint in the form of detention, house arrest, at the request of the foreigner, unless otherwise specified in legislative acts and international treaties of the Republic of Belarus, not later than one day as from the moment of detention or use in respect of him the measure of restraint in the form of taking into custody or putting under house arrest shall notify the Ministry for Foreign Affairs for further notifying the diplomatic mission or consular office of the State of citizenship or habitual residence of the foreigner, who was detained, taken into custody or put under house arrest.

The procedures of informing of the Ministry for Foreign Affairs about the detention of a foreigner or using in respect of him the measure of restraint in the form of taking into custody or putting under house arrest is determined by the Council of Ministers of the Republic of Belarus.

**Article 18.** Restriction of the rights and freedoms

Restrictions on the rights and freedoms of foreigners may be imposed only in the cases stipulated by this Law and other legislative acts of the Republic of Belarus, in the interests of national security of the Republic of Belarus, public order, for the protection of public morality, public health, rights and freedoms of citizens of the Republic of Belarus and other persons.

**Article 19.** Restriction of participation in elections and referenda

Foreigners cannot vote or be elected to elective State organs of the Republic of Belarus, as well as take part in referenda.

**Article 20.** Restriction on holding certain offices

Foreigners cannot hold offices, appointment to which, in accordance with the legislation of the Republic of Belarus is connected with belonging to the citizenship of the Republic of Belarus.

**Article 21.** Performance of military duty

Foreigners staying in the Republic of Belarus do not perform military duty.

**Article 22.** Compliance with the legislation of the Republic of Belarus and respect for its national traditions

Foreigners staying in the Republic of Belarus are obliged to observe the Constitution of the Republic of Belarus and other legislative acts of the Republic of Belarus, to respect its national traditions.

**Article 23.** Duty to register

Foreigners temporarily staying in the Republic of Belarus shall register themselves in the registration authorities in the manner prescribed by this Law, other legislative acts of the Republic of Belarus and the Rules of the Stay, unless otherwise specified in this Law.

**Article 24.** The duty of reimbursement for the upkeep of children

Foreigners staying temporarily, temporarily or permanently residing in Belarus are obliged to reimburse the costs spent by the Republic of Belarus for the upkeep of their children in public care, in the cases and according to the procedure specified by legislative acts of the Republic of Belarus.

**Article 25.** Duty to leave the Republic of Belarus

If there is no legal justification for continued stay in the Republic of Belarus foreigners must leave the Republic of Belarus by the end of the period of temporary residence or temporary residence or other periods provided in this Law.

**Article 26.** Responsibility of foreigners

Foreigners, who have committed on the territory of the Republic of Belarus a crime, administrative and other offences, shall bear responsibility in accordance with the legislative acts of the Republic of Belarus.

## CHAPTER 3 ENTRY INTO THE REPUBLIC OF BELARUS, EXIT FROM THE REPUBLIC OF BELARUS, TRANSIT PASSAGE (TRANSIT) THROUGH THE TERRITORY OF THE REPUBLIC OF BELARUS OF FOREIGNERS

**Article 27.** The Procedure for entry into the Republic of Belarus, exit from the Republic of Belarus, transit passage (transit) through the territory of the Republic of Belarus of foreigners

A foreigner may enter the Republic of Belarus, exit from the Republic of Belarus and conduct a transit passage (transit) through the territory of the Republic of Belarus by virtue of the document for travelling abroad with a visa, unless otherwise specified in this Law, other legislative acts and international treaties of the Republic of Belarus.

The President of the Republic of Belarus may establish a visa free entry regime of foreigners into the Republic of Belarus, their exit from the Republic of Belarus and the conduct of a transit passage (transit) through the territory of the Republic of Belarus.

**Article 28.** Visas

Visas are issued to foreigners by diplomatic missions or consular offices of the Republic of Belarus, the Ministry for Foreign affairs, the internal affairs organs, the organs of the Border Service of the Republic of Belarus (further - the organs of the Border Service), unless otherwise determined by legislation of the Republic of Belarus.

Types of visas and the procedure of their issue shall be determined by the Council of Ministers of the Republic of Belarus.

**Article 29.** Migration Card

A foreigner entering the Republic of Belarus shall fill out a migration card, which together with the document for travelling abroad shall be presented to an official of the organ of the Border Service at a checkpoint for passage through the State border.

When leaving the Republic of Belarus, a foreigner shall return the migration card to an official of the organ of the Border Service at a checkpoint for passage through the State border.

The official of a organ of the Border Service shall affix a marking onto the migration card certifying the entry of a foreigner into the Republic of Belarus and (or) a marking certifying his departure from the Republic of Belarus.

The form of the migration card and procedure of its use shall be determined by the Council of Ministers of the Republic of Belarus, unless otherwise determined by international treaties of the Republic of Belarus.

Legislative acts and international treaties of the Republic of Belarus may establish categories of foreigners, who are not required to fill out migration cards upon the entry into the Republic of Belarus and present them upon departure from the Republic of Belarus.

**Article 30.** Refusal of a visa for entry into the Republic of Belarus or refusal of entry into the Republic of Belarus

A foreigner may be refused a visa for entry into the Republic of Belarus or refused entry into the Republic of Belarus, if:

the foreigner at a checkpoint for passage through the State border has violated the rules of crossing the State border or customs regulations - until the violation is eliminated;

validity period of a document for travelling abroad does not exceed ninety days before the anticipated departure of a foreigner from the Republic of Belarus;

a foreigner is convicted in the Republic of Belarus or any other State for committing an offence recognised as such in accordance with the Criminal Code of the Republic of Belarus and the conviction has been cleared or settled;

the foreigner during his stay in the Republic of Belarus has repeatedly (twice or more) in the course of one year been brought to administrative responsibility and the period not expired, at the end of which he is not considered as being subjected to administrative penalty;

the foreigner subjected during his stay in the Republic of Belarus to an administrative penalty in the form of a fine, who failed to pay it within the period stipulated by legislative acts of the Republic of Belarus for the execution of the order to impose an administrative penalty in the form of a fine;

the foreigner cannot confirm the availability of the cash assets needed to cover the costs of his stay in the Republic of Belarus and exit from the Republic of Belarus, or submit assurances of presentation of such cash assets in the manner and the amount established by the Council of Ministers;

during the previous stay of the foreigner in the Republic of Belarus has expired the period of temporary stay provided for in the first and second parts of Article 39 of this Law;

there are reasonable grounds to assume that the foreigner may avoid leaving the Republic of Belarus at the end of the period of temporary stay or temporary residence;

the stay of the foreigner in the Republic of Belarus contradicts the interests of national security of the Republic of Belarus, public order, protection of morality, public health, rights and freedoms of citizens of the Republic of Belarus and other persons;

in respect of the foreigner in accordance with an international treaty of the Republic of Belarus by an authorized authority of a foreign State or an international organization there has been taken a decision to restrict his rights to enter the territory of the States-members of the international treaty or the States-members of the organization.

The foreigner is refused to be granted a visa for entry into the Republic of Belarus, except for the case provided for in the third part of this article, or the foreigner is refused an entry into the Republic of Belarus, if:

upon submitting to the relevant State organs of the Republic of Belarus of the documents necessary for obtaining a visa for entry into the Republic of Belarus or taking a decision on his entry into the Republic of Belarus, the foreigner provided false information, submitted documents and (or) information that are not conforming to the requirements of the legislation of the Republic of Belarus, including fraudulent, counterfeit or invalid documents;

the foreigner is included in the list of persons, whose entry into the Republic of Belarus is prohibited or undesirable;

the Republic of Belarus has proclaimed the foreigner inadmissible or undesirable (persona non grata);

there is the evidence available that the foreigner is or was a person carrying out an extremist, including terrorist, activities, was or is connected to extremist, including terrorist, smuggling, and (or) other activities aimed at harming the national security of the Republic of Belarus, to the illicit trade in arms, ammunition or explosives, illicit trafficking of narcotic drugs, psychotropic substances and their precursors, illegal migration of foreigners, human trafficking;

the foreigner, who is subject to compulsory health insurance in accordance with the legislative acts of the Republic of Belarus, does not have a compulsory health insurance contract with a Belarusian insurance organization or a health insurance contract entered into with a foreign insurance organization, valid on the territory of the Republic of Belarus;

the foreigner has a disease that is included in the list of diseases that pose danger to public health.

A visa for entry into the Republic of Belarus may be issued to a foreigner, who is subject to mandatory health insurance in accordance with the legislative acts of the Republic of Belarus, in the case of impossibility of the conclusion by the foreigner of the contract of compulsory medical insurance with the Belarusian insurance organization or the health insurance contract with the foreign insurance organization, valid on the territory of the Republic of Belarus.

If a decision was taken to refuse entry into the Republic of Belarus, the visa previously issued to the foreigner for the entrance into the Republic of Belarus shall be cancelled.

On the basis of the decision to refuse entry into the Republic of Belarus the foreigner in accordance with order established by the legislation of the Republic of Belarus may be included in the list of persons, whose entry into the Republic of Belarus is prohibited or undesirable.

**Article 31.** The State organs empowered to take decisions on refusal of issuing visas for entrance into the Republic of Belarus, on refusal of entrance into the Republic of Belarus and on cancellation of the visa for entrance into the Republic of Belarus

The decision to refuse issuing a visa for entrance into the Republic of Belarus may be taken by the Ministry for Foreign Affairs, the diplomatic mission or consular office of the Republic of Belarus, the organ of the Border Service.

The decision to refuse entry into the Republic of Belarus may be taken by a organ of the Border Service, organ of Internal Affairs or State security of the Republic of Belarus (hereinafter - the organ of State security).

The State organs that have taken a decision to refuse entry to the Republic of Belarus have the right to permit the foreigner to enter the Republic of Belarus for a term not exceeding one month in the manner prescribed by the Council of Ministers of the Republic of Belarus.

The decision to cancel a visa for entry into the Republic of Belarus shall be adopted by the Ministry for Foreign Affairs, the diplomatic mission or consular office of the Republic of Belarus before the entry of the foreigner into the Republic of Belarus or by the organ of the Border Service on the basis of the decision on refusal of entry into the Republic of Belarus.

The organs, which have taken decisions on refusal of issuing visas for entrance into the Republic of Belarus, on refusal of entrance into the Republic of Belarus and on cancellation of the visa for entrance into the Republic of Belarus, are not obliged to inform the foreigner, his relatives or representatives about the grounds for taking such decisions.

**Article 32.** List of persons whose entry into the Republic of Belarus is prohibited or undesirable

Terms and conditions of inclusion of foreigners in the list of persons, whose entry into the Republic of Belarus is prohibited or undesirable, and exclusion of foreigners from this list, as well as the order of keeping of such a list shall be determined by the Council of Ministers of the Republic of Belarus.

**Article 33.** Refusal to issue a visa for exit from the Republic of Belarus or refusal of the permission to leave the Republic of Belarus

A foreigner may be refused a visa to exit from the Republic of Belarus or refused the permission to leave the Republic of Belarus, if:

he is a suspect or accused in a criminal case - until the cessation of the criminal prosecution or until the entry of the sentence into legal force;

he was sentenced in the Republic of Belarus for the committing of a crime, except for convicted without establishing a punishment or a penalty in the form of deprivation of the right to occupy certain positions or engage in certain activities, - until the completion of sentence or remission of the punishment, or before the expiration of the term of a stay of execution of punishment or probation;

he has not fulfilled without reasonable excuse property, tax or other obligations to the Republic of Belarus, its administrative and territorial units, individuals and legal entities established by a legally effective court orders or writs of execution - until the performance of the obligations;

he has been brought it is in accordance with the legislative acts of the Republic of Belarus to administrative responsibility in the territory of the Republic of Belarus - until dismissal of the case on an administrative offence or enforcement of an administrative penalty;

he has debts in respect of a tax obligation established by the legislative acts of the Republic of Belarus - until the payment of the debt;

his departure is contrary to the national security interests of the Republic of Belarus - until the expiry of the circumstances preventing the exit;

it is included in the list of persons who are denied exit from the Republic of Belarus.

If a decision to refuse the exit from the Republic of Belarus, the visa previously issued to the foreigner for exit from the Republic of Belarus shall be cancelled.

On the basis of the decision to refuse the exit from the Republic of Belarus a foreigner in the manner prescribed by the legislation of the Republic of Belarus may be included in the list of persons, who are denied the exit from the Republic of Belarus.

**Article 34.** Organs that are empowered to take a decision on the refusal of issuing a visa for exit from the Republic of Belarus, on the refusal of the exit from the Republic of Belarus and the cancellation of a visa for exit from the Republic of Belarus

The decision to refuse issuing a visa fr exit from the Republic of Belarus shall taken by an organ of the internal affairs.

Decisions on refusal of the exit from the Republic of Belarus of the foreigners referred to in the second, third, fifth, seventh and eighth paragraphs of the first part of Article 33 of this Law shall be taken by an organ of the Border Service, an organ of internal affairs or an organ of State security on its own or at the request of the appropriate State organs of the Republic of Belarus.

Decisions on refusal of the exit from the Republic of Belarus of the foreigners referred to in fourth and sixth paragraphs of the first part of Article 33 of this Law shall be taken by an organ of internal affairs at the request of the appropriate State organs of the Republic of Belarus.

A decision to cancel a visa for the exit from the Republic of Belarus shall be taken by an organ of the Border Service or an organ of internal affairs.

Decisions on the refusal to issue a visa for the exit from the Republic of Belarus, on the refusal of the exit from the Republic of Belarus adopted in respect of foreigners temporarily staying or temporarily residing in the Republic of Belarus shall constitute the grounds for providing them with an extension of the period of temporary stay for a time required to eliminate the grounds for refusal to issue the visa for the exit from the Republic of Belarus or refusal of the exit from the Republic of Belarus.

**Article 35.** The list of persons who are denied exit from the Republic of Belarus

Rules of inclusion of foreigners in the list of persons who are denied exit from the Republic of Belarus, and exclusion of foreigners from this list, as well as the order of keeping of such a list shall be determined by the Council of Ministers of the Republic of Belarus.

**Article 36.** Documents for the exit from the Republic of Belarus and (or) entry into the Republic of Belarus

Foreigners may be granted documents for exiting the Republic of Belarus and (or) entry into the Republic of Belarus.

Categories of foreigners who have given papers to leave the Republic of Belarus and (or) entry into the Republic of Belarus, the types of documents and the order of their issuance, use, sharing, invalidation, withdrawal, storage, destruction, defined by laws of the Republic of Belarus.

**Article 37.** Transit passage (transit) of foreigners through the territory of the Republic of Belarus

Transit passage (transit) of foreigners through the territory of the Republic of Belarus is performed within a period not exceeding two days from the date of their entry into the Republic of Belarus, except for the cases of a forced stop, in accordance with the Rules of transit passage (transit) of foreign citizens and stateless persons through the territory of the Republic of Belarus, approved by the Council of Ministers of the Republic of Belarus.

As a forced stop shall be recognized temporary stay of foreigners on the territory of the Republic of Belarus for more than two days from the date of its entry into the Republic of Belarus due to:

natural disasters, accidents and other emergencies of natural or man-triggered character, delaying the movement of the vehicle;

need to repair the damaged vehicle;

disease or health condition, if according to a conclusion of a public health organisation of the Republic of Belarus the further travel of the foreigner and (or) the person travelling with him may pose a hazard to their life and health;

unanticipated delays in transfers from one mode of transport to another at the transfer point,

occurrence of other unforeseen circumstances that prevent the further travel of the foreigner.

In the case of a forced stop the extension of a foreigner term sojourn in the Republic of Belarus, the issuance of visa to leave the Republic of Belarus conducted by the internal affairs of the place of a forced stop on the application of a foreigner, his representative or the person next in conjunction with it.

## CHAPTER 4 STAY OF FOREIGNERS IN THE REPUBLIC OF BELARUS

**Article 38.** Regimes of stay of foreigners in the Republic of Belarus

Foreigners may stay temporarily, temporarily and permanently reside in the Republic of Belarus.

The procedure of temporary stay, temporary and permanent residence of foreigners in the Republic of Belarus established by this Law and other legislative acts of the Republic of Belarus.

**Article 39**. Temporary stay of foreigners in the Republic of Belarus

The time of temporary stay in the Republic of Belarus of a foreigner is determined by the validity term of the visa issued to him and may not exceed ninety days in a calendar year from the date of first entry into the Republic of Belarus, unless otherwise specified in this Law and international treaties of the Republic of Belarus.

The time of temporary stay in the Republic of Belarus of a foreigner, who arrived in the Republic of Belarus in a manner not requiring obtaining a visa, may not exceed ninety days in a calendar year from the date of first entry into the Republic of Belarus, unless otherwise specified in this Law and international treaties of the Republic of Belarus.

A foreigner temporarily staying in Belarus shall leave the Republic of Belarus before his visa expires or within the claimed by him period of temporary stay in the Republic of Belarus, if at the moment of the expiry of the mentioned periods the period of temporary stay of the foreigner is not extended or the temporary residence stay or not to obtain a temporary residence permit or a permit for permanent residence.

Lodging by a foreigner a complaint against the decisions of State bodies or officials of the Republic of Belarus on reducing the period of temporary stay in the Republic of Belarus, on the refusal to grant a temporary residence permit or to revoke the temporary residence permit, on the refusal to grant a permit for permanent residence or to revoke a permit for permanent residence to a superior State organ, a higher-ranking official within the time limit established by this Law for the departure of the foreigner from the Republic of Belarus or to the court after appeal of such decisions to a superior State organ, the higher-ranking official is the grounds for an extension of the temporary stay in the Republic of Belarus of the foreigner, who has lodged a complaint, for the time of consideration of the complaint.

**Article 40.** Extension of a period of temporary stay of foreigners in the Republic of Belarus

In the event of occurrence of the circumstances involving the need to extend the period of stay of a foreigner in the Republic of Belarus, the temporary stay may be extended within the limits of the period provided for in the first and second parts of Article 39 of this Law.

In case of illness, natural disasters or other unforeseen circumstances preventing the departure of a foreigner from the Republic of Belarus, the temporary stay may be extended beyond the time limit provided for in the first and second parts of Article 39 of this Law, until the cessation of these circumstances.

If the validity term of a visa issued to a foreigner has expired, upon the extension of temporary stay a visa for exit from the Republic of Belarus shall be issued to the foreigner.

Upon application for a permit for temporary or permanent residence the period of temporary stay of the foreigner in the Republic of Belarus may be extended for the period of consideration of the application.

In case of adoption of a decision on the extension of temporary stay in the Republic of Belarus the period of registration of a foreigner shall also be extended.

State bodies and other organizations of the Republic of Belarus, to which a foreigner may apply for extension of the period of temporary stay (registration), documents required for extension of the period of temporary stay (registration), a period of extension, as well as the amount of the charge levied for extension of the period of temporary stay (registration) are determined by legislative acts of the Republic of Belarus.

**Article 41.** The procedure for registration of foreigners temporarily staying in the Republic of Belarus

Foreigners, who have arrived in the Republic of Belarus, except for foreigners referred to in Article 45 of this Law, shall within five days, except for weekends, public holidays and holidays established

and declared by the President of the Republic of Belarus as legal holidays, register at the registration authority at the place of the actual temporary stay, unless otherwise specified by this Law and international treaties of the Republic of Belarus.

Foreigners temporarily staying in the Republic of Belarus are required to reside in the Republic of Belarus only at the place of temporary stay, where they are registered in the registration authorities, except for the foreigners specified in part four of this Article.

Upon a change of a place of temporary stay foreigners shall within five days, except for weekends, public holidays and holidays established and declared by the President of the Republic of Belarus as legal holidays, register at the registration authority at the new place of the temporary stay, except for the foreigners specified in part four of this Article.

Foreigners, who have arrived in Belarus for the purposes of tourism and who are travelling within the territory of the Republic of Belarus in accordance with the program of the tour, shall registered in the registration authority at the place of their initial temporary stay for the total duration of the tour.

Registration of foreigners temporarily staying in the Republic of Belarus in the registration authorities shall be performed on the basis of applications of the foreigners or requests of the host organizations.

Temporarily staying in the Republic of Belarus citizens (nationals) of the States with a visa regime for entry into the Republic of Belarus shall be registered for the time period specified in their application or request of the host organization, but no more than for the validity period of the visa.

Temporarily staying in the Republic of Belarus citizens (nationals) of the States with a visa-free regime for entry into the Republic of Belarus shall be registered for the time period not exceeding the period, specified by an international treaty of the Republic of Belarus. In the absence of such an international treaty of the Republic of Belarus or the absence in the international treaty of indication of the period of the visa-free stay, the registration shall be effected for the period specified in the application of the foreigner or the request of the host organization, but not more than for ninety days in a calendar year as from the date of the first entry into the Republic of Belarus.

Foreigners, temporarily staying in the Republic of Belarus, in respect of whom a decision on the extension of the period of temporary stay in the Republic of Belarus is adopted, shall be registered for the period of the extension of temporary stay.

A foreigner, who lodged a complaint against decisions of State organs or officials of the Republic of Belarus on reducing the period of temporary stay in the Republic of Belarus, on refusing to issue a temporary residence permit or on cancellation of the temporary residence permit, on the refusal to issue a permanent residence permit or cancellation of the permanent residence permit, on the refusal to issue a visa for the exit from the Republic of Belarus or on refusal of the permission to leave the Republic of Belarus to the superior State organ or a court within the time limit established by this Law for the departure of the foreigner from the Republic of Belarus, shall register in the registration authority at the place of the actual temporary stay for the period until the adoption of a decision on the complaint.

In the case of the adoption of a decision to cancel the temporary residence permit or permanent residence permit a foreigner shall be registered for the period provided for in this Law for the departure of the foreigner from the Republic of Belarus.

In the case of the adoption of a decision to reduce the period of temporary stay of a foreigner in the Republic of Belarus the period of his registration is reduced down to the period provided for in this Law for the departure of the foreigner from the Republic of Belarus.

State agencies and other organizations of the Republic of Belarus, to which a foreigner may apply for registration, the documents required for registration, the registration period, as well as the fees charged for registration are determined by legislative acts of the Republic of Belarus.

**Article 42.** Registration of foreigners temporarily staying in the Republic of Belarus in organs of internal affairs

In the organs of the internal affairs shall be registered foreigners temporarily staying in the Republic of Belarus, except for the foreigners referred to in Article 43 and the first and third parts of Article 44 of this Law.

**Article 43.** Registration of foreigners temporarily staying in the Republic of Belarus in a hotel, sanatorium-resort or wellness organizations

In hotels, sanatorium-resort and wellness organizations shall be registered foreigners temporarily staying in the Republic of Belarus, who have checked-in for residence in them, except for foreigners specified in parts one and three of Article 44 of this Law.

Authorized persons of hotels, sanatorium-resort and wellness organizations within one day after check-in of foreigners temporarily staying in the Republic of Belarus shall submit to an organ of internal affairs at the location of hotels, sanatorium-resort and wellness organizations information about such foreigners in the manner determined by the Ministry for Internal Affairs.

**Article 44.** Registration of foreigners temporarily residing in the Republic of Belarus in the Ministry for Foreign Affairs

In the Ministry for Foreign Affairs shall be registered guests of accredited by the Ministry for Foreign Affairs heads of diplomatic missions and consular institutions of foreign

States, missions and organs of international organizations and intergovernmental entities, if these guests live in the residences of

the heads or in premises of the mentioned missions, institutions, organs or in residential premises occupied by their employees.

In the case of residence of foreigners referred to in the first paragraph of this Article outside the residences of the heads or the premises of diplomatic missions and consular institutions of foreign States, missions and organs of international organizations and intergovernmental entities or residential premises occupied by their employees, the registration of these foreigners shall be performed according to the procedure set forth in Article 41 of this Law.

The Ministry for Foreign Affairs has the right to register of arriving to the Republic of Belarus State and public figures of foreign States and members of their families, as well as employees of international organizations and intergovernmental entities not listed in Article 45 of this Law, at the request of the diplomatic missions and consular institutions of foreign States, the host organizations.

**Article 45.** Foreigners temporarily staying in the Republic of Belarus, who are not subject to the registration in the Republic of Belarus

In the Republic of Belarus are not subject to the registration:

Heads of State and Governments of foreign States, heads and members of parliamentary, governmental and other official delegations, the technical staff of these delegations and foreigners, who arrived in the Republic of Belarus at the invitation of the President of the Republic of Belarus, the Chambers of the National Assembly of the Republic of Belarus, the Council of Ministers of the Republic of Belarus, the Constitutional Court of the Republic of Belarus, the Supreme Court of the Republic of Belarus, the Supreme Economic Court of the Republic of Belarus, the Administration of the President of the Republic of Belarus, the State Secretariat of the Security Council of the Republic of Belarus, the State Control Committee of the Republic of Belarus, the Attorney-General Office of the Republic of Belarus, the Central Commission of of the Republic of Belarus for Conduct of Elections and Republican Referenda, Republican organs of State administration, local executive and administrative organs of the Republic of Belarus, as well as their family members;

foreigners, who have arrived in Belarus by virtue of passports issued by the United Nations Organization;

heads and staff of diplomatic missions and consular institutions of foreign States, employees of the military attaches' offices, members of trade representations of foreign States in the Republic of Belarus, as well as members of their families;

heads and staff of missions and organs of international organizations and intergovernmental entities, who according to statutory documents of these organizations and entities or appropriate international treaties of the Republic of Belarus, shall enjoy the privileges and immunities, as well as members of their families;

foreigners, who have arrived in Belarus for the weekends, public holidays and holidays, established and declared by the President of the Republic of Belarus as legal holidays, and (or) for up to five

twenty-four hours during working days, if their departure from the Republic of Belarus will be performed during these days (twenty-four hours);

foreigners temporarily staying in the countryside, small towns of the Republic of Belarus on the basis of contracts for services in the field of rural and environmental tourism, concluded with an individual or peasant (farmer) household involved in such activities in accordance with the order established by legislative acts of the Republic of Belarus (hereinafter - the subjects of rural and environmental tourism), either on the basis of contracts for providing tourist services, in which services in the field of rural and environmental tourism are included;

crew members of foreign military aircrafts arriving in the Republic of Belarus according to the established order;

foreigners who are members of crews of civil aircrafts servicing international airlines, trains brigades of international rail transport, while staying in the airport or at the stations listed in a flight or train schedule;

foreigners who are members of crews of foreign vehicles and river transport performing the carriage of cargo and passengers in international traffic, while staying in towns and other settlements on the routes of transport operations, including those in other points of destinations.

foreigners who are referred to in fourth and fifth paragraphs of the first part of this article are subject to accreditation in the manner determined by the Ministry for Foreign Affairs.

foreigners, who are referred to in paragraph seven of the first part of this article, shall present to the official of an organ of the the Border Service upon leaving the Republic of Belarus a contract for provision of services in the field of rural and environmental tourism or contract for providing tourist services, in which services in the field of rural and environmental tourism are included;.

Subjects of rural and environmental tourism within one day after the arrival of foreigners referred to in paragraph seven of the first part of this Article shall submit to an organ of internal affairs at their location information on those foreigners in the manner established by the Ministry of Internal Affairs.

**Article 46.** Refusal of registration, extension and (or) reduction of the period of temporary stay in the Republic of Belarus

Registration and extension of temporary stay in the Republic of Belarus may be denied to a foreigner, and (or) the period of his stay in the Republic of Belarus may be reduced, if the grounds set forth in the first part of Article 30 of this Law are discovered.

A foreigner shall be denied the registration, the period of the temporary stay in the Republic of Belarus of the foreigner shall not be extended, and (or) shall be reduced:

if the grounds set out in the second part of Article 30 of this Law have been discovered;

if upon submitting to the relevant State organs of the Republic of Belarus of documents required for adoption of decision on registration, extension of the period of temporary stay in the Republic of Belarus a foreigner provided false information, submitted documents and (or) information that do not comply with the requirements of the legislation of the Republic of Belarus, including fraudulent, counterfeit or invalid documents;

if there are no grounds for his further stay in the Republic of Belarus;

in the case of deportation or expulsion of the foreigner.

In the case of adoption of decisions to refuse registration, extension and (or) to reduce the period of temporary stay in the Republic of Belarus the validity term of the visa issued to a foreigner, and (or) the period of his temporary stay shall be reduced, if there is no legitimate grounds for his further stay in the Republic of Belarus.

In the case, where the period of temporary stay in the Republic of Belarus has been reduced, and there is no other legitimate grounds for further stay in the Republic of Belarus, the foreigner shall leave the Republic of Belarus within ten days from the date of receipt by him of a notice about the adopted decision on reduction of the period of his temporary stay.

**Article 47.** Decision-makers to extend the period of temporary stay in the Republic of Belarus and the refusal of registration, extension and (or) reducing the period of temporary stay in the Republic of Belarus

Decisions on the extension of temporary stay of foreigners in the Republic of Belarus within the period provided for first and second parts of Article 39 of this Law shall be adopted by the registration authority and in respect of the citizens (nationals) of the visa regime of entry to the Republic of Belarus - an organ of internal affairs.

The decision to extend the temporary stay of foreigners in the Republic of Belarus over the period provided first and second parts of Article 39 of this Law, taken by the authority of the Interior.

Decisions to refuse registration, extension and (or) to reduce the period of temporary stay of foreigners in the Republic of Belarus shall be adopted:

in respect of foreigners subject to registration or accreditation, or registered or accredited by the Ministry for Foreign Affairs, as well as declared by the Republic of Belarus unacceptable or undesirable (persona non grata) - by the Ministry for Foreign Affairs;

in respect of other foreigners - by a organ of internal affairs independently or at the request of the appropriate State organs of the Republic of Belarus.

**Article 48.** Temporary residence permit

A temporary residence permit shall be issued to foreigners:

if they arrived in Belarus for receiving education or are studying on the territory of the Republic of Belarus in the institutions providing professional and vocational, specialized secondary, high and postgraduate education, advanced vocational training and retraining - for a period of study, but not more than for one year;

if they are spouses, close relatives of citizens of the Republic of Belarus or foreigners permanently residing in the Republic of Belarus - for the whole period of stay, but not more than for one year;

if they arrived in the Republic of Belarus for engaging or engaged in labour, entrepreneurial and (or) any other activity on the territory of Belarus in accordance with the legislation of Belarus - for the period of stay, but not more than for one year;

in respect of whom is established guardianship (trusteeship) of citizens of the Republic of Belarus , as well as foreigners permanently residing in the Republic of Belarus - for the period of guardianship (trusteeship), but not more than for one year;

if they are ethnic Belarusians or their blood relatives in the direct line of descent: children, grandchildren, great-grandchildren, who were born outside of the contemporary territory of the Republic of Belarus - for the whole period of stay, but not more than for one year;

if they have grounds to acquire the citizenship of the Republic of Belarus in the manner of registration - for the period of stay, but not more than for one year;

if they formerly were citizens of the Republic of Belarus - for the period of stay, but not more than for one year;

if they own residential premises in the Republic of Belarus - for the period of stay, but not more than for one year;

if they have applied in the manner established by the legislation of the Republic of Belarus for refugee status, additional protection or asylum in the Republic of Belarus - for the time of consideration of the application;

if they are granted refugee status in the Republic of Belarus - for the period not exceeding one year for obtaining of a permanent residence permit;

if they are given additional protection in the Republic of Belarus - for the period of provision of the additional protection, but not more than for one year;

if they cannot in accordance with the legislation of the Republic of Belarus be returned or expelled against their will onto the territory of a State, where their life or freedom would be endangered because of their race, religion, citizenship, nationality, belonging to a particular social group or political views, or where they are threatened with torture, or if there is no State, which has

consented to receive them, - for the period, during which the return or expulsion is impossible, but not more than for one year;

if they receive medical care as in-patient in a public health care organizations of the Republic of Belarus - for the period of treatment, but not more than for one year;

on other grounds provided by the legislation of the Republic of Belarus, including international treaties of the Republic of Belarus.

A temporary residence permit may be issued to family members (husband (wife), children, children adopted as sons (as daughters) under the age of eighteen years, persons under care) of a foreigner, who has received a temporary residence permit, if there is a legitimate source of receiving an income, providing him and his family a minimum subsistence wage established in the Republic of Belarus for the period of temporary residence in the Republic of Belarus.

A foreigner temporarily residing in the Republic of Belarus shall reside in the Republic of Belarus only at the place of temporary residence, at which he was issued a temporary residence permit.

Upon a change of a place of temporary residence a foreigner temporarily residing in the Republic of Belarus shall within five days, except for weekends, public holidays and holidays established and declared by the President of the Republic of Belarus as legal holidays, apply to an organ of internal affairs at a new place of temporary residence for making changes in the temporary residence permit.

State organs of the Republic of Belarus, to which a foreigner may apply for issuance of a temporary residence permit, documents needed for issuing the temporary residence permit, period of its issue and its validity period, as well as the charges levied for issuing the temporary residence permit are determined by legislative acts of the Republic Belarus.

A foreigner temporarily residing in the Republic of Belarus shall leave the Republic of Belarus before the expiration of the validity period of a temporary residence permit, if on the date of expiry of the mentioned period he failed to register for temporary stay or obtain a new temporary residence permit or permanent residence permit.

**Article 49.** Refusal to issue a temporary residence permit

Issuing of a temporary residence permit to a foreigner may be refused, where:

the grounds set out in the first part of Article 30 of this Law have been discovered;

the stated purpose of entry into the Republic of Belarus of the foreigner, who is a citizen (national) of the State having problems in respect of migration, is another than the ground, on the basis of which he applied for a temporary residence permit;

A temporary residence permit shall not issued to a foreigner, where:

the grounds set out in the second part of Article 30 of this Law have been discovered;

upon submitting to the relevant authorities of the Republic of Belarus of documents required for the adoption of a decision on issuing him a temporary residence permit, the foreigner provided false information, submitted documents and (or) information that are not conforming to the requirement of the legislation of the Republic of Belarus, including fraudulent, counterfeit or invalid documents;

there are no grounds for his temporary residence in the Republic of Belarus;

upon submitting to the relevant State organs of the Republic of Belarus of documents required for the adoption of the decision to issue temporary residence permits to family members of a foreigner, he could not provide evidence of his ability to support himself and his family members (husband (wife), children, children adopted as sons (as daughters) under the age of eighteen years, persons under care) in the Republic of Belarus within a minimum subsistence wage for the period of temporary residence in the Republic of Belarus, except for the case, where the foreigner is recognized disabled.

In the case of the adoption of a decision to refuse issuing a temporary residence permit the validity period of the visa issued to a foreigner, and (or) the period of registration and temporary stay shall be reduced, if there are no legitimate reason for his further stay in the Republic of Belarus.

An foreigner, in respect of whom a decision on refusal of issuing a temporary residence permit has been taken, unless there are other legitimate reasons for his further stay in the Republic of Belarus, is obliged to leave the Republic of Belarus within fifteen days from the date of receiving a notice of the decision to refuse issuing the temporary residence permit.

**Article 50.** Cancellation of a temporary residence permit

A temporary residence permit of a foreigner may be cancelled, if:

the grounds set out in the first part of Article 30 of this Law have been discovered;

a foreigner is exiting or has exited from the Republic of Belarus to a foreign State for permanent residence.

A temporary residence permit of a foreigner shall be cancelled:

if the grounds set out in the second part of Article 30 of this Law have been discovered;

where there is evidence that, upon submitting to the relevant State organs of the Republic of Belarus of the documents required for adoption of a decision on issuing him a temporary residence permit, the foreigner provided false information, submitted documents and (or) information that are not conforming to the requirements of the legislation of the Republic of Belarus, including fraudulent, counterfeit or invalid documents;

in case of deportation or expulsion of the foreigner;

in the case of expiry of the ground, in accordance with which the decision to grant a foreigner a temporary residence permit was taken.

In the case of the adoption of a decision to cancel a temporary residence permit the validity period of the visa issued to the foreigner shall be reduced, if there are no legitimate reason for his further stay in the Republic of Belarus.

If a temporary residence permit issued to a foreigner, was cancelled and there are no other legitimate grounds for his stay in the Republic of Belarus, the foreigner shall leave the Republic of Belarus within fifteen days from the date of receiving a notice of the adopted decision to cancel the temporary residence permit, if another period is not set by the legislative acts of the Republic of Belarus regulating the particulars of the legal status of the foreigners applying for the refugee status or additional protection in the Republic of Belarus, as well as foreigners, who are granted the refugee status or additional or temporary protection in the Republic of Belarus.

A foreigner, whose temporary residence permit is cancelled on the grounds specified in the first part and paragraphs two, three and five of the second part of this Article, shall register with the registration authority at the place of the actual temporary residence for the period up to the departure from the Republic of Belarus.

**Article 51.** Organs taking decisions on issuing a temporary residence permit, on refusal of issuing and cancellation of the temporary residence permit

A decision to issue a temporary residence permit shall be taken by an organ of internal affairs.

Decisions to refuse issuing and cancellation of a temporary residence permit shall be taken by an organ of internal affairs independently or at the request of the appropriate State organs of the Republic of Belarus.

**Article 52.** The document certifying in the Republic of Belarus the identity of a foreigner temporarily staying or temporarily residing in the Republic of Belarus

The document certifying in the Republic of Belarus the identity of a foreigner temporarily staying or temporarily residing in the Republic of Belarus, except for foreigners, who are granted the refugee status in the Republic of Belarus, is a document for travelling abroad.

**Article 53.** Permanent residence permit

A permanent residence permit shall be issued to the foreigners, who:

are close relatives of citizens of the Republic of Belarus permanently residing in the Republic of Belarus;

are persons, to whom a refugee status or asylum in the Republic of Belarus is granted;

have the right to family reunification;

have lived legally in the Republic of Belarus for the last seven years or more;

have the grounds to acquire the citizenship of the Republic of Belarus in the manner of registration;

held earlier the citizenship of the Republic of Belarus;

are workers and professionals who are needed for organizations of the Republic of Belarus;

possess exceptional abilities and talent, or have outstanding merits before the Republic of Belarus, the high achievements in the spheres of science, technology, culture and sports;

are the foreign investors that have made investments in the amount not less than one hundred and fifty thousand Euro in objects of investment activities in the territory of the Republic of Belarus;

are ethnic Belarusians or their blood relatives in the direct line of descent: children, grandchildren, great-grandchildren who were born outside the contemporary territory of the Republic of Belarus.

A permanent residence permit may be issued to other foreigners, who are not mentioned in the first part of this article, on the basis of a decision of the Council of Ministers of the Republic of Belarus in consultation with the President of the Republic of Belarus.

The procedure for issuing foreigners with permanent residence permits is determined by the legislative acts of the Republic of Belarus and resolutions of the Council of Ministers of the Republic of Belarus.

Procedure of registration of foreigners permanently residing in the Republic of Belarus and de-registration of them at the place of residence and place of stay in the Republic of Belarus is determined by the legislative acts of the Republic of Belarus.

**Article 54.** Immigration quota

For the purposes of State regulation of entry of foreigners for permanent residence in the Republic of Belarus the Council of Ministers of the Republic of Belarus may establish an immigration quota, which is determined separately for each State.

Foreigners having the right to family reunification may enter for permanent residence into the Republic of Belarus for the purposes of joint residence and doing the joint housekeeping beyond the established immigration quota.

The President of the Republic of Belarus may take decisions on the admission of foreigners for permanent residence into the Republic of Belarus in excess of the established immigration quota.

**Article 55**. The right to family reunification

The right to family reunification belongs to a husband (wife), minor children and children adopted as sons (as daughters), and not been married and sole children and children adopted as sons (as daughters) over eighteen years, disabled parents and adoptive parents having an invitation respectively from a husband (wife), parents, children, children adopted as sons (as daughters), being citizens of the Republic of Belarus or foreigners permanently residing in the Republic of Belarus.

In some cases the right to family reunification may be granted to other relatives of citizens of the Republic of Belarus and to foreigners permanently residing in the Republic of Belarus, not mentioned in the first part of this Article, on the condition of availability to the inviting person or the foreigner, who have applied for issuance of a permanent residence permit, of adequate housing, as well as the availability to the inviting person of a legitimate source of receiving income providing him and his family members (husband (wife), children, children adopted as sons (as daughters) under the age of eighteen years, persons under care) and the foreigner, who has applied for issuance of the permanent residence permit, a minimum subsistence wage established in the Republic of Belarus for the period of consideration of the application.

In the case of family reunification the foreigner, who has applied for the issuance of a permanent residence permit in the Republic of Belarus or the person inviting him or a person are required to submit the documents proving the right to family reunification.

**Article 56.** Refusal to issue a permanent residence permit

Issuance of a permanent residence permit to a foreigner may be refused, if:

the grounds provided for in paragraphs fourth, fifth or tenth of the first part of Article 30 of this Law have been discovered;

the stated purpose of entry into the Republic of Belarus of the foreigner, who is a citizen (national) of the State having problems in respect of migration, is another than the ground, on the basis of which he applied for a permanent residence permit;

the established immigration quota has been exhausted.

A permanent residence permit shall not be issued to a foreigner, if:

the grounds provided for in paragraphs the second - the fifth or the seventh of the second paragraph of Article 30 of this Law are discovered;

upon submitting to the relevant State organs of the Republic of Belarus of the documents necessary for taking a decision on issuance to him of the permanent residence permit, the foreigner provided false information, submitted documents and (or) information that are not conforming to the requirements of the legislation of the Republic of Belarus, including fraudulent, counterfeit or invalid documents;

there are no grounds for his permanent residence in the Republic of Belarus;

there are documents and (or) information available confirming that the marriage with a citizen of the Republic of Belarus or a foreigner permanently residing in the Republic of Belarus was effected by the foreigner solely for the purposes of obtain a permanent residence permit.

In the case of the adoption of a decision to refuse issuing a permanent residence permit the validity period of the visa issued to a foreigner, and (or) the period of registration and temporary stay shall be reduced, if there are no legitimate reason for his further stay in the Republic of Belarus.

The list of documents and (or) information provided for in the fifth paragraph of part two of this Article and the procedure of their receipt by the organs of internal affairs shall be determined by the Council of Ministers of the Republic of Belarus.

An foreigner, in respect of whom a decision on refusal of issuing a permanent residence permit has been taken, unless there are other legitimate reasons for his further stay in the Republic of Belarus, is obliged to leave the Republic of Belarus within one month from the date of receiving a notice of the decision to refuse issuing the permanent residence permit.

**Article 57.** Cancellation of permanent residence permit

A permanent residence permit issued to the foreigner may be cancelled, if:

the grounds provided for in paragraphs fourth, fifth or tenth of the first part of Article 30 of this Law have been discovered;

the foreigner has obtained a permanent residence permit in a foreign State;

the grounds, in accordance with which the decision to grant the foreigner a permanent residence permit was taken, have expired.

the foreigner resided outside the Republic of Belarus for more than one hundred eighty-three days in a calendar year;

the foreigner and his family members (husband (wife), children, children adopted as sons (as daughters) under the age of eighteen years, persons under care) permanently residing in the Republic of Belarus have no legitimate source of receiving income that provides him and his family members with the minimum subsistence wage established in the Republic of Belarus for a period longer than six months in a calendar year.

A permanent residence permit issued to the foreigner shall be cancelled:

if the grounds set out in the paragraphs from two to five of the second part of Article 30 of this Law have been discovered;

if a marriage concluded by the foreigner with a Belarusian citizen or a foreigner permanently residing in the Republic of Belarus and served as the basis or issuing a permanent residence permit was recognized null and void in the manner prescribed by legislative acts of the Republic of Belarus;

where there is evidence that, upon submitting to the relevant State organs of the Republic of Belarus of the documents required for adoption of a decision on issuing him a permanent residence permit, the foreigner provided false information, submitted documents and (or) information that are not conforming to the requirements of the legislation of the Republic of Belarus, including fraudulent, counterfeit or invalid documents;

a foreigner has exited or is exiting from the Republic of Belarus to a foreign State for permanent residence.

in the case of deportation or expulsion of the foreigner.

Cancellation of a permanent residence permit entails a reduction of the validity term of the visa issued to the foreigner, or its cancellation and (or) withdrawal of the residence permit.

In the case, where a permanent residence permit issued to a foreigner was withdrawn, and there are no other legitimate grounds for his further stay in the Republic of Belarus, the foreigner shall leave the Republic of Belarus within one month from the date of receiving a notice of the decision to cancel the permanent residence permit, if another period is not set by the legislative acts of the Republic of Belarus regulating the particulars of the legal status of the foreigners applying for the refugee status or additional protection in the Republic of Belarus, as well as foreigners, who are granted the refugee status or additional or temporary protection in the Republic of Belarus.

A foreigner, whose permanent residence permit is cancelled on the grounds specified in the first part and paragraphs from two to five of the second part of this Article, shall register with the registration authority at the place of the actual temporary residence for the period up to the departure from the Republic of Belarus.

**Article 58.** Organs taking decisions on issuing a permanent residence permit, on refusal of issuing and cancellation of the permanent residence permit

Decisions on issuance of a permanent resident permit to foreigners referred to in paragraph from two to seven and eleven of the first part of Article 53 of this Law shall be taken by an organ of internal affairs independently or at the request of the appropriate State organs of the Republic of Belarus.

Decisions on issuance of a permanent resident permit to foreigners referred to in paragraph eight of the first part of Article 53 of this Law shall be taken by an organ of internal affairs at the request of the appropriate State organs of the Republic of Belarus.

Decisions on issuance of a permanent resident permit to foreigners referred to in paragraph nine and ten of the first part of Article 53 of this Law shall be taken by the Ministry for Internal Affairs at the request of the appropriate State organs of the Republic of Belarus.

Decisions on issuance of a permanent residence permit to foreigners referred to in the second part of Article 55 of this Law shall be taken by the Ministry for Internal Affairs at the request of the inviting persons according to the procedure established by the Council of Ministers of the Republic of Belarus.

A decision to refuse issuing a permanent residence permit shall be taken by the Ministry for Internal Affairs or another organ of internal affairs independently or at the request of the appropriate State organs of the Republic of Belarus.

A decision to withdraw a permanent residence permit issued to the foreigner, in the cases provided for in paragraph four of the first part and paragraph three of the second part of Article 57 of this Law shall be adopted in judicial proceedings, in other cases stipulated by Article 57 of this Law shall be adopted by an organ of internal affairs independently or at the request of the appropriate State organs of the Republic of Belarus.

**Article 59.** Notices about decisions adopted on issues of the stay of a foreigner in the Republic of Belarus

A foreigner, in respect of whom has been taken a decision on refusal of the extension and (or) reduction of the period of temporary stay in the Republic of Belarus, the refusal to issue a temporary residence permit or cancellation of the temporary residence permit, the refusal to issue a permanent residence permit or cancellation a permanent residence permit, refusal to issue a visa for exit from the Republic of Belarus or refusal of permission to exit from the Republic of Belarus, shall be served or mailed with a notice of the decision no later than five twenty-four hours as from the day of the approval of that decision by an organ of internal affairs at the place of temporary stay, temporary residence or place of residence of the foreigner in the Republic of Belarus.

In case of sending the foreigner of the notice about a decision referred to in the first part of this Article, the foreigner is considered informed of the adoption of this decision after three twenty-four hours as from the day of sending of that notice.

**Article 60.** Residence permit

An foreigner, who has reached the age of sixteen and received in due course a permanent residence permit, shall have a residence permit.

The procedure for issuing, using, exchange, invalidation, withdrawal, storage, destruction of the residence permit is determined by the legislative acts of the Republic of Belarus.

**Article 61.** Centralized record keeping on foreigners

In order to keep records on foreigners temporarily staying, temporarily and permanently residing in the Republic of Belarus, a central data bank for keeping records on foreigners staying in the Republic of Belarus is to be created.

The procedures for establishing and maintaining a central data bank for keeping records on foreigners staying in the Republic of Belarus and the use of the information contained in this data bank shall be established by the Council of Ministers of the Republic of Belarus.

**Article 62.** The control over the stay of foreigners in the Republic of Belarus

The control over temporary stay, temporary and permanent residence of foreigners in the Republic of Belarus, as well as transit passage (transit) of foreigners through the territory of the Republic of Belarus shall be performed by the organs of internal affairs in collaboration with the organs of State security, organs of the Border Service and the Ministry for Foreign Affairs.

Foreigners at the request of officials of the organs of internal affairs, the organs of State security, the organs of the Border Services shall submit a document for travelling abroad, other documents stipulated by the legislation of the Republic of Belarus, which prove that they stay in the Republic of Belarus lawfully, as well as provide explanations relating to their stay in the Republic of Belarus.

**Article 63.** Identification of personality of a foreigner without a document for travelling abroad

With respect to a foreigner staying in the Republic of Belarus and not possessing a document for travelling abroad the organs of internal affairs shall perform identification of personality according to the procedure established by the Council of Ministers of the Republic of Belarus.

In the case, where after the conduct of identification of personality the identity of the foreigner has been established, the organs of internal affairs shall issued him a certificate, the form of which is approved by the Council of Ministers of the Republic of Belarus. The certificate confirms the identity of the foreigner until issuance to him of a document for travelling abroad or a document for the exit from the Republic of Belarus.

## CHAPTER 5 DEPORTATION. EXPULSION

**Article 64.** Deportation

Foreigners may be subjected to deportation in the cases established by certain legislative acts of the Republic of Belarus, and in the manner prescribed by the Council of Ministers of the Republic of Belarus.

**Article 65.** Expulsion

A foreigner may be expelled from the Republic of Belarus in the interests of the national security of the Republic of Belarus, public order, for the protection of public morality, public health, rights and freedoms of citizens of the Republic of Belarus and other persons, if he cannot be subjected to deportation.

The decision on expulsion is taken by a organ of internal affairs or an organ of State security.

Expulsion may be effected by means of a voluntary departure of a foreigner from the Republic of Belarus or by enforcement.

The procedure of conducting of the expulsion shall be established by the Council of Ministers of the Republic of Belarus.

**Article 66.** Expulsion by means of a voluntary departure

A foreigner, in respect of whom an organ of internal affairs or an organ of State security adopted a decision on expulsion by a voluntary departure, shall within the period prescribed in the decision depart from the Republic of Belarus.

**Article 67.** Expulsion by enforcement

Expulsion by enforcement is performed, if:

there are reasons to believe that a foreigner can avoid the fulfilment of a decision on expulsion by a voluntary departure;

the foreigner has not left the Republic of Belarus within the period prescribed in the decision on expulsion by a voluntary departure.

Upon adoption of the decision on expulsion by enforcement an organ of internal affairs or an organ of State security with a sanctions from a prosecutor shall take measures to detain a foreigner for the period necessary for expulsion.

**Article 68**. Suspension and cancellation of expulsion

The expulsion shall be suspended in the cases of application of the foreigner to an appropriate State organ of the Republic of Belarus with a petition for receiving a refugee status, additional protection or asylum in the Republic of Belarus, or in the case, where a foreigner, against whom an expulsion order is adopted, is a suspect or accused in a criminal case or sentenced to an arrest, restraint of liberty or imprisonment.

Expulsion shall be suspended until the adoption of a decision on an application for the refugee status or additional protection in the Republic of Belarus, and the expiration of the period established by the legislation of the Republic of Belarus for appealing of the decision adopted on the application for provision of the refugee status or additional protection in the Republic of Belarus (in the case of non-use of the right to appeal), or until the entry into legal force of the court's decision to dismiss the complaint, or pending a decision on an application for provision of the asylum in the Republic of Belarus or until the termination of criminal prosecution, or until the entry of a court's judgement into legal force, or until the completion of penalty in the form of arrest, restraint of liberty or imprisonment.

In the case of provision to a foreigner, against whom an expulsion order is adopted, of the refugee status or additional protection or asylum in the Republic of Belarus, as well as in the case, when a

foreigner cannot be returned or deported against his will to the State, where his life or freedom would be endangered because of his race, religion, citizenship, nationality, belonging to a particular social group or political views, or where he is threatened with tortures, the expulsion shall be stopped.

**Article 69.** The costs associated with deportation or expulsion

The costs associated with deportation or expulsion shall be covered at the expense of a foreigner, the legal entity or the individual that applied for his entry into the Republic of Belarus, stay or residence in the Republic of Belarus.

In the case, where reimbursement of the costs at the expense of the persons mentioned in the first part of this article is impossible, deportation or expulsion shall be performed at the expense of the Republican budget.

**Article 70.** The consequences of deportation or expulsion

On the basis of a decision on deportation or expulsion the foreigner is included in the list of persons, whose entry into the Republic of Belarus is prohibited or undesirable.

Entry of a deported foreigners into the Republic of Belarus may be prohibited for the period from one year to five years.

Entry of an expelled foreigner into the Republic of Belarus may be prohibited for a period from one year to ten years.

In the case of deportation or expulsion of a foreigner onto his document for travel abroad shall be affixed the appropriate mark. The form of the mark and the procedure for affixing it by the organ that has taken the decision on deportation or expulsion, shall be determined by the Council of Ministers of the Republic of Belarus.

## CHAPTER 6 APPEALING AGAINST DECISIONS AND ACTION (OMISSIONS) OF STATE ORGANS AND OFFICIALS OF THE REPUBLIC OF BELARUS

**Article 71.** The right to appeal decisions and actions (omissions) of State organs and officials of the Republic of Belarus

Foreigners as well as their representatives have the right to appeal decisions and actions (omissions) of State organs and officials of the Republic of Belarus related to the implementation of this Law to a superior State organ or the superior official.

Challenging in the court of decisions and actions (omissions) of State organs and officials of the Republic of Belarus related to the implementation of this Law shall be performed in accordance with the civil procedural legislation of the Republic of Belarus after the appeal of such decisions and actions (omissions) to the superior State organ or the superior officer.

**Article 72.** Appealing of the decisions of State organs and officials of the Republic of Belarus to the superior State organ or the superior official

Complaints of foreigners against the decisions of State organs or officials of the Republic of Belarus to refuse registration, renewal and or) on reducing the period of temporary stay in the Republic of Belarus, on the refusal to issue a temporary residence permit or cancellation of the temporary residence permit, on the refusal to issue a permanent residence permit or on cancellation of the permanent residence permit, on the refusal to issue a visa for the exit from the Republic of Belarus or refusal of permission to leave the Republic of Belarus can be filed to a superior State organ or a higher-ranking official within one year from the date of adoption of such decisions.

Complaints of foreigners on the decisions of State organs or officials of the Republic of Belarus about expulsion can be submitted to a superior State organ or higher-ranking official within one month from the foreigner's acquaintance with this decision.

The complaints of foreigners on the decisions specified in parts one and two of this article shall be considered within one month from the date of their filing.

Appeals against decisions of State organs and officials of the Republic of Belarus under part two of this article do not constitute grounds for the stay of foreigners in the Republic of Belarus.

## CHAPTER 7 FINAL PROVISIONS

**Article 73.** Introduction of amendments and additions to some Laws of the Republic of Belarus

1. To introduce into the Criminal Code of the Republic of Belarus of July 16, 1999 (the National Register of Legal Acts of the Republic of Belarus, 2000, No. 77-78, 2 / 71, 2008, No. 14, 2 / 1412) the following amendments and additions:

1.1. Part 2 of Article 115 shall read as follows:

2. The fact of detention of a foreign citizen or a stateless persons shall be notified by the organ that conducts criminal proceedings and made an arrest at the request of the foreign citizen or the stateless persons to the Ministry for Foreign Affairs of the Republic of Belarus no later than twenty-four hours after the arrest for the purpose of further notification of a diplomatic mission or consular office of the State of the citizenship or habitual residence of the detained foreign citizen or stateless person.";

1.2. Article 125 shall be amended with part 5 that reads as follows:

5. The application of a measure of restraint in the form of house arrest in respect of a foreign citizen or stateless persons shall be notified by the organ conducting criminal proceedings to the Ministry for Foreign Affairs of the Republic of Belarus at the request of the foreign citizen or the stateless person, no later than one day after the enforcing of the measure of restraint in the form of house arrest for further notification of a diplomatic mission or consular institutions of the state of the citizenship or habitual residence of the foreign citizen or stateless person placed under house arrest.";

1.3. Part 8 of Article 126 shall read as follows:

8. About the application of a measure of restraint in the form of taking into custody as prosecuting organ or a court shall notify the persons specified in part 1 of Article 115 of the present Code, as well as in the case of the application of such a measure of restraint in respect of persons, whose children remained without the care of parents, not later than on the next day after adoption of the mentioned decision shall notify the department (division) of education of a district or municipal executive committee, local administration of city district at the place of residence of these persons for ensuring State protection of the children, upon application of this measure of restraint in respect of a pensioner - shall notify the organ paying him a retirement pension, upon application of this measure of restraint in respect of a foreigner or a stateless persons at the request of a foreign citizen or stateless person shall notify about this the Ministry for Foreign Affairs of the Republic of Belarus not later than one day after the application of the measure of restraint in the form of taking into custody for the further notification of a diplomatic mission or consular office of the State of citizenship or habitual residence of the detained foreign citizen or a stateless person. ".

2. Introduce into the Law of the Republic of Belarus of 1 August 2002 "On Citizenship of the Republic of Belarus" (the National Register of Legal Acts of the Republic of Belarus, 2002, No. 88, 2/885, 2006, No. 106, 2 / 1231) the following amendments and additions:

2.1. in the first part of Article 7 the words "change of citizenship of the spouses" shall be substituted for "acquiring by the spouses of citizenship of the Republic of Belarus or its termination;

2.2. the first part of Article 9 after the word "citizenship" shall be amended with the words "(nationality) (hereinafter, unless otherwise indicated - citizenship);

2.3. fourth paragraph of Article 13 after the words "of State, by citizens" shall be amended the words "(by nationals)";

2.4. in Article 14:

in part one:

the second paragraph two shall read as follows:

"Observes and respects the Constitution of the Republic of Belarus, other acts of legislation of the Republic of Belarus, undertakes to continue to observe and respect the Constitution of the Republic of Belarus and other acts of legislation of the Republic of Belarus";

the fifth paragraph shall read as follows:

"has a legitimate source of receiving income, providing him and to incapacitated family members under his care minimum living wage established in the Republic of Belarus";

In the second part, the words "recognized them as refugees according to the order established by the legislation of the Republic of Belarus" and "recognition of them as refugees" shall be substituted by the words "to whom the status of the refugee in the Republic of Belarus is granted" and "granting them the status of refugee";

2.5. in Article 16:

in the title, the word "of rejection" with "of refusal to consider";

in the first paragraph the word "shall be rejected" by "shall not be considered";

in the third paragraph the words "serious or particularly serious" shall be deleted;

after the sixth paragraph the article shall be amended by the paragraph that reads as follows:

"Repeatedly (three or more times) is brought to administrative responsibility on the territory of the Republic of Belarus - until the expiration of the time period, after which he would not be considered as subjected to administrative penalty;"

the seventh and eighth paragraphs shall respectively be considered as the eighth and ninth paragraphs;

the Article shall be amended with the second part that reads as follows:

"If the grounds specified the first paragraph of this Article are present, the statement of acquisition of citizenship of the Republic of Belarus together with all documents submitted shall be returned without consideration.";

2.6. Article 18 shall read as follows:

"Article 18. Renunciation of citizenship of the Republic of Belarus

A citizen of the Republic of Belarus, who has reached the age of 18, has the right to apply for renunciation of citizenship of the Republic of Belarus.

A citizen of the Republic of Belarus, who is under 18 years of age, may be permitted to renounce the citizenship of the Republic of Belarus upon a request of the parents (the single parent).

Renunciation of Citizenship of the Republic of Belarus is exercised in the manner prescribed by the President of the Republic of Belarus, and in the absence of the grounds provided for in Article 20 of this Law.";

2.7. third paragraph of Article 20 after the words "the Republic of Belarus, its" shall be amended with the words "administrative-territorial units";

2.8. in Article 22:

part two shall be deleted;

part three shall be considered part two;

2.9. out of the part three of Article 2, the words "in the age of 16 years" shall be deleted;

2.10. in Article 26 the second sentence shall be deleted;

2.11. paragraph two of Article 31, paragraph two of Article 32, the title and part three of Article 34, the title of chapter 8, articles 37 and 38 after the word "citizenship" shall be amended with the words "the Republic of Belarus";

2.12. in Article 33:

the title and the third part after the word "citizenship" shall be amended with the words "the Republic of Belarus";

part two after the words "on the issues of citizenship" shall be amended with the words "the Republic of Belarus".

**Article 74.** Recognition as null and void of some legislative acts of the Republic of Belarus and some of its individual provisions

To declare null and void:

Law of the Republic of Belarus of June 3, 1993 "On the Legal Status of Foreign Citizens and Stateless Persons in the Republic of Belarus" (the Gazette of the Supreme Council of the Republic of Belarus, 1993, No. 21, Article 250);

Article 1 of the Law of the Republic of Belarus of July 18, 2000 "On introduction of amendments and additions into some legislative acts of the Republic of Belarus" (the National Register of Legal Acts of the Republic of Belarus, 2000, No.73, 2 / 197);

Law of the Republic of Belarus of January 4, 2003 "On introduction amendments and additions into some legislative acts of the Republic of Belarus in connection with accession of the Republic of Belarus to the Convention Relating to the Status of Refugees and Protocol Relating to the Status of Refugees" (the National Register of Legal Acts of the Republic of Belarus, 2003, N 8, 2 / 927);

Law of the Republic of Belarus of July 19, 2005 "On introduction of amendments and additions into the Law of the Republic of Belarus"On Legal Status of Foreign Citizens and Stateless Persons in the Republic of Belarus" (the National Register of Legal Acts of the Republic of Belarus, 2005, No. 121, 2 / 1138 );

Article 6 of the Law of the Republic of Belarus of December 26, 2007 "On introduction of amendments and additions into some legislative acts of the Republic of Belarus and recognizing as null and void of some legislative acts of the Republic of Belarus and individual provisions of the laws of the Republic of Belarus on insurance issues" (the National Register of Legal Acts of the Republic of Belarus, 2007 PM, No. 305, 2 / 1397);

fourth paragraph of Article 56 of the Law of the Republic of Belarus of June 23, 2008 "On granting foreign citizens and stateless persons a refugee status, additional and temporary protection in the Republic of Belarus" (the National Register of Legal Acts of the Republic of Belarus, 2008, No. 158, 2/1451)

Resolution of the Supreme Council of the Republic of Belarus of June 3, 1993 "On promulgation of the Law of the Republic of Belarus "On Legal Status of Foreign Citizens and Stateless Persons in the Republic of Belarus" (the Gazette of the Supreme Council of the Republic of Belarus, 1993, No. 21, Art. 251) .

**Article 75.** Measures to implement the provisions of this Law

The Council of Ministers of the Republic of Belarus within six months' term shall:

in collaboration with the National Centre of Legislation and Legal Research of the Republic of Belarus prepare and submit according to the established procedure proposals on amendment legislation of the Republic of Belarus in order to bring them in conformity with this Law;

bring decisions of the Government of the Republic of Belarus in conformity with this Law;

ensure that the Republican organs of State administration subordinated to the Government of the Republic of Belarus bring their normative legal acts in conformity with this Law;

take other measures necessary to implement the provisions of this Law.

**Article 76.** Entry into force of this Law

This Law shall enter into force six months after its official publication, except for this Article and Article 75, which enter into force from the date of the official publication of this Law.

The President of the Republic of Belarus A. Lukashenko

# ON THE LEGAL STATUS OF FOREIGN CITIZENS AND STATELESS PERSONS IN THE REPUBLIC OF BELARUS

**THE LAW OF THE REPUBLIC OF BELARUS OF JANUARY 4, 2010 NO. 105-Z**
Adopted by the House of Representatives on December 11, 2009

Approved by the Council of the Republic on December 17, 2009

The present law is intended for defining the legal status of foreign citizens and stateless persons in the Republic of Belarus, including the establishment of the procedure of their entry into the Republic of Belarus, stay in the Republic of Belarus and the departure from the Republic of Belarus, as well as for regulating other relations connected with the presence of these persons in the Republic of Belarus.

## CHAPTER 1 GENERAL PROVISIONS

**Article 1.** Key terms used in this Law and their definitions

For the purposes of this Law the following key terms and their definitions are used:

close relatives - parents, adoptive parents, children, adopted as sons (adopted as daughters), full brothers and sisters, grandmother, grandfather, grandchildren;

permit for residence in the Republic of Belarus (hereinafter - the residence permit) - an identity document of a foreign citizen, or stateless person (hereinafter, unless otherwise specified in this Law - the foreigner) on the territory of the Republic of Belarus and certifying the receipt by the foreigner of the permission for permanent residence in the Republic of Belarus (hereinafter - the permanent residence permit);

the visa of the Republic of Belarus (hereinafter - the visa) - permit, which gives a foreigner the right to cross the State border of the Republic of Belarus (hereinafter - the State border) for the purpose of entering the Republic of Belarus and (or) departure from the Republic of Belarus, stay in the Republic of Belarus or transit passage (transit) through the territory of the Republic of Belarus within the period specified in the permit, and which has been issued in accordance with order established by the legislation of the Republic of Belarus;

foreigner temporarily staying in Belarus - a person, who arrived in the Republic of Belarus for a period not exceeding ninety days in a calendar year as from the date of first entry into the Republic of Belarus on the basis of a visa or in the manner not requiring receiving the visa, and not having the permit for temporary residence in the Republic Belarus (hereinafter - the temporary residence permit) or the permanent residence permit, unless otherwise specified in this Law and international treaties of the Republic of Belarus;

foreigner temporarily residing in the Republic of Belarus - a person who has received a temporary residence permit in the manner prescribed by legislative acts of the Republic of Belarus;

deportation from the Republic of Belarus (hereinafter - the deportation) - expulsion of a foreigner out of the Republic of Belarus in accordance with this Law;

document for travel abroad - a valid passport or other document substituting it, intended for travelling abroad and issued by the relevant authority of the State of citizenship or habitual residence of the foreigner or by an international organization;

immigration quota - the maximum annual limit of admission of foreigners for permanent residence into the Republic of Belarus;

foreign citizen - a person who is not a citizen of the Republic of Belarus and has the evidence of his belonging to a citizenship (nationality) (hereinafter, unless otherwise specified in this Law - the citizenship) of another State;

stateless person - a person, who are not a citizen of the Republic of Belarus and has no proof of his belonging to the citizenship of another State;

migration card - a document containing information about the foreigner entering the Republic of Belarus and leaving the Republic of Belarus, and serving the purpose of exercising control over his temporary stay or temporary residence in the Republic of Belarus;

authorities registering foreigners temporarily staying in the Republic of Belarus (hereinafter - the registration authorities) - the Ministry for Foreign Affairs of the Republic of Belarus (hereinafter - the Ministry for Foreign Affairs), internal affairs organs of the Republic of Belarus (further - the internal affairs organs), a hotel, sanatorium, health resort or wellness organization;

foreigner permanently residing in the Republic of Belarus - a person, who has received the permanent residence permit and the residence permit in the manner prescribed by legislative acts of the Republic of Belarus and resolutions of the Council of Ministers of the Republic of Belarus;

temporary residence permit - a document which gives foreigners the right to reside in the Republic of Belarus during the period of its validity and issued in the manner prescribed by the legislation of the Republic of Belarus;

permanent residence permit - a decision of the Ministry for Internal Affairs of the Republic of Belarus (hereinafter - the Ministry for Internal Affairs) and other internal affairs organs, which entitles foreigners to the right of permanent residence in the Republic of Belarus;

Registration of a foreigner temporarily staying in the Republic of Belarus - fixing in the prescribed manner by the registration authorities of the information about the place and time of temporary stay of a foreigner in the Republic of Belarus;

transit passage (transit) of a foreigner through the territory of the Republic of Belarus - the entry of the foreigner into the Republic of Belarus from one State to follow a fixed route through the territory of the Republic of Belarus and exit of the foreigner from the Republic of Belarus to another State.

**Article 2.** Citizenship of foreign citizens, who have multiple nationality

Foreign nationals, who possess the nationality of two or more States, are considered in the Republic of Belarus citizens of the State, using the documents for travel abroad of which they entered into the Republic of Belarus.

**Article 3.** The Legislation of the Republic of Belarus on the legal status of foreigners in the Republic of Belarus

The legislation of the Republic of Belarus on the legal status of foreigners in the Republic of Belarus is based on the Constitution of the Republic of Belarus and consists of this Law and other legislative acts of the Republic of Belarus, including international treaties of the Republic of Belarus.

If an international treaty of the Republic of Belarus establishes other rules than those provided for in this Law, the rules of the international treaty shall be applied.

**Article 4.** Basic principles of the legal status of foreigners in the Republic of Belarus

Foreigners in the Republic of Belarus shall enjoy rights and liberties and fulfil duties on a par with citizens of the Republic of Belarus, unless otherwise specified in the Constitution of the Republic of Belarus, this Law and other legislative acts and international treaties of the Republic of Belarus.

Peculiarities of the legal status of foreigners applying for a refugee status, or additional protection or asylum in the Republic of Belarus, as well as foreigners, who are granted the refugee status, or additional or temporary protection or asylum in the Republic of Belarus, are governed by the specific legislative acts of the Republic of Belarus.

If another State restricts or violates universally accepted rules of the legal status of foreign citizens in respect of citizens of the Republic of Belarus, the Republic of Belarus may impose retaliatory restrictions on the rights and freedoms of citizens (nationals) of that State. Such restrictions, if they are introduced, shall not apply to foreigners listed in the second part of this article.

**Article 5.** Responsibility for violation of this Law

Persons guilty of violation of this Law shall be held liable in accordance with the legislative acts of the Republic of Belarus.

**Article 6.** Funding and material and technical support of activities provided for in this Law

Funding and material and technical support of activities provided for in this Law shall be performed at the expense of the funds of the Republican budget allocated for the upkeep of the relevant Republican organs of the State administration of the Republic of Belarus, and other sources in accordance with the legislation of the Republic of Belarus.

## CHAPTER 2 RIGHTS, FREEDOMS, DUTIES AND RESPONSIBILITY OF FOREIGNERS IN THE REPUBLIC OF BELARUS

**Article 7.** Individual rights and freedoms

Foreigners in the Republic of Belarus in accordance with the Constitution of the Republic of Belarus and other legislative acts of the Republic of Belarus shall enjoy guaranteed inviolability of person and residence and other personal rights and freedoms.

**Article 8.** Movement and choice of the place of stay (residence) within the territory of the Republic of Belarus

Foreigners shall have the right to move freely and choose freely their place of stay (residence) within the territory of the Republic of Belarus in accordance with this Law and other legislative acts of the Republic of Belarus.

The order of movement of foreigners and choice by them of the place of stay (residence) within the territory of the Republic of Belarus is determined by this Law and the Rules of Stay of Foreign Citizens and Stateless Persons in the Republic of Belarus that are approved by the Council of Ministers of the Republic of Belarus (hereinafter - the Rules of the Stay).

Foreigners are entitled to travel freely within the territory of the Republic of Belarus except for places, visit to which require a special permit issued by authorized State organs or other organizations of the Republic of Belarus, and facilities, entering the territory of which and stay on it requires a special permit issued by administrations of these facilities.

A list of the places, for visiting which foreigners will need the special permit, and the facilities, for entry into the territory of which and stay on it foreigners need the special permit, as well as the list

of State organs and other organizations of the Republic of Belarus authorized to issue such permits is determined by the Council of Ministers of the Republic of Belarus.

**Article 9**. Participation in political parties and other public associations

Foreigners may join trade unions and other public associations created and operating on the territory of the Republic of Belarus, if such possibility is provided for in their charters.

Foreigners cannot be members of political parties and other public associations, established and operating on the territory of the Republic of Belarus and having political objectives.

**Article 10.** Socio-economic rights

Foreigners residing in the Republic of Belarus have all socio-economic rights enjoyed by citizens of the Republic of Belarus, including the right to social security.

Socio-economic rights of foreigners temporarily staying or temporarily residing in the Republic of Belarus are determined by legislative acts and international treaties of the Republic of Belarus.

**Article 11.** Performance of labour, business and other activities in the Republic of Belarus

Foreigners permanently residing in the Republic of Belarus are entitled to conduct labour and entrepreneurial activities on a par with citizens of the Republic of Belarus in the manner prescribed by legislative acts of the Republic of Belarus, subject to the limitations provided for in articles 19 and 20 of this Law.

The order of performance of labour activities by foreigners temporarily staying or temporarily residing in the Republic of Belarus shall be determined by special legislative acts of the Republic of Belarus.

Foreigners temporarily staying or temporarily residing in the Republic of Belarus are not entitled to conduct in the Republic of Belarus entrepreneurial activities without establishment of a legal entity, unless otherwise specified in legislative acts and international treaties of the Republic of Belarus.

Other activities shall be performed by foreigners in the manner prescribed by the legislation of the Republic of Belarus.

**Article 12.** Property and personal non-property rights

Foreigners in the Republic of Belarus are entitled to own property, inherit it or leave it by will, enjoy other property and personal rights in the manner prescribed by the legislation of the Republic of Belarus, including international treaties of the Republic of Belarus.

**Article 13.** Right to health care

Foreigners permanently residing in the Republic of Belarus have the right to access publicly available health care on a par with citizens of the Republic of Belarus, unless otherwise specified in legislative acts and international treaties of the Republic of Belarus.

Foreigners temporarily staying or temporarily residing in the Republic of Belarus are entitled to access publicly available health care at their own expense, expense of legal entities or other sources of funding, unless otherwise specified in legislative acts and international treaties of the Republic of Belarus.

The procedure and conditions for compulsory health insurance of foreigners entering the Republic of Belarus for a temporary stay or temporary residence are determined by legislative acts of the Republic of Belarus.

**Article 14.** Right to education

Foreigners permanently residing in the Republic of Belarus have the equal right to eduction on a par with citizens of the Republic of Belarus, unless otherwise provided for in legislative acts and international treaties of the Republic of Belarus.

Foreigners temporarily staying or temporarily residing in the Republic of Belarus have the right to receive education in the Republic of Belarus in accordance with international treaties of the Republic of Belarus or on the basis of agreements on education, concluded with educational institutions or scientific organizations of the Republic of Belarus, in the manner prescribed by the legislation of the Republic of Belarus, including international treaties of the Republic of Belarus.

Minor foreigners temporarily residing in the Republic of Belarus foreign minors are eligible for receiving preschool and general secondary education on a par with a minor citizens of the Republic of Belarus.

**Article 15.** The right to preserve national culture and respect the national dignity

Foreigners in the Republic of Belarus shall have the right to maintain and develop its national language and culture, follow national traditions and customs in accordance with the laws of the Republic of Belarus.

An insult to ethnic dignity of foreigners entails responsibility in accordance with the legislative acts of the Republic of Belarus.

**Article 16.** Protecting the rights and freedoms

Foreigners in the Republic of Belarus shall enjoy all the legal remedies for protection of the rights and freedoms of the person provided by the legislation of the Republic of Belarus.

**Article 17.** Notification about detention, the use of a measure of restraint in the form taking into custody, putting under house arrest

Foreigners, who are detained, taken in custody or put under house arrest, shall be notified without delay by the organ, that detained them or used a measure of restraint in the form of taking into custody or putting under house arrest, in a language that they understand about the reasons for their detention or using in respect of them the measure of restraint in the form of taking into custody or putting under house arrest and about the rights that they have according to the legislation of the Republic of Belarus.

The organ that detained a foreigner or used in respect of him the measure of restraint in the form of detention, house arrest, at the request of the foreigner, unless otherwise specified in legislative acts and international treaties of the Republic of Belarus, not later than one day as from the moment of detention or use in respect of him the measure of restraint in the form of taking into custody or putting under house arrest shall notify the Ministry for Foreign Affairs for further notifying the diplomatic mission or consular office of the State of citizenship or habitual residence of the foreigner, who was detained, taken into custody or put under house arrest.

The procedures of informing of the Ministry for Foreign Affairs about the detention of a foreigner or using in respect of him the measure of restraint in the form of taking into custody or putting under house arrest is determined by the Council of Ministers of the Republic of Belarus.

**Article 18.** Restriction of the rights and freedoms

Restrictions on the rights and freedoms of foreigners may be imposed only in the cases stipulated by this Law and other legislative acts of the Republic of Belarus, in the interests of national security of the Republic of Belarus, public order, for the protection of public morality, public health, rights and freedoms of citizens of the Republic of Belarus and other persons.

**Article 19.** Restriction of participation in elections and referenda

Foreigners cannot vote or be elected to elective State organs of the Republic of Belarus, as well as take part in referenda.

**Article 20.** Restriction on holding certain offices

Foreigners cannot hold offices, appointment to which, in accordance with the legislation of the Republic of Belarus is connected with belonging to the citizenship of the Republic of Belarus.

**Article 21.** Performance of military duty

Foreigners staying in the Republic of Belarus do not perform military duty.

**Article 22.** Compliance with the legislation of the Republic of Belarus and respect for its national traditions

Foreigners staying in the Republic of Belarus are obliged to observe the Constitution of the Republic of Belarus and other legislative acts of the Republic of Belarus, to respect its national traditions.

**Article 23.** Duty to register

Foreigners temporarily staying in the Republic of Belarus shall register themselves in the registration authorities in the manner prescribed by this Law, other legislative acts of the Republic of Belarus and the Rules of the Stay, unless otherwise specified in this Law.

**Article 24.** The duty of reimbursement for the upkeep of children

Foreigners staying temporarily, temporarily or permanently residing in Belarus are obliged to reimburse the costs spent by the Republic of Belarus for the upkeep of their children in public care, in the cases and according to the procedure specified by legislative acts of the Republic of Belarus.

**Article 25.** Duty to leave the Republic of Belarus

If there is no legal justification for continued stay in the Republic of Belarus foreigners must leave the Republic of Belarus by the end of the period of temporary residence or temporary residence or other periods provided in this Law.

**Article 26.** Responsibility of foreigners

Foreigners, who have committed on the territory of the Republic of Belarus a crime, administrative and other offences, shall bear responsibility in accordance with the legislative acts of the Republic of Belarus.

## CHAPTER 3 ENTRY INTO THE REPUBLIC OF BELARUS, EXIT FROM THE REPUBLIC OF BELARUS, TRANSIT PASSAGE (TRANSIT) THROUGH THE TERRITORY OF THE REPUBLIC OF BELARUS OF FOREIGNERS

**Article 27.** The Procedure for entry into the Republic of Belarus, exit from the Republic of Belarus, transit passage (transit) through the territory of the Republic of Belarus of foreigners

A foreigner may enter the Republic of Belarus, exit from the Republic of Belarus and conduct a transit passage (transit) through the territory of the Republic of Belarus by virtue of the document for travelling abroad with a visa, unless otherwise specified in this Law, other legislative acts and international treaties of the Republic of Belarus.

The President of the Republic of Belarus may establish a visa free entry regime of foreigners into the Republic of Belarus, their exit from the Republic of Belarus and the conduct of a transit passage (transit) through the territory of the Republic of Belarus.

**Article 28.** Visas

Visas are issued to foreigners by diplomatic missions or consular offices of the Republic of Belarus, the Ministry for Foreign affairs, the internal affairs organs, the organs of the Border Service of the Republic of Belarus (further - the organs of the Border Service), unless otherwise determined by legislation of the Republic of Belarus.

Types of visas and the procedure of their issue shall be determined by the Council of Ministers of the Republic of Belarus.

**Article 29.** Migration Card

A foreigner entering the Republic of Belarus shall fill out a migration card, which together with the document for travelling abroad shall be presented to an official of the organ of the Border Service at a checkpoint for passage through the State border.

When leaving the Republic of Belarus, a foreigner shall return the migration card to an official of the organ of the Border Service at a checkpoint for passage through the State border.

The official of a organ of the Border Service shall affix a marking onto the migration card certifying the entry of a foreigner into the Republic of Belarus and (or) a marking certifying his departure from the Republic of Belarus.

The form of the migration card and procedure of its use shall be determined by the Council of Ministers of the Republic of Belarus, unless otherwise determined by international treaties of the Republic of Belarus.

Legislative acts and international treaties of the Republic of Belarus may establish categories of foreigners, who are not required to fill out migration cards upon the entry into the Republic of Belarus and present them upon departure from the Republic of Belarus.

**Article 30.** Refusal of a visa for entry into the Republic of Belarus or refusal of entry into the Republic of Belarus

A foreigner may be refused a visa for entry into the Republic of Belarus or refused entry into the Republic of Belarus, if:

the foreigner at a checkpoint for passage through the State border has violated the rules of crossing the State border or customs regulations - until the violation is eliminated;

validity period of a document for travelling abroad does not exceed ninety days before the anticipated departure of a foreigner from the Republic of Belarus;

a foreigner is convicted in the Republic of Belarus or any other State for committing an offence recognised as such in accordance with the Criminal Code of the Republic of Belarus and the conviction has been cleared or settled;

the foreigner during his stay in the Republic of Belarus has repeatedly (twice or more) in the course of one year been brought to administrative responsibility and the period not expired, at the end of which he is not considered as being subjected to administrative penalty;

the foreigner subjected during his stay in the Republic of Belarus to an administrative penalty in the form of a fine, who failed to pay it within the period stipulated by legislative acts of the Republic of Belarus for the execution of the order to impose an administrative penalty in the form of a fine;

the foreigner cannot confirm the availability of the cash assets needed to cover the costs of his stay in the Republic of Belarus and exit from the Republic of Belarus, or submit assurances of presentation of such cash assets in the manner and the amount established by the Council of Ministers;

during the previous stay of the foreigner in the Republic of Belarus has expired the period of temporary stay provided for in the first and second parts of Article 39 of this Law;

there are reasonable grounds to assume that the foreigner may avoid leaving the Republic of Belarus at the end of the period of temporary stay or temporary residence;

the stay of the foreigner in the Republic of Belarus contradicts the interests of national security of the Republic of Belarus, public order, protection of morality, public health, rights and freedoms of citizens of the Republic of Belarus and other persons;

in respect of the foreigner in accordance with an international treaty of the Republic of Belarus by an authorized authority of a foreign State or an international organization there has been taken a decision to restrict his rights to enter the territory of the States-members of the international treaty or the States-members of the organization.

The foreigner is refused to be granted a visa for entry into the Republic of Belarus, except for the case provided for in the third part of this article, or the foreigner is refused an entry into the Republic of Belarus, if:

upon submitting to the relevant State organs of the Republic of Belarus of the documents necessary for obtaining a visa for entry into the Republic of Belarus or taking a decision on his entry into the Republic of Belarus, the foreigner provided false information, submitted documents and (or) information that are not conforming to the requirements of the legislation of the Republic of Belarus, including fraudulent, counterfeit or invalid documents;

the foreigner is included in the list of persons, whose entry into the Republic of Belarus is prohibited or undesirable;

the Republic of Belarus has proclaimed the foreigner inadmissible or undesirable (persona non grata);

there is the evidence available that the foreigner is or was a person carrying out an extremist, including terrorist, activities, was or is connected to extremist, including terrorist, smuggling, and (or) other activities aimed at harming the national security of the Republic of Belarus, to the illicit trade in arms, ammunition or explosives, illicit trafficking of narcotic drugs, psychotropic substances and their precursors, illegal migration of foreigners, human trafficking;

the foreigner, who is subject to compulsory health insurance in accordance with the legislative acts of the Republic of Belarus, does not have a compulsory health insurance contract with a Belarusian insurance organization or a health insurance contract entered into with a foreign insurance organization, valid on the territory of the Republic of Belarus;

the foreigner has a disease that is included in the list of diseases that pose danger to public health.

A visa for entry into the Republic of Belarus may be issued to a foreigner, who is subject to mandatory health insurance in accordance with the legislative acts of the Republic of Belarus, in the case of impossibility of the conclusion by the foreigner of the contract of compulsory medical insurance with the Belarusian insurance organization or the health insurance contract with the foreign insurance organization, valid on the territory of the Republic of Belarus.

If a decision was taken to refuse entry into the Republic of Belarus, the visa previously issued to the foreigner for the entrance into the Republic of Belarus shall be cancelled.

On the basis of the decision to refuse entry into the Republic of Belarus the foreigner in accordance with order established by the legislation of the Republic of Belarus may be included in the list of persons, whose entry into the Republic of Belarus is prohibited or undesirable.

**Article 31.** The State organs empowered to take decisions on refusal of issuing visas for entrance into the Republic of Belarus, on refusal of entrance into the Republic of Belarus and on cancellation of the visa for entrance into the Republic of Belarus

The decision to refuse issuing a visa for entrance into the Republic of Belarus may be taken by the Ministry for Foreign Affairs, the diplomatic mission or consular office of the Republic of Belarus, the organ of the Border Service.

The decision to refuse entry into the Republic of Belarus may be taken by a organ of the Border Service, organ of Internal Affairs or State security of the Republic of Belarus (hereinafter - the organ of State security).

The State organs that have taken a decision to refuse entry to the Republic of Belarus have the right to permit the foreigner to enter the Republic of Belarus for a term not exceeding one month in the manner prescribed by the Council of Ministers of the Republic of Belarus.

The decision to cancel a visa for entry into the Republic of Belarus shall be adopted by the Ministry for Foreign Affairs, the diplomatic mission or consular office of the Republic of Belarus before the entry of the foreigner into the Republic of Belarus or by the organ of the Border Service on the basis of the decision on refusal of entry into the Republic of Belarus.

The organs, which have taken decisions on refusal of issuing visas for entrance into the Republic of Belarus, on refusal of entrance into the Republic of Belarus and on cancellation of the visa for entrance into the Republic of Belarus, are not obliged to inform the foreigner, his relatives or representatives about the grounds for taking such decisions.

**Article 32.** List of persons whose entry into the Republic of Belarus is prohibited or undesirable

Terms and conditions of inclusion of foreigners in the list of persons, whose entry into the Republic of Belarus is prohibited or undesirable, and exclusion of foreigners from this list, as well as the order of keeping of such a list shall be determined by the Council of Ministers of the Republic of Belarus.

**Article 33.** Refusal to issue a visa for exit from the Republic of Belarus or refusal of the permission to leave the Republic of Belarus

A foreigner may be refused a visa to exit from the Republic of Belarus or refused the permission to leave the Republic of Belarus, if:

he is a suspect or accused in a criminal case - until the cessation of the criminal prosecution or until the entry of the sentence into legal force;

he was sentenced in the Republic of Belarus for the committing of a crime, except for convicted without establishing a punishment or a penalty in the form of deprivation of the right to occupy certain positions or engage in certain activities, - until the completion of sentence or remission of the punishment, or before the expiration of the term of a stay of execution of punishment or probation;

he has not fulfilled without reasonable excuse property, tax or other obligations to the Republic of Belarus, its administrative and territorial units, individuals and legal entities established by a legally effective court orders or writs of execution - until the performance of the obligations;

he has been brought it is in accordance with the legislative acts of the Republic of Belarus to administrative responsibility in the territory of the Republic of Belarus - until dismissal of the case on an administrative offence or enforcement of an administrative penalty;

he has debts in respect of a tax obligation established by the legislative acts of the Republic of Belarus - until the payment of the debt;

his departure is contrary to the national security interests of the Republic of Belarus - until the expiry of the circumstances preventing the exit;

it is included in the list of persons who are denied exit from the Republic of Belarus.

If a decision to refuse the exit from the Republic of Belarus, the visa previously issued to the foreigner for exit from the Republic of Belarus shall be cancelled.

On the basis of the decision to refuse the exit from the Republic of Belarus a foreigner in the manner prescribed by the legislation of the Republic of Belarus may be included in the list of persons, who are denied the exit from the Republic of Belarus.

**Article 34.** Organs that are empowered to take a decision on the refusal of issuing a visa for exit from the Republic of Belarus, on the refusal of the exit from the Republic of Belarus and the cancellation of a visa for exit from the Republic of Belarus

The decision to refuse issuing a visa fr exit from the Republic of Belarus shall taken by an organ of the internal affairs.

Decisions on refusal of the exit from the Republic of Belarus of the foreigners referred to in the second, third, fifth, seventh and eighth paragraphs of the first part of Article 33 of this Law shall be taken by an organ of the Border Service, an organ of internal affairs or an organ of State security on its own or at the request of the appropriate State organs of the Republic of Belarus.

Decisions on refusal of the exit from the Republic of Belarus of the foreigners referred to in fourth and sixth paragraphs of the first part of Article 33 of this Law shall be taken by an organ of internal affairs at the request of the appropriate State organs of the Republic of Belarus.

A decision to cancel a visa for the exit from the Republic of Belarus shall be taken by an organ of the Border Service or an organ of internal affairs.

Decisions on the refusal to issue a visa for the exit from the Republic of Belarus, on the refusal of the exit from the Republic of Belarus adopted in respect of foreigners temporarily staying or temporarily residing in the Republic of Belarus shall constitute the grounds for providing them with an extension of the period of temporary stay for a time required to eliminate the grounds for refusal to issue the visa for the exit from the Republic of Belarus or refusal of the exit from the Republic of Belarus.

**Article 35.** The list of persons who are denied exit from the Republic of Belarus

Rules of inclusion of foreigners in the list of persons who are denied exit from the Republic of Belarus, and exclusion of foreigners from this list, as well as the order of keeping of such a list shall be determined by the Council of Ministers of the Republic of Belarus.

**Article 36.** Documents for the exit from the Republic of Belarus and (or) entry into the Republic of Belarus

Foreigners may be granted documents for exiting the Republic of Belarus and (or) entry into the Republic of Belarus.

Categories of foreigners who have given papers to leave the Republic of Belarus and (or) entry into the Republic of Belarus, the types of documents and the order of their issuance, use, sharing, invalidation, withdrawal, storage, destruction, defined by laws of the Republic of Belarus.

**Article 37.** Transit passage (transit) of foreigners through the territory of the Republic of Belarus

Transit passage (transit) of foreigners through the territory of the Republic of Belarus is performed within a period not exceeding two days from the date of their entry into the Republic of Belarus, except for the cases of a forced stop, in accordance with the Rules of transit passage (transit) of foreign citizens and stateless persons through the territory of the Republic of Belarus, approved by the Council of Ministers of the Republic of Belarus.

As a forced stop shall be recognized temporary stay of foreigners on the territory of the Republic of Belarus for more than two days from the date of its entry into the Republic of Belarus due to:

natural disasters, accidents and other emergencies of natural or man-triggered character, delaying the movement of the vehicle;

need to repair the damaged vehicle;

disease or health condition, if according to a conclusion of a public health organisation of the Republic of Belarus the further travel of the foreigner and (or) the person travelling with him may pose a hazard to their life and health;

unanticipated delays in transfers from one mode of transport to another at the transfer point,

occurrence of other unforeseen circumstances that prevent the further travel of the foreigner.

In the case of a forced stop the extension of a foreigner term sojourn in the Republic of Belarus, the issuance of visa to leave the Republic of Belarus conducted by the internal affairs of the place of a forced stop on the application of a foreigner, his representative or the person next in conjunction with it.

## CHAPTER 4 STAY OF FOREIGNERS IN THE REPUBLIC OF BELARUS

**Article 38.** Regimes of stay of foreigners in the Republic of Belarus

Foreigners may stay temporarily, temporarily and permanently reside in the Republic of Belarus.

The procedure of temporary stay, temporary and permanent residence of foreigners in the Republic of Belarus established by this Law and other legislative acts of the Republic of Belarus.

**Article 39**. Temporary stay of foreigners in the Republic of Belarus

The time of temporary stay in the Republic of Belarus of a foreigner is determined by the validity term of the visa issued to him and may not exceed ninety days in a calendar year from the date of first entry into the Republic of Belarus, unless otherwise specified in this Law and international treaties of the Republic of Belarus.

The time of temporary stay in the Republic of Belarus of a foreigner, who arrived in the Republic of Belarus in a manner not requiring obtaining a visa, may not exceed ninety days in a calendar year from the date of first entry into the Republic of Belarus, unless otherwise specified in this Law and international treaties of the Republic of Belarus.

A foreigner temporarily staying in Belarus shall leave the Republic of Belarus before his visa expires or within the claimed by him period of temporary stay in the Republic of Belarus, if at the moment of the expiry of the mentioned periods the period of temporary stay of the foreigner is not extended or the temporary residence stay or not to obtain a temporary residence permit or a permit for permanent residence.

Lodging by a foreigner a complaint against the decisions of State bodies or officials of the Republic of Belarus on reducing the period of temporary stay in the Republic of Belarus, on the refusal to grant a temporary residence permit or to revoke the temporary residence permit, on the refusal to grant a permit for permanent residence or to revoke a permit for permanent residence to a superior State organ, a higher-ranking official within the time limit established by this Law for the departure of the foreigner from the Republic of Belarus or to the court after appeal of such decisions to a superior State organ, the higher-ranking official is the grounds for an extension of the temporary stay in the Republic of Belarus of the foreigner, who has lodged a complaint, for the time of consideration of the complaint.

**Article 40.** Extension of a period of temporary stay of foreigners in the Republic of Belarus

In the event of occurrence of the circumstances involving the need to extend the period of stay of a foreigner in the Republic of Belarus, the temporary stay may be extended within the limits of the period provided for in the first and second parts of Article 39 of this Law.

In case of illness, natural disasters or other unforeseen circumstances preventing the departure of a foreigner from the Republic of Belarus, the temporary stay may be extended beyond the time limit provided for in the first and second parts of Article 39 of this Law, until the cessation of these circumstances.

If the validity term of a visa issued to a foreigner has expired, upon the extension of temporary stay a visa for exit from the Republic of Belarus shall be issued to the foreigner.

Upon application for a permit for temporary or permanent residence the period of temporary stay of the foreigner in the Republic of Belarus may be extended for the period of consideration of the application.

In case of adoption of a decision on the extension of temporary stay in the Republic of Belarus the period of registration of a foreigner shall also be extended.

State bodies and other organizations of the Republic of Belarus, to which a foreigner may apply for extension of the period of temporary stay (registration), documents required for extension of the period of temporary stay (registration), a period of extension, as well as the amount of the charge levied for extension of the period of temporary stay (registration) are determined by legislative acts of the Republic of Belarus.

**Article 41.** The procedure for registration of foreigners temporarily staying in the Republic of Belarus

Foreigners, who have arrived in the Republic of Belarus, except for foreigners referred to in Article 45 of this Law, shall within five days, except for weekends, public holidays and holidays established

and declared by the President of the Republic of Belarus as legal holidays, register at the registration authority at the place of the actual temporary stay, unless otherwise specified by this Law and international treaties of the Republic of Belarus.

Foreigners temporarily staying in the Republic of Belarus are required to reside in the Republic of Belarus only at the place of temporary stay, where they are registered in the registration authorities, except for the foreigners specified in part four of this Article.

Upon a change of a place of temporary stay foreigners shall within five days, except for weekends, public holidays and holidays established and declared by the President of the Republic of Belarus as legal holidays, register at the registration authority at the new place of the temporary stay, except for the foreigners specified in part four of this Article.

Foreigners, who have arrived in Belarus for the purposes of tourism and who are travelling within the territory of the Republic of Belarus in accordance with the program of the tour, shall registered in the registration authority at the place of their initial temporary stay for the total duration of the tour.

Registration of foreigners temporarily staying in the Republic of Belarus in the registration authorities shall be performed on the basis of applications of the foreigners or requests of the host organizations.

Temporarily staying in the Republic of Belarus citizens (nationals) of the States with a visa regime for entry into the Republic of Belarus shall be registered for the time period specified in their application or request of the host organization, but no more than for the validity period of the visa.

Temporarily staying in the Republic of Belarus citizens (nationals) of the States with a visa-free regime for entry into the Republic of Belarus shall be registered for the time period not exceeding the period, specified by an international treaty of the Republic of Belarus. In the absence of such an international treaty of the Republic of Belarus or the absence in the international treaty of indication of the period of the visa-free stay, the registration shall be effected for the period specified in the application of the foreigner or the request of the host organization, but not more than for ninety days in a calendar year as from the date of the first entry into the Republic of Belarus.

Foreigners, temporarily staying in the Republic of Belarus, in respect of whom a decision on the extension of the period of temporary stay in the Republic of Belarus is adopted, shall be registered for the period of the extension of temporary stay.

A foreigner, who lodged a complaint against decisions of State organs or officials of the Republic of Belarus on reducing the period of temporary stay in the Republic of Belarus, on refusing to issue a temporary residence permit or on cancellation of the temporary residence permit, on the refusal to issue a permanent residence permit or cancellation of the permanent residence permit, on the refusal to issue a visa for the exit from the Republic of Belarus or on refusal of the permission to leave the Republic of Belarus to the superior State organ or a court within the time limit established by this Law for the departure of the foreigner from the Republic of Belarus, shall register in the registration authority at the place of the actual temporary stay for the period until the adoption of a decision on the complaint.

In the case of the adoption of a decision to cancel the temporary residence permit or permanent residence permit a foreigner shall be registered for the period provided for in this Law for the departure of the foreigner from the Republic of Belarus.

In the case of the adoption of a decision to reduce the period of temporary stay of a foreigner in the Republic of Belarus the period of his registration is reduced down to the period provided for in this Law for the departure of the foreigner from the Republic of Belarus.

State agencies and other organizations of the Republic of Belarus, to which a foreigner may apply for registration, the documents required for registration, the registration period, as well as the fees charged for registration are determined by legislative acts of the Republic of Belarus.

**Article 42.** Registration of foreigners temporarily staying in the Republic of Belarus in organs of internal affairs

In the organs of the internal affairs shall be registered foreigners temporarily staying in the Republic of Belarus, except for the foreigners referred to in Article 43 and the first and third parts of Article 44 of this Law.

**Article 43.** Registration of foreigners temporarily staying in the Republic of Belarus in a hotel, sanatorium-resort or wellness organizations

In hotels, sanatorium-resort and wellness organizations shall be registered foreigners temporarily staying in the Republic of Belarus, who have checked-in for residence in them, except for foreigners specified in parts one and three of Article 44 of this Law.

Authorized persons of hotels, sanatorium-resort and wellness organizations within one day after check-in of foreigners temporarily staying in the Republic of Belarus shall submit to an organ of internal affairs at the location of hotels, sanatorium-resort and wellness organizations information about such foreigners in the manner determined by the Ministry for Internal Affairs.

**Article 44.** Registration of foreigners temporarily residing in the Republic of Belarus in the Ministry for Foreign Affairs

In the Ministry for Foreign Affairs shall be registered guests of accredited by the Ministry for Foreign Affairs heads of diplomatic missions and consular institutions of foreign States, missions and organs of international organizations and intergovernmental entities, if these guests live in the residences of

the heads or in premises of the mentioned missions, institutions, organs or in residential premises occupied by their employees.

In the case of residence of foreigners referred to in the first paragraph of this Article outside the residences of the heads or the premises of diplomatic missions and consular institutions of foreign States, missions and organs of international organizations and intergovernmental entities or residential premises occupied by their employees, the registration of these foreigners shall be performed according to the procedure set forth in Article 41 of this Law.

The Ministry for Foreign Affairs has the right to register of arriving to the Republic of Belarus State and public figures of foreign States and members of their families, as well as employees of international organizations and intergovernmental entities not listed in Article 45 of this Law, at the request of the diplomatic missions and consular institutions of foreign States, the host organizations.

**Article 45.** Foreigners temporarily staying in the Republic of Belarus, who are not subject to the registration in the Republic of Belarus

In the Republic of Belarus are not subject to the registration:

Heads of State and Governments of foreign States, heads and members of parliamentary, governmental and other official delegations, the technical staff of these delegations and foreigners, who arrived in the Republic of Belarus at the invitation of the President of the Republic of Belarus, the Chambers of the National Assembly of the Republic of Belarus, the Council of Ministers of the Republic of Belarus, the Constitutional Court of the Republic of Belarus, the Supreme Court of the Republic of Belarus, the Supreme Economic Court of the Republic of Belarus, the Administration of the President of the Republic of Belarus, the State Secretariat of the Security Council of the Republic of Belarus, the State Control Committee of the Republic of Belarus, the Attorney-General Office of the Republic of Belarus, the Central Commission of of the Republic of Belarus for Conduct of Elections and Republican Referenda, Republican organs of State administration, local executive and administrative organs of the Republic of Belarus, as well as their family members;

foreigners, who have arrived in Belarus by virtue of passports issued by the United Nations Organization;

heads and staff of diplomatic missions and consular institutions of foreign States, employees of the military attaches' offices, members of trade representations of foreign States in the Republic of Belarus, as well as members of their families;

heads and staff of missions and organs of international organizations and intergovernmental entities, who according to statutory documents of these organizations and entities or appropriate international treaties of the Republic of Belarus, shall enjoy the privileges and immunities, as well as members of their families;

foreigners, who have arrived in Belarus for the weekends, public holidays and holidays, established and declared by the President of the Republic of Belarus as legal holidays, and (or) for up to five

twenty-four hours during working days, if their departure from the Republic of Belarus will be performed during these days (twenty-four hours);

foreigners temporarily staying in the countryside, small towns of the Republic of Belarus on the basis of contracts for services in the field of rural and environmental tourism, concluded with an individual or peasant (farmer) household involved in such activities in accordance with the order established by legislative acts of the Republic of Belarus (hereinafter - the subjects of rural and environmental tourism), either on the basis of contracts for providing tourist services, in which services in the field of rural and environmental tourism are included;

crew members of foreign military aircrafts arriving in the Republic of Belarus according to the established order;

foreigners who are members of crews of civil aircrafts servicing international airlines, trains brigades of international rail transport, while staying in the airport or at the stations listed in a flight or train schedule;

foreigners who are members of crews of foreign vehicles and river transport performing the carriage of cargo and passengers in international traffic, while staying in towns and other settlements on the routes of transport operations, including those in other points of destinations.

foreigners who are referred to in fourth and fifth paragraphs of the first part of this article are subject to accreditation in the manner determined by the Ministry for Foreign Affairs.

foreigners, who are referred to in paragraph seven of the first part of this article, shall present to the official of an organ of the the Border Service upon leaving the Republic of Belarus a contract for provision of services in the field of rural and environmental tourism or contract for providing tourist services, in which services in the field of rural and environmental tourism are included;.

Subjects of rural and environmental tourism within one day after the arrival of foreigners referred to in paragraph seven of the first part of this Article shall submit to an organ of internal affairs at their location information on those foreigners in the manner established by the Ministry of Internal Affairs.

**Article 46.** Refusal of registration, extension and (or) reduction of the period of temporary stay in the Republic of Belarus

Registration and extension of temporary stay in the Republic of Belarus may be denied to a foreigner, and (or) the period of his stay in the Republic of Belarus may be reduced, if the grounds set forth in the first part of Article 30 of this Law are discovered.

A foreigner shall be denied the registration, the period of the temporary stay in the Republic of Belarus of the foreigner shall not be extended, and (or) shall be reduced:

if the grounds set out in the second part of Article 30 of this Law have been discovered;

if upon submitting to the relevant State organs of the Republic of Belarus of documents required for adoption of decision on registration, extension of the period of temporary stay in the Republic of Belarus a foreigner provided false information, submitted documents and (or) information that do not comply with the requirements of the legislation of the Republic of Belarus, including fraudulent, counterfeit or invalid documents;

if there are no grounds for his further stay in the Republic of Belarus;

in the case of deportation or expulsion of the foreigner.

In the case of adoption of decisions to refuse registration, extension and (or) to reduce the period of temporary stay in the Republic of Belarus the validity term of the visa issued to a foreigner, and (or) the period of his temporary stay shall be reduced, if there is no legitimate grounds for his further stay in the Republic of Belarus.

In the case, where the period of temporary stay in the Republic of Belarus has been reduced, and there is no other legitimate grounds for further stay in the Republic of Belarus, the foreigner shall leave the Republic of Belarus within ten days from the date of receipt by him of a notice about the adopted decision on reduction of the period of his temporary stay.

**Article 47.** Decision-makers to extend the period of temporary stay in the Republic of Belarus and the refusal of registration, extension and (or) reducing the period of temporary stay in the Republic of Belarus

Decisions on the extension of temporary stay of foreigners in the Republic of Belarus within the period provided for first and second parts of Article 39 of this Law shall be adopted by the registration authority and in respect of the citizens (nationals) of the visa regime of entry to the Republic of Belarus - an organ of internal affairs.

The decision to extend the temporary stay of foreigners in the Republic of Belarus over the period provided first and second parts of Article 39 of this Law, taken by the authority of the Interior.

Decisions to refuse registration, extension and (or) to reduce the period of temporary stay of foreigners in the Republic of Belarus shall be adopted:

in respect of foreigners subject to registration or accreditation, or registered or accredited by the Ministry for Foreign Affairs, as well as declared by the Republic of Belarus unacceptable or undesirable (persona non grata) - by the Ministry for Foreign Affairs;

in respect of other foreigners - by a organ of internal affairs independently or at the request of the appropriate State organs of the Republic of Belarus.

**Article 48.** Temporary residence permit

A temporary residence permit shall be issued to foreigners:

if they arrived in Belarus for receiving education or are studying on the territory of the Republic of Belarus in the institutions providing professional and vocational, specialized secondary, high and postgraduate education, advanced vocational training and retraining - for a period of study, but not more than for one year;

if they are spouses, close relatives of citizens of the Republic of Belarus or foreigners permanently residing in the Republic of Belarus - for the whole period of stay, but not more than for one year;

if they arrived in the Republic of Belarus for engaging or engaged in labour, entrepreneurial and (or) any other activity on the territory of Belarus in accordance with the legislation of Belarus - for the period of stay, but not more than for one year;

in respect of whom is established guardianship (trusteeship) of citizens of the Republic of Belarus , as well as foreigners permanently residing in the Republic of Belarus - for the period of guardianship (trusteeship), but not more than for one year;

if they are ethnic Belarusians or their blood relatives in the direct line of descent: children, grandchildren, great-grandchildren, who were born outside of the contemporary territory of the Republic of Belarus - for the whole period of stay, but not more than for one year;

if they have grounds to acquire the citizenship of the Republic of Belarus in the manner of registration - for the period of stay, but not more than for one year;

if they formerly were citizens of the Republic of Belarus - for the period of stay, but not more than for one year;

if they own residential premises in the Republic of Belarus - for the period of stay, but not more than for one year;

if they have applied in the manner established by the legislation of the Republic of Belarus for refugee status, additional protection or asylum in the Republic of Belarus - for the time of consideration of the application;

if they are granted refugee status in the Republic of Belarus - for the period not exceeding one year for obtaining of a permanent residence permit;

if they are given additional protection in the Republic of Belarus - for the period of provision of the additional protection, but not more than for one year;

if they cannot in accordance with the legislation of the Republic of Belarus be returned or expelled against their will onto the territory of a State, where their life or freedom would be endangered because of their race, religion, citizenship, nationality, belonging to a particular social group or political views, or where they are threatened with torture, or if there is no State, which has

consented to receive them, - for the period, during which the return or expulsion is impossible, but not more than for one year;

if they receive medical care as in-patient in a public health care organizations of the Republic of Belarus - for the period of treatment, but not more than for one year;

on other grounds provided by the legislation of the Republic of Belarus, including international treaties of the Republic of Belarus.

A temporary residence permit may be issued to family members (husband (wife), children, children adopted as sons (as daughters) under the age of eighteen years, persons under care) of a foreigner, who has received a temporary residence permit, if there is a legitimate source of receiving an income, providing him and his family a minimum subsistence wage established in the Republic of Belarus for the period of temporary residence in the Republic of Belarus.

A foreigner temporarily residing in the Republic of Belarus shall reside in the Republic of Belarus only at the place of temporary residence, at which he was issued a temporary residence permit.

Upon a change of a place of temporary residence a foreigner temporarily residing in the Republic of Belarus shall within five days, except for weekends, public holidays and holidays established and declared by the President of the Republic of Belarus as legal holidays, apply to an organ of internal affairs at a new place of temporary residence for making changes in the temporary residence permit.

State organs of the Republic of Belarus, to which a foreigner may apply for issuance of a temporary residence permit, documents needed for issuing the temporary residence permit, period of its issue and its validity period, as well as the charges levied for issuing the temporary residence permit are determined by legislative acts of the Republic Belarus.

A foreigner temporarily residing in the Republic of Belarus shall leave the Republic of Belarus before the expiration of the validity period of a temporary residence permit, if on the date of expiry of the mentioned period he failed to register for temporary stay or obtain a new temporary residence permit or permanent residence permit.

**Article 49.** Refusal to issue a temporary residence permit

Issuing of a temporary residence permit to a foreigner may be refused, where:

the grounds set out in the first part of Article 30 of this Law have been discovered;

the stated purpose of entry into the Republic of Belarus of the foreigner, who is a citizen (national) of the State having problems in respect of migration, is another than the ground, on the basis of which he applied for a temporary residence permit;

A temporary residence permit shall not issued to a foreigner, where:

the grounds set out in the second part of Article 30 of this Law have been discovered;

upon submitting to the relevant authorities of the Republic of Belarus of documents required for the adoption of a decision on issuing him a temporary residence permit, the foreigner provided false information, submitted documents and (or) information that are not conforming to the requirement of the legislation of the Republic of Belarus, including fraudulent, counterfeit or invalid documents;

there are no grounds for his temporary residence in the Republic of Belarus;

upon submitting to the relevant State organs of the Republic of Belarus of documents required for the adoption of the decision to issue temporary residence permits to family members of a foreigner, he could not provide evidence of his ability to support himself and his family members (husband (wife), children, children adopted as sons (as daughters) under the age of eighteen years, persons under care) in the Republic of Belarus within a minimum subsistence wage for the period of temporary residence in the Republic of Belarus, except for the case, where the foreigner is recognized disabled.

In the case of the adoption of a decision to refuse issuing a temporary residence permit the validity period of the visa issued to a foreigner, and (or) the period of registration and temporary stay shall be reduced, if there are no legitimate reason for his further stay in the Republic of Belarus.

An foreigner, in respect of whom a decision on refusal of issuing a temporary residence permit has been taken, unless there are other legitimate reasons for his further stay in the Republic of Belarus, is obliged to leave the Republic of Belarus within fifteen days from the date of receiving a notice of the decision to refuse issuing the temporary residence permit.

**Article 50.** Cancellation of a temporary residence permit

A temporary residence permit of a foreigner may be cancelled, if:

the grounds set out in the first part of Article 30 of this Law have been discovered;

a foreigner is exiting or has exited from the Republic of Belarus to a foreign State for permanent residence.

A temporary residence permit of a foreigner shall be cancelled:

if the grounds set out in the second part of Article 30 of this Law have been discovered;

where there is evidence that, upon submitting to the relevant State organs of the Republic of Belarus of the documents required for adoption of a decision on issuing him a temporary residence permit, the foreigner provided false information, submitted documents and (or) information that are not conforming to the requirements of the legislation of the Republic of Belarus, including fraudulent, counterfeit or invalid documents;

in case of deportation or expulsion of the foreigner;

in the case of expiry of the ground, in accordance with which the decision to grant a foreigner a temporary residence permit was taken.

In the case of the adoption of a decision to cancel a temporary residence permit the validity period of the visa issued to the foreigner shall be reduced, if there are no legitimate reason for his further stay in the Republic of Belarus.

If a temporary residence permit issued to a foreigner, was cancelled and there are no other legitimate grounds for his stay in the Republic of Belarus, the foreigner shall leave the Republic of Belarus within fifteen days from the date of receiving a notice of the adopted decision to cancel the temporary residence permit, if another period is not set by the legislative acts of the Republic of Belarus regulating the particulars of the legal status of the foreigners applying for the refugee status or additional protection in the Republic of Belarus, as well as foreigners, who are granted the refugee status or additional or temporary protection in the Republic of Belarus.

A foreigner, whose temporary residence permit is cancelled on the grounds specified in the first part and paragraphs two, three and five of the second part of this Article, shall register with the registration authority at the place of the actual temporary residence for the period up to the departure from the Republic of Belarus.

**Article 51.** Organs taking decisions on issuing a temporary residence permit, on refusal of issuing and cancellation of the temporary residence permit

A decision to issue a temporary residence permit shall be taken by an organ of internal affairs.

Decisions to refuse issuing and cancellation of a temporary residence permit shall be taken by an organ of internal affairs independently or at the request of the appropriate State organs of the Republic of Belarus.

**Article 52.** The document certifying in the Republic of Belarus the identity of a foreigner temporarily staying or temporarily residing in the Republic of Belarus

The document certifying in the Republic of Belarus the identity of a foreigner temporarily staying or temporarily residing in the Republic of Belarus, except for foreigners, who are granted the refugee status in the Republic of Belarus, is a document for travelling abroad.

**Article 53.** Permanent residence permit

A permanent residence permit shall be issued to the foreigners, who:

are close relatives of citizens of the Republic of Belarus permanently residing in the Republic of Belarus;

are persons, to whom a refugee status or asylum in the Republic of Belarus is granted;

have the right to family reunification;

have lived legally in the Republic of Belarus for the last seven years or more;

have the grounds to acquire the citizenship of the Republic of Belarus in the manner of registration;

held earlier the citizenship of the Republic of Belarus;

are workers and professionals who are needed for organizations of the Republic of Belarus;

possess exceptional abilities and talent, or have outstanding merits before the Republic of Belarus, the high achievements in the spheres of science, technology, culture and sports;

are the foreign investors that have made investments in the amount not less than one hundred and fifty thousand Euro in objects of investment activities in the territory of the Republic of Belarus;

are ethnic Belarusians or their blood relatives in the direct line of descent: children, grandchildren, great-grandchildren who were born outside the contemporary territory of the Republic of Belarus.

A permanent residence permit may be issued to other foreigners, who are not mentioned in the first part of this article, on the basis of a decision of the Council of Ministers of the Republic of Belarus in consultation with the President of the Republic of Belarus.

The procedure for issuing foreigners with permanent residence permits is determined by the legislative acts of the Republic of Belarus and resolutions of the Council of Ministers of the Republic of Belarus.

Procedure of registration of foreigners permanently residing in the Republic of Belarus and de-registration of them at the place of residence and place of stay in the Republic of Belarus is determined by the legislative acts of the Republic of Belarus.

**Article 54.** Immigration quota

For the purposes of State regulation of entry of foreigners for permanent residence in the Republic of Belarus the Council of Ministers of the Republic of Belarus may establish an immigration quota, which is determined separately for each State.

Foreigners having the right to family reunification may enter for permanent residence into the Republic of Belarus for the purposes of joint residence and doing the joint housekeeping beyond the established immigration quota.

The President of the Republic of Belarus may take decisions on the admission of foreigners for permanent residence into the Republic of Belarus in excess of the established immigration quota.

**Article 55**. The right to family reunification

The right to family reunification belongs to a husband (wife), minor children and children adopted as sons (as daughters), and not been married and sole children and children adopted as sons (as daughters) over eighteen years, disabled parents and adoptive parents having an invitation respectively from a husband (wife), parents, children, children adopted as sons (as daughters), being citizens of the Republic of Belarus or foreigners permanently residing in the Republic of Belarus.

In some cases the right to family reunification may be granted to other relatives of citizens of the Republic of Belarus and to foreigners permanently residing in the Republic of Belarus, not mentioned in the first part of this Article, on the condition of availability to the inviting person or the foreigner, who have applied for issuance of a permanent residence permit, of adequate housing, as well as the availability to the inviting person of a legitimate source of receiving income providing him and his family members (husband (wife), children, children adopted as sons (as daughters) under the age of eighteen years, persons under care) and the foreigner, who has applied for issuance of the permanent residence permit, a minimum subsistence wage established in the Republic of Belarus for the period of consideration of the application.

In the case of family reunification the foreigner, who has applied for the issuance of a permanent residence permit in the Republic of Belarus or the person inviting him or a person are required to submit the documents proving the right to family reunification.

**Article 56.** Refusal to issue a permanent residence permit

Issuance of a permanent residence permit to a foreigner may be refused, if:

the grounds provided for in paragraphs fourth, fifth or tenth of the first part of Article 30 of this Law have been discovered;

the stated purpose of entry into the Republic of Belarus of the foreigner, who is a citizen (national) of the State having problems in respect of migration, is another than the ground, on the basis of which he applied for a permanent residence permit;

the established immigration quota has been exhausted.

A permanent residence permit shall not be issued to a foreigner, if:

the grounds provided for in paragraphs the second - the fifth or the seventh of the second paragraph of Article 30 of this Law are discovered;

upon submitting to the relevant State organs of the Republic of Belarus of the documents necessary for taking a decision on issuance to him of the permanent residence permit, the foreigner provided false information, submitted documents and (or) information that are not conforming to the requirements of the legislation of the Republic of Belarus, including fraudulent, counterfeit or invalid documents;

there are no grounds for his permanent residence in the Republic of Belarus;

there are documents and (or) information available confirming that the marriage with a citizen of the Republic of Belarus or a foreigner permanently residing in the Republic of Belarus was effected by the foreigner solely for the purposes of obtain a permanent residence permit.

In the case of the adoption of a decision to refuse issuing a permanent residence permit the validity period of the visa issued to a foreigner, and (or) the period of registration and temporary stay shall be reduced, if there are no legitimate reason for his further stay in the Republic of Belarus.

The list of documents and (or) information provided for in the fifth paragraph of part two of this Article and the procedure of their receipt by the organs of internal affairs shall be determined by the Council of Ministers of the Republic of Belarus.

An foreigner, in respect of whom a decision on refusal of issuing a permanent residence permit has been taken, unless there are other legitimate reasons for his further stay in the Republic of Belarus, is obliged to leave the Republic of Belarus within one month from the date of receiving a notice of the decision to refuse issuing the permanent residence permit.

**Article 57.** Cancellation of permanent residence permit

A permanent residence permit issued to the foreigner may be cancelled, if:

the grounds provided for in paragraphs fourth, fifth or tenth of the first part of Article 30 of this Law have been discovered;

the foreigner has obtained a permanent residence permit in a foreign State;

the grounds, in accordance with which the decision to grant the foreigner a permanent residence permit was taken, have expired.

the foreigner resided outside the Republic of Belarus for more than one hundred eighty-three days in a calendar year;

the foreigner and his family members (husband (wife), children, children adopted as sons (as daughters) under the age of eighteen years, persons under care) permanently residing in the Republic of Belarus have no legitimate source of receiving income that provides him and his family members with the minimum subsistence wage established in the Republic of Belarus for a period longer than six months in a calendar year.

A permanent residence permit issued to the foreigner shall be cancelled:

if the grounds set out in the paragraphs from two to five of the second part of Article 30 of this Law have been discovered;

if a marriage concluded by the foreigner with a Belarusian citizen or a foreigner permanently residing in the Republic of Belarus and served as the basis or issuing a permanent residence permit was recognized null and void in the manner prescribed by legislative acts of the Republic of Belarus;

where there is evidence that, upon submitting to the relevant State organs of the Republic of Belarus of the documents required for adoption of a decision on issuing him a permanent residence permit, the foreigner provided false information, submitted documents and (or) information that are not conforming to the requirements of the legislation of the Republic of Belarus, including fraudulent, counterfeit or invalid documents;

a foreigner has exited or is exiting from the Republic of Belarus to a foreign State for permanent residence.

in the case of deportation or expulsion of the foreigner.

Cancellation of a permanent residence permit entails a reduction of the validity term of the visa issued to the foreigner, or its cancellation and (or) withdrawal of the residence permit.

In the case, where a permanent residence permit issued to a foreigner was withdrawn, and there are no other legitimate grounds for his further stay in the Republic of Belarus, the foreigner shall leave the Republic of Belarus within one month from the date of receiving a notice of the decision to cancel the permanent residence permit, if another period is not set by the legislative acts of the Republic of Belarus regulating the particulars of the legal status of the foreigners applying for the refugee status or additional protection in the Republic of Belarus, as well as foreigners, who are granted the refugee status or additional or temporary protection in the Republic of Belarus.

A foreigner, whose permanent residence permit is cancelled on the grounds specified in the first part and paragraphs from two to five of the second part of this Article, shall register with the registration authority at the place of the actual temporary residence for the period up to the departure from the Republic of Belarus.

**Article 58.** Organs taking decisions on issuing a permanent residence permit, on refusal of issuing and cancellation of the permanent residence permit

Decisions on issuance of a permanent resident permit to foreigners referred to in paragraph from two to seven and eleven of the first part of Article 53 of this Law shall be taken by an organ of internal affairs independently or at the request of the appropriate State organs of the Republic of Belarus.

Decisions on issuance of a permanent resident permit to foreigners referred to in paragraph eight of the first part of Article 53 of this Law shall be taken by an organ of internal affairs at the request of the appropriate State organs of the Republic of Belarus.

Decisions on issuance of a permanent resident permit to foreigners referred to in paragraph nine and ten of the first part of Article 53 of this Law shall be taken by the Ministry for Internal Affairs at the request of the appropriate State organs of the Republic of Belarus.

Decisions on issuance of a permanent residence permit to foreigners referred to in the second part of Article 55 of this Law shall be taken by the Ministry for Internal Affairs at the request of the inviting persons according to the procedure established by the Council of Ministers of the Republic of Belarus.

A decision to refuse issuing a permanent residence permit shall be taken by the Ministry for Internal Affairs or another organ of internal affairs independently or at the request of the appropriate State organs of the Republic of Belarus.

A decision to withdraw a permanent residence permit issued to the foreigner, in the cases provided for in paragraph four of the first part and paragraph three of the second part of Article 57 of this Law shall be adopted in judicial proceedings, in other cases stipulated by Article 57 of this Law shall be adopted by an organ of internal affairs independently or at the request of the appropriate State organs of the Republic of Belarus.

**Article 59.** Notices about decisions adopted on issues of the stay of a foreigner in the Republic of Belarus

A foreigner, in respect of whom has been taken a decision on refusal of the extension and (or) reduction of the period of temporary stay in the Republic of Belarus, the refusal to issue a temporary residence permit or cancellation of the temporary residence permit, the refusal to issue a permanent residence permit or cancellation a permanent residence permit, refusal to issue a visa for exit from the Republic of Belarus or refusal of permission to exit from the Republic of Belarus, shall be served or mailed with a notice of the decision no later than five twenty-four hours as from the day of the approval of that decision by an organ of internal affairs at the place of temporary stay, temporary residence or place of residence of the foreigner in the Republic of Belarus.

In case of sending the foreigner of the notice about a decision referred to in the first part of this Article, the foreigner is considered informed of the adoption of this decision after three twenty-four hours as from the day of sending of that notice.

**Article 60.** Residence permit

An foreigner, who has reached the age of sixteen and received in due course a permanent residence permit, shall have a residence permit.

The procedure for issuing, using, exchange, invalidation, withdrawal, storage, destruction of the residence permit is determined by the legislative acts of the Republic of Belarus.

**Article 61.** Centralized record keeping on foreigners

In order to keep records on foreigners temporarily staying, temporarily and permanently residing in the Republic of Belarus, a central data bank for keeping records on foreigners staying in the Republic of Belarus is to be created.

The procedures for establishing and maintaining a central data bank for keeping records on foreigners staying in the Republic of Belarus and the use of the information contained in this data bank shall be established by the Council of Ministers of the Republic of Belarus.

**Article 62.** The control over the stay of foreigners in the Republic of Belarus

The control over temporary stay, temporary and permanent residence of foreigners in the Republic of Belarus, as well as transit passage (transit) of foreigners through the territory of the Republic of Belarus shall be performed by the organs of internal affairs in collaboration with the organs of State security, organs of the Border Service and the Ministry for Foreign Affairs.

Foreigners at the request of officials of the organs of internal affairs, the organs of State security, the organs of the Border Services shall submit a document for travelling abroad, other documents stipulated by the legislation of the Republic of Belarus, which prove that they stay in the Republic of Belarus lawfully, as well as provide explanations relating to their stay in the Republic of Belarus.

**Article 63.** Identification of personality of a foreigner without a document for travelling abroad

With respect to a foreigner staying in the Republic of Belarus and not possessing a document for travelling abroad the organs of internal affairs shall perform identification of personality according to the procedure established by the Council of Ministers of the Republic of Belarus.

In the case, where after the conduct of identification of personality the identity of the foreigner has been established, the organs of internal affairs shall issued him a certificate, the form of which is approved by the Council of Ministers of the Republic of Belarus. The certificate confirms the identity of the foreigner until issuance to him of a document for travelling abroad or a document for the exit from the Republic of Belarus.

## CHAPTER 5 DEPORTATION. EXPULSION

**Article 64.** Deportation

Foreigners may be subjected to deportation in the cases established by certain legislative acts of the Republic of Belarus, and in the manner prescribed by the Council of Ministers of the Republic of Belarus.

**Article 65.** Expulsion

A foreigner may be expelled from the Republic of Belarus in the interests of the national security of the Republic of Belarus, public order, for the protection of public morality, public health, rights and freedoms of citizens of the Republic of Belarus and other persons, if he cannot be subjected to deportation.

The decision on expulsion is taken by a organ of internal affairs or an organ of State security.

Expulsion may be effected by means of a voluntary departure of a foreigner from the Republic of Belarus or by enforcement.

The procedure of conducting of the expulsion shall be established by the Council of Ministers of the Republic of Belarus.

**Article 66.** Expulsion by means of a voluntary departure

A foreigner, in respect of whom an organ of internal affairs or an organ of State security adopted a decision on expulsion by a voluntary departure, shall within the period prescribed in the decision depart from the Republic of Belarus.

**Article 67.** Expulsion by enforcement

Expulsion by enforcement is performed, if:

there are reasons to believe that a foreigner can avoid the fulfilment of a decision on expulsion by a voluntary departure;

the foreigner has not left the Republic of Belarus within the period prescribed in the decision on expulsion by a voluntary departure.

Upon adoption of the decision on expulsion by enforcement an organ of internal affairs or an organ of State security with a sanctions from a prosecutor shall take measures to detain a foreigner for the period necessary for expulsion.

**Article 68**. Suspension and cancellation of expulsion

The expulsion shall be suspended in the cases of application of the foreigner to an appropriate State organ of the Republic of Belarus with a petition for receiving a refugee status, additional protection or asylum in the Republic of Belarus, or in the case, where a foreigner, against whom an expulsion order is adopted, is a suspect or accused in a criminal case or sentenced to an arrest, restraint of liberty or imprisonment.

Expulsion shall be suspended until the adoption of a decision on an application for the refugee status or additional protection in the Republic of Belarus, and the expiration of the period established by the legislation of the Republic of Belarus for appealing of the decision adopted on the application for provision of the refugee status or additional protection in the Republic of Belarus (in the case of non-use of the right to appeal), or until the entry into legal force of the court's decision to dismiss the complaint, or pending a decision on an application for provision of the asylum in the Republic of Belarus or until the termination of criminal prosecution, or until the entry of a court's judgement into legal force, or until the completion of penalty in the form of arrest, restraint of liberty or imprisonment.

In the case of provision to a foreigner, against whom an expulsion order is adopted, of the refugee status or additional protection or asylum in the Republic of Belarus, as well as in the case, when a

foreigner cannot be returned or deported against his will to the State, where his life or freedom would be endangered because of his race, religion, citizenship, nationality, belonging to a particular social group or political views, or where he is threatened with tortures, the expulsion shall be stopped.

**Article 69.** The costs associated with deportation or expulsion

The costs associated with deportation or expulsion shall be covered at the expense of a foreigner, the legal entity or the individual that applied for his entry into the Republic of Belarus, stay or residence in the Republic of Belarus.

In the case, where reimbursement of the costs at the expense of the persons mentioned in the first part of this article is impossible, deportation or expulsion shall be performed at the expense of the Republican budget.

**Article 70.** The consequences of deportation or expulsion

On the basis of a decision on deportation or expulsion the foreigner is included in the list of persons, whose entry into the Republic of Belarus is prohibited or undesirable.

Entry of a deported foreigners into the Republic of Belarus may be prohibited for the period from one year to five years.

Entry of an expelled foreigner into the Republic of Belarus may be prohibited for a period from one year to ten years.

In the case of deportation or expulsion of a foreigner onto his document for travel abroad shall be affixed the appropriate mark. The form of the mark and the procedure for affixing it by the organ that has taken the decision on deportation or expulsion, shall be determined by the Council of Ministers of the Republic of Belarus.

## CHAPTER 6 APPEALING AGAINST DECISIONS AND ACTION (OMISSIONS) OF STATE ORGANS AND OFFICIALS OF THE REPUBLIC OF BELARUS

**Article 71.** The right to appeal decisions and actions (omissions) of State organs and officials of the Republic of Belarus

Foreigners as well as their representatives have the right to appeal decisions and actions (omissions) of State organs and officials of the Republic of Belarus related to the implementation of this Law to a superior State organ or the superior official.

Challenging in the court of decisions and actions (omissions) of State organs and officials of the Republic of Belarus related to the implementation of this Law shall be performed in accordance with the civil procedural legislation of the Republic of Belarus after the appeal of such decisions and actions (omissions) to the superior State organ or the superior officer.

**Article 72.** Appealing of the decisions of State organs and officials of the Republic of Belarus to the superior State organ or the superior official

Complaints of foreigners against the decisions of State organs or officials of the Republic of Belarus to refuse registration, renewal and or) on reducing the period of temporary stay in the Republic of Belarus, on the refusal to issue a temporary residence permit or cancellation of the temporary residence permit, on the refusal to issue a permanent residence permit or on cancellation of the permanent residence permit, on the refusal to issue a visa for the exit from the Republic of Belarus or refusal of permission to leave the Republic of Belarus can be filed to a superior State organ or a higher-ranking official within one year from the date of adoption of such decisions.

Complaints of foreigners on the decisions of State organs or officials of the Republic of Belarus about expulsion can be submitted to a superior State organ or higher-ranking official within one month from the foreigner's acquaintance with this decision.

The complaints of foreigners on the decisions specified in parts one and two of this article shall be considered within one month from the date of their filing.

Appeals against decisions of State organs and officials of the Republic of Belarus under part two of this article do not constitute grounds for the stay of foreigners in the Republic of Belarus.

## CHAPTER 7 FINAL PROVISIONS

**Article 73.** Introduction of amendments and additions to some Laws of the Republic of Belarus

1. To introduce into the Criminal Code of the Republic of Belarus of July 16, 1999 (the National Register of Legal Acts of the Republic of Belarus, 2000, No. 77-78, 2 / 71, 2008, No. 14, 2 / 1412) the following amendments and additions:

1.1. Part 2 of Article 115 shall read as follows:

2. The fact of detention of a foreign citizen or a stateless persons shall be notified by the organ that conducts criminal proceedings and made an arrest at the request of the foreign citizen or the stateless persons to the Ministry for Foreign Affairs of the Republic of Belarus no later than twenty-four hours after the arrest for the purpose of further notification of a diplomatic mission or consular office of the State of the citizenship or habitual residence of the detained foreign citizen or stateless person.";

1.2. Article 125 shall be amended with part 5 that reads as follows:

5. The application of a measure of restraint in the form of house arrest in respect of a foreign citizen or stateless persons shall be notified by the organ conducting criminal proceedings to the Ministry for Foreign Affairs of the Republic of Belarus at the request of the foreign citizen or the stateless person, no later than one day after the enforcing of the measure of restraint in the form of house arrest for further notification of a diplomatic mission or consular institutions of the state of the citizenship or habitual residence of the foreign citizen or stateless person placed under house arrest.";

1.3. Part 8 of Article 126 shall read as follows:

8. About the application of a measure of restraint in the form of taking into custody as prosecuting organ or a court shall notify the persons specified in part 1 of Article 115 of the present Code, as well as in the case of the application of such a measure of restraint in respect of persons, whose children remained without the care of parents, not later than on the next day after adoption of the mentioned decision shall notify the department (division) of education of a district or municipal executive committee, local administration of city district at the place of residence of these persons for ensuring State protection of the children, upon application of this measure of restraint in respect of a pensioner - shall notify the organ paying him a retirement pension, upon application of this measure of restraint in respect of a foreigner or a stateless persons at the request of a foreign citizen or stateless person shall notify about this the Ministry for Foreign Affairs of the Republic of Belarus not later than one day after the application of the measure of restraint in the form of taking into custody for the further notification of a diplomatic mission or consular office of the State of citizenship or habitual residence of the detained foreign citizen or a stateless person. ".

2. Introduce into the Law of the Republic of Belarus of 1 August 2002 "On Citizenship of the Republic of Belarus" (the National Register of Legal Acts of the Republic of Belarus, 2002, No. 88, 2/885, 2006, No. 106, 2 / 1231) the following amendments and additions:

2.1. in the first part of Article 7 the words "change of citizenship of the spouses" shall be substituted for "acquiring by the spouses of citizenship of the Republic of Belarus or its termination;

2.2. the first part of Article 9 after the word "citizenship" shall be amended with the words "(nationality) (hereinafter, unless otherwise indicated - citizenship);

2.3. fourth paragraph of Article 13 after the words "of State, by citizens" shall be amended the words "(by nationals)";

2.4. in Article 14:

in part one:

the second paragraph two shall read as follows:

"Observes and respects the Constitution of the Republic of Belarus, other acts of legislation of the Republic of Belarus, undertakes to continue to observe and respect the Constitution of the Republic of Belarus and other acts of legislation of the Republic of Belarus";

the fifth paragraph shall read as follows:

"has a legitimate source of receiving income, providing him and to incapacitated family members under his care minimum living wage established in the Republic of Belarus";

In the second part, the words "recognized them as refugees according to the order established by the legislation of the Republic of Belarus" and "recognition of them as refugees" shall be substituted by the words "to whom the status of the refugee in the Republic of Belarus is granted" and "granting them the status of refugee";

2.5. in Article 16:

in the title, the word "of rejection" with "of refusal to consider";

in the first paragraph the word "shall be rejected" by "shall not be considered";

in the third paragraph the words "serious or particularly serious" shall be deleted;

after the sixth paragraph the article shall be amended by the paragraph that reads as follows:

"Repeatedly (three or more times) is brought to administrative responsibility on the territory of the Republic of Belarus - until the expiration of the time period, after which he would not be considered as subjected to administrative penalty;"

the seventh and eighth paragraphs shall respectively be considered as the eighth and ninth paragraphs;

the Article shall be amended with the second part that reads as follows:

"If the grounds specified the first paragraph of this Article are present, the statement of acquisition of citizenship of the Republic of Belarus together with all documents submitted shall be returned without consideration.";

2.6. Article 18 shall read as follows:

"Article 18. Renunciation of citizenship of the Republic of Belarus

A citizen of the Republic of Belarus, who has reached the age of 18, has the right to apply for renunciation of citizenship of the Republic of Belarus.

A citizen of the Republic of Belarus, who is under 18 years of age, may be permitted to renounce the citizenship of the Republic of Belarus upon a request of the parents (the single parent).

Renunciation of Citizenship of the Republic of Belarus is exercised in the manner prescribed by the President of the Republic of Belarus, and in the absence of the grounds provided for in Article 20 of this Law.";

2.7. third paragraph of Article 20 after the words "the Republic of Belarus, its" shall be amended with the words "administrative-territorial units";

2.8. in Article 22:

part two shall be deleted;

part three shall be considered part two;

2.9. out of the part three of Article 2, the words "in the age of 16 years" shall be deleted;

2.10. in Article 26 the second sentence shall be deleted;

2.11. paragraph two of Article 31, paragraph two of Article 32, the title and part three of Article 34, the title of chapter 8, articles 37 and 38 after the word "citizenship" shall be amended with the words "the Republic of Belarus";

2.12. in Article 33:

the title and the third part after the word "citizenship" shall be amended with the words "the Republic of Belarus";

part two after the words "on the issues of citizenship" shall be amended with the words "the Republic of Belarus".

**Article 74.** Recognition as null and void of some legislative acts of the Republic of Belarus and some of its individual provisions

To declare null and void:

Law of the Republic of Belarus of June 3, 1993 "On the Legal Status of Foreign Citizens and Stateless Persons in the Republic of Belarus" (the Gazette of the Supreme Council of the Republic of Belarus, 1993, No. 21, Article 250);

Article 1 of the Law of the Republic of Belarus of July 18, 2000 "On introduction of amendments and additions into some legislative acts of the Republic of Belarus" (the National Register of Legal Acts of the Republic of Belarus, 2000, No.73, 2 / 197);

Law of the Republic of Belarus of January 4, 2003 "On introduction amendments and additions into some legislative acts of the Republic of Belarus in connection with accession of the Republic of Belarus to the Convention Relating to the Status of Refugees and Protocol Relating to the Status of Refugees" (the National Register of Legal Acts of the Republic of Belarus, 2003, N 8, 2 / 927);

Law of the Republic of Belarus of July 19, 2005 "On introduction of amendments and additions into the Law of the Republic of Belarus"On Legal Status of Foreign Citizens and Stateless Persons in the Republic of Belarus" (the National Register of Legal Acts of the Republic of Belarus, 2005, No. 121, 2 / 1138 );

Article 6 of the Law of the Republic of Belarus of December 26, 2007 "On introduction of amendments and additions into some legislative acts of the Republic of Belarus and recognizing as null and void of some legislative acts of the Republic of Belarus and individual provisions of the laws of the Republic of Belarus on insurance issues" (the National Register of Legal Acts of the Republic of Belarus, 2007 PM, No. 305, 2 / 1397);

fourth paragraph of Article 56 of the Law of the Republic of Belarus of June 23, 2008 "On granting foreign citizens and stateless persons a refugee status, additional and temporary protection in the Republic of Belarus" (the National Register of Legal Acts of the Republic of Belarus, 2008, No. 158, 2/1451)

Resolution of the Supreme Council of the Republic of Belarus of June 3, 1993 "On promulgation of the Law of the Republic of Belarus "On Legal Status of Foreign Citizens and Stateless Persons in the Republic of Belarus" (the Gazette of the Supreme Council of the Republic of Belarus, 1993, No. 21, Art. 251) .

**Article 75.** Measures to implement the provisions of this Law

The Council of Ministers of the Republic of Belarus within six months' term shall:

in collaboration with the National Centre of Legislation and Legal Research of the Republic of Belarus prepare and submit according to the established procedure proposals on amendment legislation of the Republic of Belarus in order to bring them in conformity with this Law;

bring decisions of the Government of the Republic of Belarus in conformity with this Law;

ensure that the Republican organs of State administration subordinated to the Government of the Republic of Belarus bring their normative legal acts in conformity with this Law;

take other measures necessary to implement the provisions of this Law.

**Article 76.** Entry into force of this Law

This Law shall enter into force six months after its official publication, except for this Article and Article 75, which enter into force from the date of the official publication of this Law.

The President of the Republic of Belarus A. Lukashenko

## LAW ON IMMIGRATION

## ON APPROVAL OF REGULATION ON STAY OF FOREIGN CITIZENS AND PERSONS WITHOUT CITIZENSHIP IN THE REPUBLIC OF BELARUS[2]

In accordance with the Law of the Republic of Belarus of 29 December, 1998 "On Immigration", the Council of Ministers of the Republic of Belarus RESOLVES that:

1. The attached Regulation on Stay of Foreign Citizens and Persons without Citizenship in the Republic of Belarus shall be approved.

2. The Resolution of the Cabinet of Ministers of the Republic of Belarus of 26 January, 1996 No. 64 "On Approval of Regulation on Stay of Foreign Citizens and Persons without Citizenship in the Republic of Belarus" shall be considered invalid (see Collection of Decrees of the President and Resolutions of the Cabinet of Ministers of the Republic of Belarus, 1996, Vol. 3, Art.68).

S. Ling
Prime Minister of the Republic of Belarus
APPROVED
Resolution of the Council of Ministers
of the Republic of Belarus
25 October, 1999, No. 1654

---

[2] Resolution 1654 of the Council of Ministers on Stay of Foreign Citizens and Persons Without Citizenship in the Republic of Belarus *(1999)*

## GENERAL PROVISIONS

1. This Regulation has been developed in accordance with the Law of the Republic of Belarus "On Legal Status of Foreign Citizens and Persons without Citizenship in the Republic of Belarus", Law of the Republic of Belarus "On Immigration" and other acts of legislation of the Republic of Belarus.

2. Foreign citizens and persons without citizenship (hereinafter, if other is not stipulated, – foreigners) in the Republic of Belarus shall be registered in order established by this Regulation, they shall have with them valid passports or documents replacing them (hereinafter – passports) and they shall present them at request of competent agencies.

3. Officials of legal entities that receive foreigners or individual businessmen receiving foreigners (hereinafter, if other is not stipulated, -- receiving organization) shall ensure timely explanation to the foreigners their rights and duties stipulated by the Constitution of the Republic of Belarus, Law of the Republic of Belarus "On Legal Status of Foreign Citizens and Persons without Citizenship in the Republic of Belarus", Law of the Republic of Belarus "On Immigration", this Regulation, other acts of the legislation of the Republic of Belarus; they shall ensure timely execution of legal standards stipulated in relation to the foreigners, they perform proper control of foreigners received by them and they are also responsible for timely compilation of documents for stay in the Republic of Belarus, movement through the territory of the country and exit from the Republic of Belarus on the expiry of the time of stay in the Republic, as established for foreigners.

4. Those persons who have invited foreigners to the Republic of Belarus for personal affairs and who have provided them with accommodation in the Republic of Belarus, shall take measures to register these foreigners on time, to perform their residence registration and de-registration, they shall be responsible for compliance with these requirements.

Those persons who have provided housing, means of transportation or who have provided other services to foreigners residing on the territory of the Republic of Belarus in violation of these Regulation or Regulation on Transit Passage of Foreign Citizens and Persons without Citizenship, shall be held responsible in accordance with the legislation of the Republic of Belarus.

5. The control over implementation of this Regulation shall be performed by agencies of the interior in co-operation with agencies of State Security, along with Border Troops of the Republic of Belarus – in control points on the State Border of the Republic of Belarus.

## ENTRY OF FOREIGNERS INTO THE REPUBLIC OF BELARUS AND THEIR DEPARTURE

6. Foreigners enter the Republic of Belarus and depart from the Republic of Belarus through control points on the State Border of the Republic of Belarus that are open for international communication, by passports issued by competent agencies of the country

of their citizenship or permanent place of residence with visas of the Republic of Belarus obtained in established order, unless another method of entry is stipulated by international agreement of the Republic of Belarus with the proper country.

7. The order of issuance of visas of the Republic of Belarus is stipulated by the Instruction on Order of Issuance of Visas of the Republic of Belarus to Foreign Citizens and Persons without Citizenship, approved by the Ministry of Foreign Affairs of the Republic of Belarus, Ministry of Interior Affairs of the Republic of Belarus and the State Committee of Border Troops of the Republic of Belarus.

8. A foreigner entering the Republic of Belarus shall possess means sufficient to cover expenses on his/her stay on its territory and for departure from the Republic of Belarus, he/she shall present at request of officials of the Border Troops of the Republic of Belarus these means, permission to enter another country or permission to return to the country of his/her citizenship or permanent place of residence.

9. The availability of means stipulated by paragraph 8 of this Regulation shall be supported by presentation of:

national currency of the Republic of Belarus or foreign currency quoted by the National Bank of the Republic of Belarus;

document that allows receipt of means of payment;

invitation for temporary entry into the Republic of Belarus documented by agencies of the interior of the Republic of Belarus;

document supporting reservation and payment in the Republic of Belarus of a place of residence and payment for food;

letter from the receiving organization guaranteeing payment of all expenses of the foreigner in the Republic of Belarus and his/her departure form the territory of the Republic of Belarus;

means of transportation or travel tickets to the country of his/her citizenship or permanent place of residence or to a third country.

At entering the Republic of Belarus a foreigner shall possess means at the amount equivalent to no less than 50 minimum wages established in the Republic of Belarus per each month of stay. At foreigner's entrance for a period of less than 1 month, the amount of means at his/her disposal must be no less than 1 minimum wage per each day of stay.

10. A foreigner may be refused from entry into the territory of the Republic of Belarus for reasons stipulated by the legislation of the Republic of Belarus.

The refusal from foreigner's entry into the territory of the Republic of Belarus shall be recorded in his/her passport by making a proper note in it. The form of note and order of its entry shall be defined by the State Committee of Border Troops of the Republic of Belarus.

11. The rules of inclusion of foreigners into the List of Persons Whose Entry into the Republic of Belarus is Prohibited or Undesirable, as well as the maintenance of that list shall be stipulated by the Instruction on the Order of Entry of Foreigners into the List of Persons Whose Entry into the Republic of Belarus is Prohibited or Undesirable that shall be approved by the Committee of State Security of the Republic of Belarus, State Committee of Border Troops of the Republic of Belarus, Ministry of Foreign Affairs and Ministry of Internal Affairs of the Republic of Belarus.

12. The right of foreigner for departure from the Republic of Belarus may be limited for reasons stipulated by the legislation of the Republic of Belarus.

## THE ORDER OF TEMPORARY STAY OF FOREIGNERS IN THE REPUBLIC OF BELARUS

13. Foreigners who stay temporarily in the Republic of Belarus reside on the territory of the Republic of Belarus with a document (note) of registration or with a permission for temporary stay, documented in order established by this Regulation.

14. In order to document registration, at arrival in the Republic of Belarus, foreigners shall within 3 days except official holidays and weekends, present their passports at agencies authorized to perform registration located at the place of residence of the foreigner (hereinafter, if other is not stipulated, -- agencies of registration).

Foreigners shall reside in the Republic of Belarus only in place of residence where they are registered by agencies of registration.

At change of place of residence, a foreigner shall register within 3 days in agencies of registration at his/her new place of residence.

A state fee in order and at amount established by the legislation of the Republic of Belarus shall be imposed on foreigners for registration and extension of the period of validity of registration.

15. The following persons are exempt from registration:

15.1. heads of state and governments of foreign countries, heads and members of parliamentary, governmental and departmental delegations who have arrived in the Republic of Belarus by invitations from the President of the Republic of Belarus, National Assembly of the Republic of Belarus, Council of Ministers of the Republic of Belarus, republican agencies of state administration, local executive and administrative agencies of the Republic of Belarus, technical personnel of these delegations, family members of the above listed persons;

15.2. persons who have arrived in the Republic of Belarus by passports issued by the Organization of United Nations;

15.3. persons who have arrived in the Republic of Belarus for holidays or weekends or for a period of no longer than 3 days and who shall depart from the Republic of Belarus within these days;

15.4. crew members of foreign military aircraft who have arrived in the Republic of Belarus in the established order;

15.5. persons who are part of crews of civil aircraft of international airlines, train crews of international railroad communication, at their stay in airport or at the stations indicated in current timetable;

15.6. persons who are part of crews of international cargo and passenger automotive vehicles that conduct transit of cargo and passengers in international communication, or staying in cities or settlements on the route of transit including destination points.

16. The Ministry of Foreign Affairs of the Republic of Belarus shall register:

16.1. heads and members of foreign diplomatic representations and consular establishments, employees of offices of military attaché, trade representations of foreign countries in the Republic of Belarus as well as spouse, children, parents who live together with the above persons, guests of heads and employees of foreign diplomatic representations and consular establishments if these guests shall live in their residences or on the territory of the subject representations and establishments;

16.2. employees (including members of their families) of representations of international organizations in the Republic of Belarus who in accordance with charter documents of those organizations or in accordance with international treaties have privileges and immunity, and also members of their families.

The above persons who have passed registration shall be issued diplomatic, service or consular cards.

Foreigners listed in this paragraph are exempt from registration in hotels and agencies of the interior at the place of residence.

17. The Ministry of Foreign Affairs of the Republic of Belarus shall have the right to carry out, when necessary, registration of state and social leaders of foreign countries and members of their families who have arrived in the Republic of Belarus when it is requested by receiving organizations, diplomatic representations or consular establishments, and also to register employees of international organizations not listed in paragraphs 15, 16 of this Regulation. In these cases foreigners are exempt from registration in hotels and agencies of the interior.

18. All foreigners residing in hotels shall register there.

19. All foreigners except those listed in paragraphs 15 –18 of this Regulation shall register at agencies of the interior.

20. The registration of foreigners in agencies of the interior or in hotels shall be based on personal requests of foreigners or written requests of receiving organizations, permanent foreign representations in the Republic of Belarus for the period of residence of foreigners indicated in requests, tours, invitations.

However, citizens of countries with visa mode of entry into the territory of the Republic of Belarus, shall be registered for the period indicated in their personal requests or written requests of receiving organizations but not exceeding the period of validity of visa of the Republic of Belarus.

Citizens of countries with visaless mode of entry into the territory of the Republic of Belarus shall be registered for a period not exceeding the time stipulated by the international agreement of the Republic of Belarus with the proper country. In case of absence of indication of such time of visaless stay, the registration shall be made for a period indicated in the personal request of the foreigner or in the written request of the receiving organization but not exceeding 90 days per year.

Upon registration of foreigners, administration of hotels shall forward in the established order appropriate information to agencies of the interior at the location of the hotel.

21. Foreigners shall depart from the Republic of Belarus or extend the period of validity of registration or document in the established order permission for temporary stay in the Republic of Belarus by obtaining, if necessary, appropriate visa of the Republic of Belarus before the time of expiry of registration.

22. Permission for temporary stay is a document or an appropriate note in a foreigner's passport that supports the fact of registration of the foreigner at agencies of the interior and his/her right for temporary stay on the territory of the Republic of Belarus for the period of validity of the permission.

23. The permission for temporary stay in the Republic of Belarus shall be issued by agencies of the interior to foreigners who have arrived in the Republic of Belarus for a period exceeding 90 days per year:

for studying in educational institutions of the Republic of Belarus – for the duration of study, but no longer than 1 year;

to visit close relatives – citizens of the Republic of Belarus who permanently reside in the Republic of Belarus – for the time of stay but no longer than 1 year;

for conduct of work, administrative or other activities on the territory of the Republic of Belarus in order established by legislation – for the period of stay but no longer than 1 year;

persons who have submitted application for asylum or refugee status in order established by legislation – for the period of review of their applications;

persons who possess property by the right of private property and who reside in it – for the period of stay, but no longer than 180 days;

persons who have a document that supports the holder's right to enter the Republic of Belarus, stay in the Republic of Belarus and departure from the Republic of Belarus – for the period of its validity;

for other reasons stipulated by legislation of the Republic of Belarus.

24. The permission for temporary stay shall be issued to foreigners registered at agencies of the interior in the order established by this Regulation.

25. A foreigner may be refused from extension of period of registration or issuance of permission for temporary stay and he/she may be ordered to leave the territory of the Republic of Belarus, if:

there have been found reason according to which he/she may have been refused from entry into the territory of the Republic of Belarus;

there have been established facts of the foreigner's violation of legislation on legal status of foreign citizens and persons without citizenship in the Republic of Belarus, customs, currency or other legislation.

The refusal to extend the period of validity of registration or to issue permission for temporary residence shall be documented as a corresponding conclusion of an agency of the interior and it shall be reflected by a proper note in the foreigner's passport. The form of the note and order of its entry shall be defined by the Ministry of Interior Affairs of the Republic of Belarus.

26. Extension or refusal to extend the period of registration of foreigners registered at the Ministry of Foreign Affairs of the Republic of Belarus shall be conducted by this Ministry.

## ISSUANCE OF PERMISSIONS FOR PERMANENT RESIDENCE AND RESIDENCE PERMITS IN THE REPUBLIC OF BELARUS

27. Written requests for receipt of permission for permanent residence in the Republic of Belarus shall be submitted ahead of time by foreigners staying in the Republic of Belarus to agencies of the interior at place of temporary residence, by persons who stay abroad – to diplomatic representations or consular establishments of the Republic of Belarus.

28. In order to obtain permission for permanent residence in the Republic of Belarus, a foreigner shall submit the following documents to agency of the interior at the

prospective place of residence or to diplomatic representation, consular establishments of the Republic of Belarus abroad:

written request with detailed information about activities that he/she plans to engage in the Republic of Belarus, availability of means for entry into the Republic of Belarus and for staying on its territory until job employment and possibility of transfer of these means to the Republic of Belarus;

passport issued by the country of his/her citizenship or country of his/her permanent residence;

document on previous convictions;

medical certificate of health;

other documents to be listed by the Ministry of Internal Affairs of the Republic of Belarus and the Ministry of Foreign Affairs of the Republic of Belarus.

29. Before a decision on the foreigner's request for permission for permanent residence in the Republic of Belarus has been made, the agency of the interior shall perform inspection of reasons for satisfaction of the request for permission for permanent residence in the Republic of Belarus or for refusal to issue such a permission.

In case of absence of information about the previous convictions of the foreigner's applying for permission for permanent residence in the Republic of Belarus, the agency of the interior may inquire this information from competent agencies of the country of his/her citizenship or permanent place of residence.

30. Decision on foreigner's request for permission for permanent residence in the Republic of Belarus shall be made by the head of the agency of the interior at the place of the foreigner's permanent place of residence in the Republic of Belarus.

A negative decision shall be made only if there are reasons to refuse permission for permanent residence in the Republic of Belarus stipulated by Article 14 of the Law of the Republic of Belarus "On Immigration" and in case of absence of reasons for satisfaction of the request for permission for permanent residence.

A written notification about the decision made shall be sent to the foreigner temporarily residing in the Republic of Belarus no later than within 10 days after the decision has been made.

The Consular Department of the Ministry of Foreign Affairs of the Republic of Belarus shall notify a foreigner residing abroad of the decision made by the agency of the interior within 10 days after the decision has been made, through a diplomatic representation or consular establishment of the Republic of Belarus abroad.

Diplomatic representation or consular establishment of the Republic of Belarus abroad shall issue immigrant visa to foreigner who has received permission for entry into the Republic of Belarus for permanent residence.

31. Foreigners who have received in the established order permission for permanent residence in the Republic of Belarus shall be issued proper residence permits.

32. Foreign citizens permanently residing in the Republic of Belarus shall be issued residence permits for persons without citizenship only upon presentation of a document stating that competent agencies of the country of their residence have allowed them to leave citizenship of their country or that they have lost their citizenship.

33. A residence permit for a person without citizenship shall be replaced by residence permit of a foreign citizen if its holder can present at agencies of the interior a passport or any other document that supports the fact of the acquisition by the requestor of citizenship of a country.

34. Foreigners permanently residing in the Republic of Belarus are subject to residence registration at their places of permanent residence and de-registration at the place of permanent residence in the order established for citizens of the Republic of Belarus.

35. In cases stipulated by legislation of the Republic of Belarus permission for permanent residence of a foreigner in the Republic of Belarus may be cancelled by the agency of the interior at the place of permanent residence of its territory of the foreigner independently or by report of an involved agency.

When decision on cancellation of permission for permanent residence of foreigner in the Republic of Belarus is made in legal form, the agency of the interior at the place of permanent residence of the foreigner shall prepare necessary materials and forward them in the established order to the court in charge of this issue.

36. Before a decision on cancellation of permission for permanent residence in the Republic of Belarus has been made, the court or agency of the interior shall send to the foreigner a notification that shall list the reasons for review of that issue, time and place of review.

37. A foreigner whose permission for permanent residence in the Republic of Belarus has been cancelled, shall leave the territory of the Republic of Belarus within 1 month after the day of his/her notification about that decision.

The period of stay of a foreigner whose permission for permanent residence in the Republic of Belarus has been cancelled may be extended if the foreigner appeals against the decision on cancellation of his/her permission for permanent residence in the Republic of Belarus in court (for the time of review of his/her appeal) or if he/she has other reasons stipulated by the legislation of the Republic of Belarus for temporary stay on the territory of the Republic of Belarus.

38. Permission for permanent residence in the Republic of Belarus may be granted for family reunification to close relatives of citizens of the Republic of Belarus and immigrants in the order established by the Ministry of Internal Affairs of the Republic of Belarus.

The order of presentation of appropriate documents for making such decisions shall be defined by the Ministry of Internal Affairs of the Republic of Belarus.

**Movement of foreigners through the territory**

**of the Republic of Belarus and their selection of place of residence in the Republic of Belarus**

39. Foreigners may freely move through the territory of the Republic of Belarus with the exception of places visits of which require a special permission (pass) issued by agencies of the interior.

40. Entry (temporary stay and residence) of foreigners into border zone is prohibited with the exception of cases when:

invitations, telegrams received by foreigners indicate points located in that zone;

the foreigners have received passes from agencies of the interior for entry into border zone.

41. Foreigners who have changed their place of residence in the Republic of Belarus in violation of this Regulation shall return to their former place of residence at demand of agencies of the interior.

42. A foreigner shall inform the agencies of the interior of the Republic of Belarus about all changes of his/her place of residence within 10 days.

## RESPONSIBILITY FOR VIOLATION OF THIS REGULATION.

**Reduction of term of stay of foreigners in the Republic of Belarus**

43. For violation of this Regulation foreigners shall be liable in accordance with legislation of the Republic of Belarus.

Violation of this Regulation by persons who must follow its requirements (including persons who have invited foreigners to the Republic of Belarus for personal affairs or who provide services to them) entails liability in accordance with legislation of the Republic of Belarus.

44. Reduction of the period of stay of foreigners in the Republic of Belarus may be made for reasons stipulated by the legislation of the Republic of Belarus.

The order and rules of eviction of foreigners from the territory of the Republic of Belarus shall be defined by the legislation of the Republic of Belarus.

45. The decision on reduction of the period of stay of foreigners in the Republic of Belarus shall be made by the agency of the interior.

After a decision on reduction of the period of stay of a foreigner in the Republic of Belarus has been made, a proper note shall be made in his/her passport. The form of note and order of its entry shall be defined by the Ministry of Internal Affairs of the Republic of Belarus.

46. The decision on reduction of the period of stay in relation to a foreigner who has a visa of the Republic of Belarus involves cancellation of the corresponding visa of the Republic of Belarus or reduction of the time of its validity.

The decision on reduction of the period of stay of a foreigner who has registration or permission for temporary stay involves cancellation of registration or reduction of the time of its validity.

A foreigner in whose relation a decision on reduction of the period of his/her stay in the Republic of Belarus has been made, shall leave the territory of the Republic of Belarus within the time indicated by the agency of the interior.

47. A foreigner has the right to appeal against a decision on reduction of the period of his/her stay in the Republic of Belarus in the order established by legislation.

48. During the review of the case on violation of legislation on immigration of the Republic of Belarus by a foreigner, the agency of the interior has the right to temporarily withdraw passport from the foreigner who has violated immigration legislation if he/she does not have a permanent place of residence in the Republic of Belarus.

After closing the case on violation of immigration legislation or this Regulation, the passport shall be returned to its holder.

49. The means coming to the republican budget from collection of fees from foreigners who have violated legislation of the Republic of Belarus on immigration shall be later forwarded to agencies of the interior for financing their expenses related to review and execution of cases on violation of immigration legislation.

The order of forwarding of the above said means to agencies of the interior shall be defined by the Ministry of Finances of the Republic of Belarus and the Ministry of Interior Affairs of the Republic of Belarus.

50.Foreigners may pay fees imposed on them for violation of immigration legislation in freely convertible currency at the day of payment exchange rate established by the National Bank of the Republic of Belarus.

# PROVISION ON ORDER OF DEPORTATION OF FOREIGN CITIZENS AND PERSONS WITHOUT CITIZENSHIP IN THE REPUBLIC OF BELARUS

## GENERAL PROVISIONS

1.This Provision has been developed in accordance with the Law of the Republic of Belarus "On Legal Status of Foreign Citizens and Persons without Citizenship in the Republic of Belarus", Law of the Republic of Belarus "On Immigration", Law of the Republic of Belarus "On State Border of the Republic of Belarus", and other legislative acts of the Republic of Belarus. It establishes the order of deportation, order of reimbursement of expenses related to deportation of foreign citizens and persons without citizenship in the Republic of Belarus (hereinafter – foreigners).

2. Deportation is compulsory eviction of a foreigner outside the Republic of Belarus in accordance with the legislation of the Republic of Belarus. Deportation (hereinafter – eviction or deportation) is a procedure related to organization of compulsory departure of a foreigner from the territory of the Republic of Belarus applied to persons who have entered the Republic of Belarus or are in the Republic of Belarus without proper visa or with invalid visa of the Republic of Belarus, also to persons in relation to whom there has been made a decision on cancellation of permission for permanent residence in the Republic of Belarus or who have been refused from further permission for staying on its territory.

3. Eviction in simplified order (hereinafter – transfer) is a procedure related to organization by the Border Troops of the Republic of Belarus (hereinafter – Border Troops) of an official transfer of foreigners -- trespassers of the State Border of the Republic of Belarus to authorities of neighboring country.

The procedure of transfer shall be applied to foreigners who have crossed or have attempted to cross the State Border of the Republic of Belarus in violation of the legislation of the Republic of Belarus from territories of foreign countries and in regard to whom there are no grounds for bringing to criminal or administrative responsibility and who do not use the right for obtaining asylum or refugee status. The decision on transfer of this category of foreigners shall be made by the State Committee of Border Troops of the Republic of Belarus based on reports of the Border Troops unit commanders.

The order of transfer of foreigner is defined in agreement with representatives of authorities of the foreign country in the course of work with mandatory execution of a proper receipt and transfer document.

If transfer of foreigner to authorities of a foreign country is not stipulated by an international treaty of the Republic of Belarus with that country, the Border Troops shall transfer trespassers of the State Border of the Republic of Belarus to agencies of the interior for eviction outside the Republic of Belarus.

4. The decision on eviction is a resolution of an agency of the interior or an agency of the State Security on deportation of a foreigner for reasons stipulated by the legislation of the Republic of Belarus.

In the decision on eviction, the order of departure, time of departure of the foreigner from the territory of the Republic of Belarus, country of destination and the order of appeal against the decision, shall be defined.

The order of departure of the foreigner from the territory of the Republic of Belarus may be either voluntary or compulsory (under escort).

5. A decision on eviction of foreigner legally residing on the territory of the Republic of Belarus shall involve cancellation of the foreigner's visa of the Republic of Belarus, registration, permission for temporary stay or permission for permanent residence in the Republic of Belarus.

6. Eviction of foreigners from the territory of the Republic of Belarus shall be carried out by employees of the agency that made the decision on deportation, in an order agreed upon with the Border Troops, at control points of the State Border of the Republic of Belarus.

7. Foreigners evicted from the territory of the Republic of Belarus shall be refused from entry into the Republic of Belarus for a period stipulated by the legislation, an appropriate note shall be entered in the decision on eviction and the Ministry of Foreign Affairs of the Republic of Belarus and the State Committee on Border Troops of the Republic of Belarus shall be notified.

8. Foreigners detained by agencies of the interior, State Security or Border Troops on the territory of the Republic of Belarus without passports or documents replacing them (hereinafter – passports) shall be forwarded in the established order to reception and distribution centers of the agencies of the interior or to special facilities of the Border Troops for identification of personality for a time stipulated by the legislation of the Republic of Belarus. Upon identification of personality of the foreigner, decisions on him/her shall be made in accordance with the legislation of the Republic of Belarus.

Foreigners detained administratively by Border Troops for violation of the State Border of the Republic of Belarus and for related delinquencies, shall be kept in specially equipped facilities of the Border Troops for identification of personality and initial investigation.

9. Detention for identification of personality or deportation shall not be made in relation to the following foreigners:

those who are under 16 years old or those who are above 60 years old; those who are conspicuously disabled;

pregnant women.

10. In case of receipt from a detained foreigner of an application for refugee status in the Republic of Belarus, the agency conducting detention shall within 3 days inform a regional migration agency about the desire of that foreigner to be recognized as refugee, for review of the subject of registration of application. If the regional migration agency has made a decision to register the foreigner's application, that foreigner shall be transferred to the regional migration agency.

11. Expenses related to maintenance of a foreigner in the reception and distribution center of the agency of the interior or in special facilities of the Border Troops shall be paid for from the foreigner's means, his/her property or the republican budget.

## ORDER OF MAKING DECISION ON EVICTION.

**Procedure of Eviction**

12. The decision on eviction of foreigners shall be made by agencies of the interior or State Security of the Republic of Belarus independently or upon reports of involved agencies.

Appropriate materials (copies of materials) supporting presence of legal grounds for making a resolution on deportation of a foreigner shall be attached to reports of involved agencies on the need of deportation of a foreigner.

13. Before making a decision on eviction of a foreigner, an agency of the interior or agency of State Security shall send to the foreigner a notification in which it shall describe the reasons for deportation, place and time of review of that case and also it shall explain the right for presence of that foreigner during review of his/her case. In case of default, also in case of absence at the allowed place of residence, the question on deportation of the foreigner may be reviewed without his/her presence. Foreigners, in regard to whom a case of deportation is reviewed, must reside on the territory of the Republic of Belarus only at the place of residence allowed by the agencies that review the case on deportation of the foreigner.

14. Agency of the interior or agency of State Security shall define in the resolution on deportation of a foreigner the method of eviction (departure) of the foreigner outside the Republic of Belarus (the foreigner shall be evicted in a compulsory manner (under escort) including detention for a period needed for eviction, the foreigner voluntarily leaves the territory of the Republic of Belarus at his/her personal means within the period defined in the resolution on eviction). In case of need of detention of a foreigner for further eviction from the Republic of Belarus, the resolution on eviction shall be approved by a public prosecutor at the place of residence or detention of the foreigner.

15. Voluntary departure of a foreigner shall not be allowed in the following cases:

if there are reasons to believe that the foreigner may evade execution of the decision on eviction or he/she has evaded voluntary departure from the Republic of Belarus within the period indicated in the decision on eviction;

deportation of the foreigner is related to his/her illegal activities or is in relation to actions aimed at undermining the national security of the Republic of Belarus or to other actions that represent social danger for the Republic of Belarus; the foreigner has made a gross violation of the legislation on immigration or other legislation and there are no grounds to bring him/her to criminal responsibility; a foreigner without permission for temporary stay or for permanent residence in the Republic of Belarus was received by agencies of the interior from proper agencies of another country for further deportation in accordance with an international treaty on transfer and receipt of persons (readmission) concluded by the Republic of Belarus with a third country.

16. After a decision on eviction, transfer or non admission of a foreigner through the State Border of the Republic of Belarus, a proper note shall be entered in his/her passport. The form of note and order of its entry shall be defined by the Ministry of the Interior of the Republic of Belarus, Committee of State Security of the Republic of Belarus or by the State Committee of Border Troops of the Republic of Belarus.

17. Upon detention of a foreigner with a view of his/her eviction from the territory of the Republic of Belarus, the agency that has made the resolution on his/her eviction, shall:

within 3 days notify the proper diplomatic representation or consular establishment of the country of the foreigner's citizenship or permanent place of residence through the Consular Department of the Ministry of Foreign Affairs of the Republic of Belarus;

inform the State Committee of Border Troops of the Republic of Belarus about the control point where the procedure of eviction shall be conducted, including date and time of its execution;

take necessary measures to ensure safety of the foreigner's property;

inform the foreigner in a language that he/she understands about legal grounds of his/her detention, his/her rights and duties, order of his/her deportation from the territory of the Republic of Belarus, inquiries and requests made in his/her regard.

18. Foreigners subject to eviction from the territory of the Republic of Belarus shall, in agreement with an official of the agency that has made the decision on eviction, shall be allowed to have visitors, to make telephone calls to representatives of diplomatic representations or consular establishments of the country of their citizenship or permanent place of residence.

19. Foreigners in regard to whom a decision on eviction under escort has been made, may be evicted to the country of their citizenship or permanent place of residence, to countries from where they had arrived in the Republic of Belarus, to countries that would like to admit them and apply for their extradition.

20. The procedure of eviction of a foreigner may be postponed in the following cases:

if the application for refugee status or asylum has been accepted for review in accordance with the legislation of the Republic of Belarus – until a decision on his/her application is made;

if the foreigner has made a demand in court for review of decision on deportation. In this case he/she may be discharged on security the size of which shall not exceed twice the size of the means necessary for eviction of the foreigner from the territory of Belarus. The decision on security shall be made by the head of the agency that has made the resolution on deportation. The security amount shall be paid by a person authorized by the foreigner or it shall be taken from the means of the foreigner, in the national currency of the Republic of Belarus or in a foreign currency quoted by the National Bank of the Republic of Belarus and it shall be temporarily enclosed with the materials of the case. If the foreigner upon discharge has evaded deportation, the security paid by him/her shall be spent by agencies of the interior or State Security on execution of measures related to eviction of the foreigner from the territory of the Republic of Belarus. The remainder of the security amount paid by the foreigner shall be forwarded to the republican budget in the order established by the Ministry of the Interior of the Republic of Belarus, Committee of State Security of the Republic of Belarus and Ministry of Finances of the Republic of Belarus.

21. If application for refugee status is received after decision on eviction of foreigner has been made, the agency of the interior or agency of state security that has made the decision on deportation, shall inform the regional migration agency about the desire of the foreigner to be recognized as refugee. If the regional migration agency has consequently made a decision to register the foreigner's application for refugee status, the procedure of deportation shall be postponed and he/she shall be forwarded to the regional migration agency for resolution of the subject of provision of refugee status to him/her.

22. Employees of the agency that has made the decision on eviction of foreigner shall escort the deported foreigner until the control point at the State Border of the Republic of Belarus, the escort shall be removed when the foreigner crosses the State Border of the Republic of Belarus.

In agreement with authorized agencies of both countries or in compliance with international treaties of the Republic of Belarus with other countries, transfer and admission of such persons may be conducted at control points on the State Border of the Republic of Belarus at mandatory presence of a representative of the Border Troops with compilation of a document on admission and transfer.

## EXPENSES RELATED TO THE PROCEDURE OF EVICTION

23. Expenses related to eviction of foreigners from the territory of the Republic of Belarus shall be defrayed:

by citizens of the Republic of Belarus or foreigners who have applied at proper agencies for entrance of the evicted foreigner into the territory of the Republic of Belarus; deported foreigners; legal entities that have applied for entry into the Republic of Belarus of the foreigner subject to deportation.

If expenses related to eviction of foreigner from the territory of the Republic of Belarus may not be covered by means of physical or legal entities stipulated in this paragraph, these expenses shall be defrayed by agencies of the interior or agencies of State Security from the republican budget or from the budget of the country applying for extradition of the foreigner.

24. The estimate of expenses related to eviction of foreigner from the territory of the Republic of Belarus shall include expenses related to:

acquisition of travel documents for the foreigner and persons accompanying him/her; maintenance of the foreigner in reception and distribution center, temporary isolator ward, special center of the agencies of the interior or special facilities of Border Troops; compilation of documents and performance of other actions related to eviction and other expenses incurred. The control of expenses shall be conducted by agencies of the interior, State Security and Border Troops, report on them shall be made in 2 original copies in the form established by the Ministry of the Interior of the Republic of Belarus, Committee of State Security of the Republic of Belarus or by the State Committee of Border Troops of the Republic of Belarus. The foreigner shall sign for notification about the amount of expenses related to his/her eviction (transfer) from the territory of Belarus. If the foreigner refuses to agree with the amount sent to him for reimbursement, a note shall be entered in the Act indicating reasons of refusal.

25. Foreigners subject to eviction from the territory of the Republic of Belarus may pay the expenses on deportation either in the national currency of the Republic of Belarus or in a foreign currency at the day of payment exchange rate established by the National Bank of the Republic of Belarus.

26. If a foreigner refuses to defray expenses on his/her eviction from the territory of the Republic of Belarus, appropriate amounts may be recovered from him/her in legal form. In order to support the claim, the court may sequestrate the foreigner's property. If during detention or later, the foreigner subject to deportation is found to have means for defraying the expenses, they shall be sequestrated for provision of execution of resolution on eviction in accordance with the estimate of expenses.

27. In case of refusal of the legal or physical entity who has applied for entry of the foreigner into the Republic of Belarus to defray expenses of agencies of the interior, State Security or Border Troops on his/her eviction, these expenses may be recovered from them in legal form. Documentation for recovery of expenses in legal form include resolution of an agency of the interior or agency of State Security on eviction or resolution of Border Troops on transfer of foreigner approved by the Public Prosecutor, Act of Incurred Expenses.

# BUSINESS TRAVEL TO BELARUS

## BUSINESS CUSTOMS

Business customs in Belarus are generally identical to those in Russia.

Like in Russia, obtaining an appointment can be difficult, so persistence and patience are essential. Appointments should be scheduled far in advance and, if possible, confirmed.

Scheduling a business trip to Belarus in July and August may not be a good idea, because this is the time of the year many people take their vacations.

An old Russian proverb says - "People meet you depending on how you're dressed and they say good bye depending on how wise you seem." Belarusian businesspeople pay a lot of attention to how they and their potential partners are dressed. Casual wear is unacceptable at business meetings.

## TRAVEL

Travelers entering Belarus by air with more than 50 kilograms of luggage (110 pounds) will be charged Euro 2 per kilogram in excess of that limit. The fee must be paid in dollars or Euros. Travelers should declare all electrical and electronic equipment or devices upon entry; failure to do so will require the traveler to pay up to 30 percent customs duty on these items upon departure. Travelers should complete two customs declarations at the time of entry and should retain one copy and produce it at the time of exit in order to prove that items were not acquired while in Belarus.

Belarus requires all foreign nationals (other than accredited diplomats) entering the country to purchase medical insurance at the port-of-entry regardless of any other insurance they might have. Costs for this insurance will vary according to the length of stay. (Subject to change, current information puts costs at $1.00 for a one-or two-day stay, $15.00 for a stay up to 30-31 days, and $85.00 for a stay of one year.)
A presidential decree adopted in June 2005 requires citizens of foreign countries to pay a one-time fee when entering/exiting Belarus. The entry/exit tax currently amounts to approximately $3.00 per person. Travelers should receive a receipt and produce this document at the request of Border Control Officers at border crossing points. Diplomats and their family members, as well as members of official delegations and representatives of international organizations, are exempt from the duty.

U.S. citizens traveling through Belarus to other countries are strongly reminded that there is a transit visa requirement for entering and leaving Belarus. Transit visas should be obtained prior to any journey that requires travel through Belarus. Commonwealth of Independent States (CIS) and Russian visas are no substitute for this transit visa. Most travel agencies, including those in Russia and CIS countries as well as train ticket sales personnel, are often not aware of this visa requirement and may not seek a transit visa for a traveler unless instructed by the traveler to do so. U.S. citizens traveling to Belarus via Russia are reminded that they must possess a Russian transit visa in addition to their

Belarusian visa. The Russian Embassy generally does not issue transit or tourist visas to Americans in Belarus.

U.S. citizens attempting to transit Belarus without a valid Belarusian transit visa have been denied entry into the country and forcibly removed from trains. In some instances, local border and train authorities have threatened passengers who did not possess a valid transit visa with jail or extorted "fines." American citizens are advised not to pay any border or train officials for transit visas or "transit visa fines" as these officials are not authorized to issue such visas. Americans finding themselves in Belarus without transit visas should, if confronted by border or train personnel, demand to be put in contact with consular officials at the U.S. Embassy in Minsk. Travelers who enter and then leave Belarus in a private vehicle at two different points are often required to pay a "green" tax, or ecology tax, which is levied by the regional authorities.

In addition to the above, the Belarusian government sometimes enforces a requirement for special permits to travel in "protected border zones." The Government of Belarus has not provided information defining the parameters of those zones. Travelers should be alert for warning signs, road barriers, and/or border guard posts, and are advised not to cross into such areas without permission.

For Customs Information see http://travel.state.gov/travel/cis_pa_tw/cis/cis_1468.html.

## VISA REQUIREMENTS

A passport and visa are required. A visa must be obtained before entering Belarus. Travelers who do not have a visa cannot register at hotels. U.S. citizens residing in Belarus are required to register with the local office of visas and registration (OVIR) within three working days after arrival. Failure to do so can result in fines and visits from local law enforcement authorities. U.S. citizens staying in hotels are automatically registered at check-in. Visa validity dates are strictly enforced; travelers should request sufficient time to allow for delays in arrival and departure.

U.S. Companies that require travel of foreign businesspersons to the United States should be advised that security options are handled via an interagency process. Visa applicants should go to the following links.

State Department Visa Website: http://travel.state.gov/visa/index.html

United States Visas.gov: http://www.unitedstatesvisas.gov/

For the most current visa information, contact the Embassy of Belarus at 1619 New Hampshire Avenue, N.W., Washington, DC 20009, tel. 202-986-1606, fax: 202-986-1805, email: consul@belarusembassy.org, or visit the Embassy web site at http://www.belarusembassy.org/.

## TELECOMMUNICATIONS

Telecommunication services are fairly reliable in Belarus. The Belarusian Ministry of Communications pursues a "socially-oriented" policy. Its priorities are: extension of fixed-line telephony in rural regions and low tariffs. The state - owned Beltelecom holds a monopoly as the only provider of fixed line telephony services in Belarus. Being a monopolist, Beltelecom keeps prices for international calls very high.

At present, there are three GSM mobile phone services providers in Belarus and one CDMA-450 mobile phone services provider. Internet access is readily available, though mostly consists of slow dial-up connections. High speed internet is available in some areas.

Beltelecom is active in the Internet access services market, providing such services as dial-up access (analogous and ISDN) and digital dedicated lines access. In February 2002 Beltelecom launched an IP-telephony service, but licenses for secondary provides forbid IP telephony services. Old analog PBX's are being extensively replaced by digital ones throughout the country and the quality of regular telephone lines is improving.

## TRANSPORTATION

While in a foreign country, U.S. citizens may encounter road conditions that differ significantly from those in the United States. The information below concerning Belarus is provided for general reference only, and may not be totally accurate in a particular location or circumstance.

Individual U.S. state drivers' licenses are not recognized in Belarus unless accompanied by an international drivers' license. When U.S. state licenses are used in conjunction with an international drivers' license, U.S. citizens may drive in Belarus for up to three months. U.S. citizens should, therefore, always carry with them their passports to prove date of entry into the country in the event that police stop them. After residing in Belarus for three months, one may apply for a local driver's license. Drivers will be required to successfully complete a two-part test in Russian. The first part is a computer-based multiple-choice test on local driving rules. The second part of the test is a driving test. To receive a local driver's license, drivers will also need to complete a medical exam at a special medical clinic, which will include a general physical, a chest x-ray, and an eye exam.

Driving with caution is urged at all times. Radio dispatched taxi services are generally reliable, arrive promptly once called and usually offer the lowest fare. Most radio-dispatched taxis are metered, although fares can vary greatly and are considerably higher in the late evening and overnight hours. Unmetered taxis and private autos are also available; however, using such taxis is not recommended, as they are often more expensive for foreigners and less safe. In the event a traveler must use such a taxi, he or she should not travel alone and should agree to the price of the trip before getting into the vehicle.

Minsk has a clean, safe, and efficient subway system that easily reaches most of the city's core. Service is stopped briefly during the early morning hours, but otherwise runs regularly throughout the day. Ticket prices are extremely low by western standards.

Though their routes are extensive, buses and trolleys lack cooling capabilities and are usually crowded.

Travelers on all public transportation should be wary of pickpockets and other petty crime. For travelers interested in car rental, only AVIS currently operates in Minsk. In general, rental car networks in Belarus are not well developed.

Travelers may experience significant delays (of several hours) in crossing the border by road into neighboring countries.

Please refer to our Road Safety page for more information at http://travel.state.gov/travel/tips/safety/safety_1179.html or visit the website of the Republic of Belarus National Tourism Agency at http://www.touragency.by/.

**AVIATION SAFETY OVERSIGHT:** As there is no direct commercial air service between the United States and Belarus, the U.S. Federal Aviation Administration (FAA) has not assessed Belarus' Civil Aviation Authority for compliance with ICAO international aviation safety standards. For more information, travelers may visit the FAA's Internet web site at http://www.faa.gov/safety/programs_initiatives/oversight/iasa.

**SPECIAL CIRCUMSTANCES:** Traveler's checks are not widely accepted in Belarus. Most hotels accept either American Express or Visa credit cards. In addition, one hotel in Minsk, "Planeta," provides cash from Visa credit cards during business hours. Travelers face arrest if they attempt to buy items with currency other than Belarusian rubles. Authorized currency exchange centers are widely available throughout major cities. ATMs are also available for use. Travelers should be aware that there is a high incidence of credit card fraud in Belarus. If they choose to use credit cards, they should regularly check their account status to ensure its integrity.

## LANGUAGE

Both Belarusian and Russian are official languages. Russian is widely spoken throughout the country, particularly in the cities. Many business people in Belarus speak English or some other European language.

## HEALTH

Medical care in Belarus is limited. Basic medical supplies, including anesthetics, vaccines and antibiotics are not always readily available. Elderly travelers and those with existing health problems may be at risk due to inadequate medical facilities. Information on vaccinations and other health precautions, such as safe food and water precautions and insect bite protection, may be obtained from the Centers for Disease Control and Prevention's hotline for international travelers at 1-877-FYI-TRIP (1-877-394-8747) or via the CDC's Internet site at http://www.cdc.gov/travel. For information about outbreaks of infectious diseases abroad consult the World Health Organization's

(WHO) website at http://www.who.int/en. Further health information for travelers is available at http://www.who.int/ith.

The U.S. Department of State strongly urges Americans to consult with their medical insurance company prior to traveling abroad to confirm whether their policy applies overseas and whether it will cover emergency expenses such as a medical evacuation. Please see the information on medical insurance overseas at http://travel.state.gov/travel/cis_pa_tw/cis/cis_1470.html.

### LOCAL TIME, BUSINESS HOURS, AND HOLIDAYS

RETURN TO TOP

Standard time zone: UTC/GMT +2 hours. Regular business hours: 9:00 - 18:00. The list of Belarusian holidays includes:

| | |
|---|---|
| New Year | January 1 |
| Orthodox Christmas | January 7 |
| Orthodox New Year | January 14 |
| International Women's Day | March 8 |
| Constitution Day | March 15 |
| International Labor Day | May 1 |
| Victory Day | May 9 |
| Independence Day | July 3 |
| Catholic Christmas | December 25 |
| Catholic Easter | Movable |
| Orthodox Easter | Movable |
| Radunitsa | First Tuesday after Orthodox Easter |
| Commemoration Day | 9 days after Orthodox Easter |

### TEMPORARY ENTRY OF MATERIALS AND PERSONAL BELONGINGS

For detailed information on entry of materials and personal belonging to Belarus please see the link of the State Customs Committee of Belarus.
http://gtk.gov.by/index.php?ch=399

## INFORMATION RESOURCES OF THE REPUBLIC OF BELARUS

### FREE ECONOMIC ZONES

Minsk
www.fezminsk.by

Brest
www.fezbrest.com

Vitebsk
www.fez-vitebsk.com

Grodno invest
www.invest.grodno.by

Gomel-Raton
www.gomelraton.com

Mogilev
www.region.mogilev.by

## GOVERNMENT AGENCIES

Official site of state bodies of the Republic of Belarus
www.main.gov.by

Presidential Administration of the Republic of Belarus
www.president.gov.by

Council of the Republic of the National Assembly of the Republic of Belarus
www.sovrep.gov.by

Chamber of Representatives of the National Assembly of the Republic of Belarus
www.house.gov.by

Council of Ministers Official Site of the Government of Belarus
www.government.by

Constitutional Court of the Republic of Belarus
http://ncpi.gov.by/constsud/

Supreme Economic Court of the Republic of Belarusь
www.court.by

The National Bank of the Republic of Belarus
www.nbrb.by

Ministry of architecture and construction of the Republic of Belarus
www.minstroyarch.gov.by

Ministry of Internal Affairs of the Republic of Belarus
http://mvd-belarus.nsys.by/

Ministry of Health of the Republic of Belarus
www.minzdrav.by

MFA Ministry of Foreign Affairs of the Republic of Belarus
www.mfa.gov.by

Ministry of Information of the Republic of Belarus

www.mininform.gov.by

Ministry of Culture of the Republic of Belarus
www.kultura.by

Ministry of Defense of the Republic of Belarus
www.mod.mil.by

Ministry of Education of the Republic of Belarus
www.minedu.unibel.by

Ministry of Taxes and Collection of the Republic of Belarus
www.nalog.by

Ministry of Rescue of the Republic of Belarus
www.rescue01.gov.by

Ministry of Natural Resources and Environmental Protection of the Republic of Belarus
www.minpriroda.by

Ministry of Posts and Telecommunications of the Republic of Belarus
www.mpt.gov.by

Ministry of Agriculture and Food of the Republic of Belarus
http://mshp.minsk.by/

Ministry of Sport and Tourism of the Republic of Belarus
www.mst.by

Ministry of Statistics and Analysis of the Republic of Belarus
http://www.president.gov.by/Minstat/

Ministry of Transportation and Communications of the Republic of Belarus
www.mintrans.by

Ministry of Finances of the Republic of Belarus
http://ncpi.gov.by/minfin

Ministry of Economy of the Republic of Belarus
www.economy.gov.by

Ministry of Justice of the Republic of Belarus
http://ncpi.gov.by/minjust/

Official Site of Minsk City Executive Committee
www.minsk.gov.by

Official Site of Vitebsk Region Administration

www.regadmin.vitebsk.by

Official Site of Mogilev Region Administration
www.region.mogilev.by

Official Site of Gomel Region Executive Committee
http://gomel-region.gov.by/

Official Site of Grodno Region Administration
www.region.grodno.by

## REPRESENTATIONS OF INTERNATIONAL ORGANISATIONS

United Nations Office in Belarus
www.un.minsk.by

World Bank in Belarus
www.worldbank.org.by

Chamber of Commerce and Industry of Belarus
http://www.cci.by

International Financial Corporation in Belarus
http://ifcln1.ifc.org/ifcext/ceu.nsf/Content/Belarus/

Executive Committee of the Commonwealth of the Independent States
www.cis.minsk.by

## OTHER BUSINESS RESOURCES

Business Belarus - Information Directory
www.b2b.by

Infoline 085 - Phone directory
www.085.by

A-Zimut - professional directory of IT companies
www.azimut.by

IT in Belarus
s.net www.it-belaru

Belarusian Export
www.export.by

Council of Entrepreneurship Development in the Republic of Belarus
www.sovpr.org

National Internet portal of judicial information of the Republic of Belarus www.pravo.by

National center for judicial information of the Republic of Belarus
http://ncpi.gov.by/

BELEXPO – Exhibitions
www.belexpo.by

MINSKEXPO - Exhibition company
www.minskexpo.com.by

International exhibitions in the Republic of Belarus
www.tc.by

Green Expo - exhibition
http://www.greenexpo.by/

**MISCELLANEOUS**

Belavia national air company
www.belavia.by

Belarusian railway
www.rw.by

National Airport
www.airport.by

All Hotels of Belarus
www.belarustravel.by
http://hotels.by.com/

Weather in Belarus
www.meteo.by

Maps of all regions and cities of the Republic of Belarus
www.emaps-online.com

Map of Minsk
www.kartaminska.by.ru

Press portfolio of Belarus
http://photo.bymedia.net/

Belarus: XXI - Photo Gallery
www.babinets.com

History of Belarus
http://albaruthenia.by.ru/

History of Belarus
www.hf.uib.no/Andre/Vesti/belohist.htm

Globe of Belarus - architectural sights of Belarus
http://globus.tut.by/

NON-PROFIT ORGANISATIONS OF THE REPUBLIC OF BELARUS

Information portal of Non-governmental organisations
www.ngo.by

Minsk Capital Association of Entrepreneurs and Employers
www.allminsk.biz

Brest Region Association of Entrepreneurs
http://spbo.iatp.by/

Vitebsk Region Association of Employers and Entrepreneurs
http://anp2003.at.tut.by/

Mogilev Region Public Association of Entrepreneurs
www.mogilevbiz.net

Rotary Club Minsk
www.rotary.org.by

Anticrisis management corporation
www.kay.by

Belarusian public association of economic lawyers
www.lex.by

# SELECTED INDUSTRIAL AND BUSINESS COMPANIES IN BELARUS

1. Belpromwest Ltd., Industrial and Finance Company

ADDRESS: per. Asanalieva, 3
220024, g. Minsk
PHONE: 017\278-4755
FAX: 017\278-6800
E-MAIL: lom@belpromwest.com
Products or services (manufactured): NACE-Code
Wholesale of metals and metal ores 5152
Products or services (export): NACE-Code
Wholesale of household appliances and radio and television goods 5143
Wholesale of metals and metal ores 5152
Wholesale of waste and scrap 5157
Wholesale of other machinery for use in industry, trade and navigation 5165
Products or services (import): NACE-Code
Wholesale of metals and metal ores 5152
Wholesale of waste and scrap 5157

---

2. ARKLOW COMPANY Foreign Enterprise

ADDRESS: Partizanskiy pr-t, 95, k.47e
220026, g. Minsk
PHONE: 017\245-0174, 245-7295
FAX: 017\285-4879
E-MAIL: arklow@fenox.com
Products or services (manufactured): NACE-Code
Sale of motor vehicle parts and accessories 5030
Wholesale of solid, liquid and gaseous fuels and related products 5151
Products or services (export): NACE-Code
Sale of motor vehicle parts and accessories 5030
Products or services (import): NACE-Code
Sale of motor vehicle parts and accessories 5030
Wholesale of solid, liquid and gaseous fuels and related products 5151

---

3. Bahco Tools, Foreign Private Trade Unitary Enterprise

ADDRESS: ul. Zm. Byaduli, 13
220034, g. Minsk
PHONE: 017\236-2046
FAX: 017\206-5758
E-MAIL: bahco.bisov@open.by
Products or services (manufactured): NACE-Code
Wholesale of hardware, plumbing and heating equipment and supplies 5154
Products or services (export): NACE-Code

Manufacture of tools 2862
Wholesale of hardware, plumbing and heating equipment and supplies 5154
Products or services (import): NACE-Code
Manufacture of tools 2862
Wholesale of hardware, plumbing and heating equipment and supplies 5154

4. Rimmis, Unitary Private Trade Enterprise

ADDRESS: per. Komissariatskiy, 5, of. 7
212030, g. Mogilyov
PHONE: 0222\221-060
FAX: 0222\221-060
E-MAIL: rimmis-by@rambler.ru
Products or services (manufactured): NACE-Code
Wholesale of machinery, equipment and supplies 516
Products or services (export): NACE-Code
Wholesale of machinery, equipment and supplies 516
Products or services (import): NACE-Code
Wholesale of machinery, equipment and supplies 516

5. Selmashcomplect, Ltd.

ADDRESS: pr. Partizanskiy, 6a, k. 405
220033, g. Minsk
PHONE: 017\219-0446
FAX: 017\219-0446
E-MAIL: selmaskomplekt@enterltd.com
Products or services (manufactured): NACE-Code
Sale of motor vehicle parts and accessories 5030
Wholesale of agricultural machinery and accessories and implements, including tractors 5166
Products or services (export): NACE-Code
Sale of motor vehicle parts and accessories 5030
Wholesale of agricultural machinery and accessories and implements, including tractors 5166
Products or services (import): NACE-Code
Sale of motor vehicle parts and accessories 5030
Wholesale of agricultural machinery and accessories and implements, including tractors 5166

6. Kantin, Ltd.

ADDRESS: ul. Brestskaya, 18, k. 31
220099, g. Minsk
PHONE: 017\277-4921, 277-4931
FAX: 017\277-4921
Products or services (manufactured): NACE-Code
Wholesale of other intermediate products 5156

Wholesale of other machinery for use in industry, trade and navigation 5165
Products or services (export):NACE-Code
Wholesale of other intermediate products 5156

Products or services (import):NACE-Code
Wholesale of other intermediate products 5156
Wholesale of other machinery for use in industry, trade and navigation 5165

7. Aitin, Trade and Production Private Unitary Enterprise

ADDRESS: ul. Zakharova, 76
220088, g. Minsk
PHONE: 017\217-0534, 236-3443
FAX: 017\217-0534
E-MAIL: aitin@aitin.com
WEB SITE: www.aitin.com
Products or services (manufactured): NACE-Code
Shaping and processing of flat glass 2612
Manufacture of lighting equipment and electric lamps 3150
Products or services (export):NACE-Code
Shaping and processing of flat glass 2612
Manufacture of lighting equipment and electric lamps 3150
Products or services (import):NACE-Code
Shaping and processing of flat glass 2612
Manufacture of lighting equipment and electric lamps 3150

8. Unitary Production Enterprise "Zabudova-Sbytkomplex" of the Open Joint Stock Company "Zabudova"

ADDRESS: ul. Zavodskaya, 1
222321, Minskaya obl., Molodechnenskiy r-on, p. Chist'
PHONE: 01773\99-235
FAX: 01773\90-348, 90-206
Products or services (manufactured): NACE-Code
Wholesale of wood and of construction materials 5153
Products or services (export):NACE-Code
Wholesale of wood and of construction materials 5153
Products or services (import):NACE-Code
Wholesale of wood and of construction materials 5153

9. Mivad, Production and Trade Private Unitary Enterprise

ADDRESS: ul. Zapadnaya, 7a, k. 6
220050, g. Minsk
PHONE: 017\211-0630
FAX: 017\211-0638
E-MAIL: mivadby@mail.ru
roducts or services (manufactured): NACE-Code

Wholesale of pharmaceutical goods 5146
Products or services (export): NACE-Code
Wholesale of pharmaceutical goods 5146
Products or services (import): NACE-Code
Wholesale of pharmaceutical goods 5146

---

10. Dmitry V. Zhigalo, Private Entepreneur

ADDRESS: ul. Kletskova, 3, k.369
230020, g. Grodno
PHONE: 01522\53-913
FAX: 01522\53-913
Products or services (manufactured): NACE-Code
Other wholesale 5170
Products or services (export): NACE-Code
Other wholesale 5170
Products or services (import): NACE-Code
Other wholesale 5170

---

11. Grokard, Trade Association Additional Liability Company

ADDRESS: a/ya 140
230013, g. Grodno
PHONE: 0152\794-779
FAX: 0152\738-174
E-MAIL: grokard@mailru.com
WEB SITE: www.grokard.mailru.com/grokard.html
Products or services (manufactured): NACE-Code
Sale of motor vehicle parts and accessories 5030
Wholesale of chemical products 5155
Wholesale of agricultural machinery and accessories and implements, including tractors 5166
Other wholesale 5170
Products or services (export): NACE-Code
Sale of motor vehicle parts and accessories 5030
Wholesale of chemical products 5155
Other wholesale 5170
Products or services (import): NACE-Code
Wholesale of agricultural machinery and accessories and implements, including tractors 5166
Other wholesale 5170

---

12. VS Trading, Ltd.

ADDRESS: ul. P. Brovki, 18, k. 102
220013, g. Minsk
PHONE: 017\206-6245
FAX: 017\268-4362

E-MAIL: alsandrpw@mail.ru
Products or services (manufactured): NACE-Code
Production, processing and preserving of meat 1511
Products or services (export): NACE-Code
Production, processing and preserving of meat 1511
Products or services (import): NACE-Code
Production, processing and preserving of meat 1511

13. Baranovichi Meat Cannery, Utility Production Unitary Enterprise

ADDRESS: ul. Komsomol'skaya, 90
225320, Brestskaya obl., g. Baranovichi
PHONE: 0163\423-266
FAX: 0163\421-915
Products or services (manufactured): NACE-Code
Production, processing and preserving of meat 1511
Production, processing and preserving of poultry meat 1512
Production of meat and poultry meat products 1513
Manufacture of prepared pet feeds 1572
Manufacture of light metal packaging 2872
Storage and warehousing 6312
Products or services (export): NACE-Code
Production, processing and preserving of meat 1511
Production of meat and poultry meat products 1513
Manufacture of prepared pet feeds 1572
Manufacture of light metal packaging 2872
Products or services (import): NACE-Code
Production, processing and preserving of meat 1511
Production, processing and preserving of poultry meat 1512
Production of meat and poultry meat products 1513

14. Brest Regional Union of Consumer Societies

ADDRESS: ul. Kuybysheva, 28-1
224016, g. Brest
PHONE: 0162\263-034
FAX: 0162\235-704, 233-905
E-MAIL: ops@bresttelecom.by
Products or services (manufactured): NACE-Code
Production of meat and poultry meat products 1513
Manufacture of fruit and vegetable juice 1532
Processing and preserving of fruit and vegetables nec 1533
Manufacture of bread; manufacture of fresh pastry goods and cakes 1581
Manufacture of macaroni, noodles and similar farinaceous products 1585
Manufacture of condiments and seasonings 1587
Production of mineral waters and soft drinks 1598
Wholesale of fruit and vegetables 5131
Wholesale of meat and meat products 5132

Wholesale of dairy produce, eggs and edible oils and fats 5133
Wholesale of sugar and chocolate and sugar confectionery 5136
Non-specialized wholesale of food, beverages and tobacco 5138
Products or services (export): NACE-Code
Production of meat and poultry meat products 1513
Manufacture of fruit and vegetable juice 1532
Processing and preserving of fruit and vegetables nec 1533
Manufacture of macaroni, noodles and similar farinaceous products 1585
Wholesale of fruit and vegetables 5131
Wholesale of meat and meat products 5132
Products or services (import): NACE-Code
Processing and preserving of fruit and vegetables nec 1533
Wholesale of fruit and vegetables 5131
Wholesale of dairy produce, eggs and edible oils and fats 5133
Wholesale of sugar and chocolate and sugar confectionery 5136
Non-specialized wholesale of food, beverages and tobacco 5138

---

15. Welz Brest, Foreign Private Unitary Transport and Trade Enterprise

ADDRESS: ul. Pushkinskaya, 19-504
224030, g. Brest
PHONE: 0162\235-265
FAX: 0162\235-484, 235-265
E-MAIL: welz@mail.ru
Products or services (manufactured): NACE-Code
Transport via railways 6010
Other land passenger transport 6024
Activities of other transport agencies 6340
Products or services (export): NACE-Code
Transport via railways 6010
Other land passenger transport 6024
Activities of other transport agencies 6340
Products or services (import): NACE-Code
Transport via railways 6010
Other land passenger transport 6024

---

16. MOGILEVTECHNOMASH Business-Innovation Complex

ADDRESS: ul.Leninskaya, 61
212030, g. Mogilyov
PHONE: 0222\231-094
FAX: 0222\321-491
E-MAIL: root@bic.belpak.mogilev.by
Products or services (manufactured): NACE-Code
Manufacture of lifting and handling equipment 2922
Manufacture of machine-tools 2940
Market research and public opinion polling 7413
Architectural and engineering activities and related technical consultancy 7420

Products or services (export): NACE-Code
Manufacture of lifting and handling equipment 2922
Manufacture of machine-tools 2940
Wholesale of machinery, equipment and supplies 516
Products or services (import): NACE-Code
Manufacture of lifting and handling equipment 2922

17. Gomselmash, Production Association

ADDRESS: ul.Shosseynaya, 41
246004, g. Gomel'
PHONE: 0232\559-693
FAX: 0232\549-193
Products or services (manufactured): NACE-Code
Manufacture of agricultural tractors 2931
Manufacture of other agricultural and forestry machinery 2932
Manufacture of bodies (coachwork) for motor vehicles; manufacture of trailers and semi-trailers 3420
Manufacture of furniture 361
Products or services (export): NACE-Code
Manufacture of agricultural tractors 2931
Manufacture of other agricultural and forestry machinery 2932
Manufacture of bodies (coachwork) for motor vehicles; manufacture of trailers and semi-trailers 3420
Manufacture of furniture 361
Products or services (import): NACE-Code
Manufacture of agricultural tractors 2931
Manufacture of other agricultural and forestry machinery 2932
Manufacture of bodies (coachwork) for motor vehicles; manufacture of trailers and semi-trailers 3420

18. Gidroprivod, Gomel Plant, Republican Unitary Enterprise

ADDRESS: per.Inzhenernyy, 3
246629, g. Gomel'
PHONE: 0232\564-064
FAX: 0232\576-835, 572-757
Products or services (manufactured): NACE-Code
Manufacture of pumps and compressors 2912
Manufacture of taps and valves 2913
Manufacture of weapons and ammunition 2960
Manufacture of brooms and brushes 3662
Other manufacturing nec 3663
Products or services (export): NACE-Code
Manufacture of pumps and compressors 2912
Manufacture of taps and valves 2913
Manufacture of weapons and ammunition 2960
Manufacture of brooms and brushes 3662

Other manufacturing nec 3663
Products or services (import): NACE-Code
Manufacture of pumps and compressors 2912
Manufacture of taps and valves 2913
Manufacture of weapons and ammunition 2960
Manufacture of brooms and brushes 3662
Other manufacturing nec 3663

19. Gomel Starting Engines Plant, Republican Unitary Enterprise

ADDRESS: ul.Barykina, 150
246027, g. Gomel'
PHONE: 0232\494-304
FAX: 0232\494-328
Products or services (manufactured): NACE-Code
Manufacture of wire products 2873
Manufacture of pumps and compressors 2912
Manufacture of bearings, gears, gearing and driving elements 2914
Manufacture of electric motors, generators and transformers 3110
Manufacture of motor vehicles 3410
Manufacture of parts and accessories for motor vehicles and their engines 3430
Products or services (export): NACE-Code
Manufacture of wire products 2873
Manufacture of pumps and compressors 2912
Manufacture of bearings, gears, gearing and driving elements 2914
Manufacture of electric motors, generators and transformers 3110
Manufacture of motor vehicles 3410
Manufacture of parts and accessories for motor vehicles and their engines 3430
Products or services (import): NACE-Code
Manufacture of parts and accessories for motor vehicles and their engines 3430

20. Slonim Meat Processing Plant, Open Joint Stock Company

ADDRESS: ul.Chkalova, 35
231800, Grodnenskaya obl., g. Slonim
PHONE: 01562\21-275
FAX: 01562\21-331
E-MAIL: slmeat@mail.ru
Products or services (manufactured): NACE-Code
Hunting, trapping and game propagation including related service activities 15
Production, processing and preserving of meat 1511
Production, processing and preserving of poultry meat 1512
Production of meat and poultry meat products 1513
Manufacture of prepared pet feeds 1572
Products or services (export): NACE-Code
Hunting, trapping and game propagation including related service activities 15
Production, processing and preserving of meat 1511
Production, processing and preserving of poultry meat 1512

Production of meat and poultry meat products 1513
Manufacture of prepared pet feeds 1572
Products or services (import):NACE-Code
Hunting, trapping and game propagation including related service activities 15
Production, processing and preserving of meat 1511
Production, processing and preserving of poultry meat 1512

21. VolMet, Open Joint Stock Company

ADDRESS: ul.Krasnoarmeyskaya, 23
231900, Grodnenskaya obl., g. Volkovysk
PHONE: 01512\20-613
FAX: 01512\20-613, 20-812
E-MAIL: zamok@volmet.belpak.grodno.by
Products or services (manufactured): NACE-Code
Manufacture of locks and hinges 2863
Products or services (export):NACE-Code
Manufacture of locks and hinges 2863
Products or services (import):NACE-Code
Manufacture of locks and hinges 2863

22. Frezenius-Borisov-Dializotekhnik, Belarusian-German JV Ltd.

ADDRESS: ul.Chapaeva, 64-27
222120, Minskaya obl., g. Borisov
PHONE: 01777\34-265
FAX: 01777\34-265
Products or services (manufactured): NACE-Code
Manufacture of man-made fibres 2470
Manufacture of medical and surgical equipment and orthopaedic appliances 3310
Products or services (export):NACE-Code
Manufacture of medical and surgical equipment and orthopaedic appliances 3310
Products or services (import):NACE-Code
Manufacture of medical and surgical equipment and orthopaedic appliances 3310

23. Belfin, Belarusian-Finnish JV Ltd.

ADDRESS: ul.Velikaya, 1
223036, Minskaya obl., Minskiy r-on, g. Zaslavl'
PHONE: 017\239-0415
FAX: 017\210-0195
E-MAIL: belfin@iptel.by
Products or services (manufactured): NACE-Code
Wholesale of other household goods 5147
Wholesale of wood and of construction materials 5153
Wholesale of hardware, plumbing and heating equipment and supplies 5154
Wholesale of other machinery for use in industry, trade and navigation 5165
Products or services (export):NACE-Code

Wholesale of wood and of construction materials 5153
Wholesale of other machinery for use in industry, trade and navigation 5165
Products or services (import): NACE-Code
Wholesale of other household goods 5147
Wholesale of wood and of construction materials 5153
Wholesale of hardware, plumbing and heating equipment and supplies 5154
Wholesale of other machinery for use in industry, trade and navigation 5165

24. Motovelo,Open Joint Stock Company

ADDRESS: Partizanskiy pr., 8, p/ya 33
220765, g. Minsk
PHONE: 017\221-6819
FAX: 017\221-6806, 221-4318
E-MAIL: Motovelo@open.by
Products or services (manufactured): NACE-Code
Manufacture of motorcycles and bicycles 354
Manufacture of motorcycles 3541
Manufacture of bicycles 3542
Products or services (export): NACE-Code
Manufacture of motorcycles and bicycles 354
Manufacture of motorcycles 3541
Manufacture of bicycles 3542
Products or services (import): NACE-Code
Manufacture of bicycles 3542

25. Polymaster, Belarusian-Polish JV Ltd.

ADDRESS: ul.M.Bogdanovicha, 112
220040, g. Minsk
PHONE: 017\217-7080
FAX: 017\217-7081
E-MAIL: polimaster@polimaster.com
WEB SITE: www.polimaster.com
Products or services (manufactured): NACE-Code
Manufacture of instruments and appliances for measuring, checking, testing, navigating and other purposes, except industrial process control equipment 3320
Products or services (export): NACE-Code
Manufacture of instruments and appliances for measuring, checking, testing, navigating and other purposes, except industrial process control equipment 3320
Products or services (import): NACE-Code
Manufacture of instruments and appliances for measuring, checking, testing, navigating and other purposes, except industrial process control equipment 3320

26. Department for Production and Technological Procurement Limited Liability Company

ADDRESS: ul.Selitskogo, 9
220075, g. Minsk
PHONE: 017\244-2121
FAX: 017\244-6022
Products or services (manufactured): NACE-Code
Manufacture of fruit and vegetable juice 1532
Manufacture of other outerwear 1822
Manufacture of plastic products 252
MANUFACTURE OF FABRICATED METAL PRODUCTS, EXCEPT MACHINERY AND EQUIPMENT 28
Manufacture of central heating radiators and boilers 2822
Manufacture of other fabricated metal products nec 2875
Manufacture of non-domestic cooling and ventilation equipment 2923
Manufacture of insulated wire and cable 3130
Manufacture of lighting equipment and electric lamps 3150
Products or services (export): NACE-Code
Manufacture of fruit and vegetable juice 1532
Manufacture of plastic products 252
MANUFACTURE OF FABRICATED METAL PRODUCTS, EXCEPT MACHINERY AND EQUIPMENT 28
Manufacture of other fabricated metal products nec 2875
Products or services (import): NACE-Code
Manufacture of fruit and vegetable juice 1532

---

27. JAK – Automotive Technologies Ltd Joint Venture

ADDRESS: ul.3-ya Poselkovaya, 10, 3 etazh
220113, g. Minsk
PHONE: 017\262-6377
FAX: 017\265-4631
Products or services (manufactured): NACE-Code
MANUFACTURE OF FABRICATED METAL PRODUCTS, EXCEPT MACHINERY AND EQUIPMENT 28
Manufacture of electrical equipment for engines and vehicles nec 3161
Manufacture of motor vehicles 3410
Manufacture of parts and accessories for motor vehicles and their engines 3430
Manufacture of bicycles 3542
Products or services (export): NACE-Code
MANUFACTURE OF FABRICATED METAL PRODUCTS, EXCEPT MACHINERY AND EQUIPMENT 28
Manufacture of electrical equipment for engines and vehicles nec 3161
Manufacture of motor vehicles 3410
Manufacture of parts and accessories for motor vehicles and their engines 3430
Manufacture of bicycles 3542
Products or services (import): NACE-Code
MANUFACTURE OF FABRICATED METAL PRODUCTS, EXCEPT MACHINERY AND EQUIPMENT 28
Manufacture of electrical equipment for engines and vehicles nec 3161

Manufacture of parts and accessories for motor vehicles and their engines 3430
Sale of motor vehicle parts and accessories 5030

28. Minsk Plant of Special Tools and Technological Rigging, Production Republican Unitary Enterprise

ADDRESS: ul. Dolgobrodskaya, 29
220668, g. Minsk
PHONE: 017\289-9893
FAX: 017\230-1726
E-MAIL: market@sittp.belpak.minsk.by
Products or services (manufactured): NACE-Code
Manufacture of other plastic products 2524
Manufacture of tools 2862
Manufacture of other fabricated metal products nec 2875
Manufacture of machine-tools 2940
Products or services (export): NACE-Code
Manufacture of tools 2862
Manufacture of machine-tools 2940
Products or services (import): NACE-Code
Manufacture of tools 2862

29. Footwear Fashion Design House Open Joint Stock Company

ADDRESS: ul.Oktyabr'skaya, 19
220030, g. Minsk
PHONE: 017\227-7300
Products or services (manufactured): NACE-Code
Manufacture of footwear 1930
Products or services (export): NACE-Code
Manufacture of footwear 1930
Products or services (import): NACE-Code
Manufacture of footwear 1930

30. Minskoblplodoovoshchzhoz, Production Association

ADDRESS: ul.K.Chornogo, 21b
220012, g. Minsk
PHONE: 017\266-1770
FAX: 017\266-4834
E-MAIL: sales@ov.open.by
Products or services (manufactured): NACE-Code
Growing of cereals and other crops nec 0111
Growing of vegetables, horticultural specialities and nursery products 0112
Growing of fruit, nuts, beverage and spice crops 0113
Production, processing and preserving of meat 1511
Processing and preserving of fruit and vegetables nec 1533
Operation of dairies and cheese making 1551

Manufacture of condiments and seasonings 1587
Manufacture of other food products nec 1589
Manufacture of distilled potable alcoholic beverages 1591
Manufacture of cider and other fruit wines 1594
Manufacture of beer 1596
Production of mineral waters and soft drinks 1598
Manufacture of hollow glass 2613
Wholesale of food, beverages and tobacco 513
Products or services (export): NACE-Code
Growing of vegetables, horticultural specialities and nursery products 0112
Growing of fruit, nuts, beverage and spice crops 0113
Processing and preserving of fruit and vegetables nec 1533
Manufacture of distilled potable alcoholic beverages 1591
Production of mineral waters and soft drinks 1598
Products or services (import): NACE-Code
Growing of vegetables, horticultural specialities and nursery products 0112
Processing and preserving of fruit and vegetables nec 1533

---

31. KVANT State Scientific and production Enterprise

ADDRESS: ul.Starovilenskaya, 54
220002, g. Minsk
PHONE: 017\234-9041
FAX: 017\234-8297
Products or services (manufactured): NACE-Code
Recycling of metal waste and scrap 3710
Software consultancy and supply 7220
Dental practice activities 8513
Products or services (export): NACE-Code
Recycling of metal waste and scrap 3710
Products or services (import): NACE-Code
Recycling of metal waste and scrap 3710

---

32. POISK Joint-Stock Commercial Bank

ADDRESS: ul.Gamarnika, 9, korp.4
220090, g. Minsk
PHONE: 017\228-3249
FAX: 017\228-3248
Products or services (manufactured): NACE-Code
Central banking 6511
Financial leasing 6521
Administration of financial markets 6711
Security dealing activities 6712
OTHER BUSINESS ACTIVITIES 74
Products or services (export): NACE-Code
Central banking 6511
Financial leasing 6521

Administration of financial markets 6711
Security dealing activities 6712
OTHER BUSINESS ACTIVITIES 74
Products or services (import): NACE-Code
Administration of financial markets 6711
Security dealing activities 6712

33. SEMIPLAN

ADDRESS: ul.Orlovskaya, 58
220053, g. Minsk
PHONE: 017\237-7321
FAX: 017\237-3566
E-MAIL: semiplan-minolta@belsonet.net
Products or services (manufactured): NACE-Code
Wholesale of office machinery and equipment 5164
Products or services (export): NACE-Code
Wholesale of pharmaceutical goods 5146
Wholesale of other household goods 5147
Wholesale of office machinery and equipment 5164
Products or services (import): NACE-Code
Wholesale of pharmaceutical goods 5146
Wholesale of other household goods 5147
Wholesale of office machinery and equipment 5164

34. BELBUILDMATERIALS Open Joint Stock Company

ADDRESS: ul.Kazintsa, 2, k.309
220099, g. Minsk
PHONE: 017\224-1917
FAX: 017\224-6704
Products or services (manufactured): NACE-Code
Wholesale of wood and of construction materials 5153
Products or services (export): NACE-Code
WHOLESALE TRADE AND COMMISSION TRADE, EXCEPT OF MOTOR VEHICLES AND MOTORCYCLES 51
Wholesale of other household goods 5147
Wholesale of metals and metal ores 5152
Wholesale of wood and of construction materials 5153
Wholesale of hardware, plumbing and heating equipment and supplies 5154
Products or services (import): NACE-Code
WHOLESALE TRADE AND COMMISSION TRADE, EXCEPT OF MOTOR VEHICLES AND MOTORCYCLES 51
Wholesale of other household goods 5147
Wholesale of metals and metal ores 5152
Wholesale of wood and of construction materials 5153
Wholesale of hardware, plumbing and heating equipment and supplies 5154

35. ABC firm , Production and Trade Association, Additional Liability Company

ADDRESS: ul. Pobedy, 27
230026, g. Grodno
PHONE: 0152\742-040, 742-049
E-MAIL: abc@mail.grodno.by

Products or services (manufactured): NACE-Code
Growing of vegetables, horticultural specialities and nursery products 0112
Growing of fruit, nuts, beverage and spice crops 0113
Processing and preserving of fruit and vegetables nec 1533
Manufacture of condiments and seasonings 1587
Products or services (export): NACE-Code
Growing of vegetables, horticultural specialities and nursery products 0112
Growing of fruit, nuts, beverage and spice crops 0113
Processing and preserving of fruit and vegetables nec 1533
Manufacture of condiments and seasonings 1587
Products or services (import): NACE-Code
Processing and preserving of fruit and vegetables nec 1533

---

36. Metr Ltd Production and Commercial Company

ADDRESS: ul.Kazintsa, 2, kom.208
220099, g. Minsk
PHONE: 017\278-2231
FAX: 017\278-2231
Products or services (manufactured): NACE-Code
Manufacture of other agricultural and forestry machinery 2932
Products or services (export): NACE-Code
Manufacture of other agricultural and forestry machinery 2932
Wholesale of hardware, plumbing and heating equipment and supplies 5154
Wholesale of chemical products 5155
Wholesale of agricultural machinery and accessories and implements, including tractors 5166
Products or services (import): NACE-Code
Manufacture of other agricultural and forestry machinery 2932
Wholesale of hardware, plumbing and heating equipment and supplies 5154

---

37. TSANT

ADDRESS: ul.Kuntsevshchina, 6-76
220017, g. Minsk
PHONE: 017\259-8591
FAX: 017\259-8591
Products or services (manufactured): NACE-Code
MANUFACTURE OF MOTOR VEHICLES, TRAILERS AND SEMI-TRAILERS 34
Products or services (export): NACE-Code
MANUFACTURE OF MOTOR VEHICLES, TRAILERS AND SEMI-TRAILERS 34

Fishing, operation of fish hatcheries and fish farms; service activities incidental to fishing 50
Wholesale of metals and metal ores 5152
Products or services (import): NACE-Code
MANUFACTURE OF MOTOR VEHICLES, TRAILERS AND SEMI-TRAILERS 34

38. Yurditime, Additional Liability Company

ADDRESS: ul. Fabritsiusa, 9, k. 30
220000, g. Minsk
Products or services (manufactured): NACE-Code
Sale of motor vehicles 5010
Products or services (export): NACE-Code
Sale of motor vehicles 5010
Products or services (import): NACE-Code

39. USV, Production and Trade Unitary Enterprise

ADDRESS: dom b/n, liter A 3/k
223021, Minskaya obl., Minskiy r-on, p. Ozertso
PHONE: 017\507-6563, 507-6564
FAX: 017\507-6561
E-MAIL: usv@open.by
Products or services (manufactured): NACE-Code
Manufacture of bicycles 3542
Products or services (export): NACE-Code
Manufacture of bicycles 3542
Products or services (import): NACE-Code
Manufacture of bicycles 3542

40. Transexim, Ltd.

ADDRESS: ul. Rybalko, 26, a/ya 130
220033, g. Minsk
PHONE: 017\210-5400
FAX: 017\210-5390
E-MAIL: info@ferteco.net
Products or services (manufactured): NACE-Code
Sale of motor vehicles 5010
Non-specialized wholesale of food, beverages and tobacco 5138
Wholesale of machinery, equipment and supplies 516
Wholesale of construction machinery 5162
Products or services (export): NACE-Code
Sale of motor vehicles 5010
Wholesale of construction machinery 5162
Products or services (import): NACE-Code
Sale of motor vehicles 5010
Non-specialized wholesale of food, beverages and tobacco 5138

Wholesale of machinery, equipment and supplies 516

41. Platan, Ltd.

ADDRESS: ul. Oktyabr'skaya, 206
213802, Mogilyovskaya obl., g. Bobruysk
PHONE: 0225\586-718
FAX: 0225\552-066
Products or services (manufactured): NACE-Code
Manufacture of chairs and seats 3611
Sale of motor vehicles 5010
Sale of motor vehicle parts and accessories 5030
Products or services (export):NACE-Code
Manufacture of chairs and seats 3611
Sale of motor vehicles 5010
Sale of motor vehicle parts and accessories 5030
Products or services (import):NACE-Code
Sale of motor vehicles 5010
Sale of motor vehicle parts and accessories 5030

42. Beltransauto, Novopotsk Autotransport Enterprise Ltd.

ADDRESS: ul. Pushkina, 16
211400, Vitebskaya obl., Polotskiy r-on, g. Novopolotsk
PHONE: 0214\446-048
FAX: 0214\446-009
E-MAIL: beltransauto@tut.by
Products or services (manufactured): NACE-Code
Wholesale of chemical products 5155
Other scheduled passenger land transport 6021
Other land passenger transport 6024
Products or services (export):NACE-Code
Wholesale of chemical products 5155
Products or services (import):NACE-Code
Wholesale of chemical products 5155

43. Allegro, Production and Commercial Firm, Ltd.

ADDRESS: ul. Parkovaya, 16a
211440, Vitebskaya obl., Polotskiy r-on, g. Novopolotsk
PHONE: 02145\58-632, 56-072
FAX: 02145\17-677
E-MAIL: ooo_allegro@tut.by
Products or services (manufactured): NACE-Code
Wholesale of non-agricultural intermediate products, waste and scrap 515
Wholesale of solid, liquid and gaseous fuels and related products 5151
Wholesale of chemical products 5155
Products or services (export):NACE-Code

Wholesale of solid, liquid and gaseous fuels and related products 5151
Wholesale of chemical products 5155
Products or services (import): NACE-Code
Wholesale of non-agricultural intermediate products, waste and scrap 515
Wholesale of solid, liquid and gaseous fuels and related products 5151

---

44. Ganna K. Rusak, Private Enterpreneur

ADDRESS: ul. Kabushkina, 80
225320, Brestskaya obl., g. Baranovichi
PHONE: 0163\425-257
FAX: 0163\424-438
E-MAIL: 6300867@tut.by
Products or services (manufactured): NACE-Code
Non-specialized wholesale of food, beverages and tobacco 5138
Wholesale of household goods 514
Wholesale of chemical products 5155
Wholesale of other intermediate products 5156
Products or services (export): NACE-Code
Non-specialized wholesale of food, beverages and tobacco 5138
Wholesale of household goods 514
Wholesale of chemical products 5155
Wholesale of other intermediate products 5156
Products or services (import): NACE-Code
Non-specialized wholesale of food, beverages and tobacco 5138
Wholesale of household goods 514
Wholesale of chemical products 5155
Wholesale of other intermediate products 5156

---

45. Technoshans, Closed Joint Stock Company

ADDRESS: ul. Bogdanovicha, 78, k. 1a
220100, g. Minsk
PHONE: 017\239-3956
FAX: 017\231-4339
Products or services (manufactured): NACE-Code
Manufacture of instruments and appliances for measuring, checking, testing, navigating and other purposes, except industrial process control equipment 3320
Wholesale of other household goods 5147
Wholesale of hardware, plumbing and heating equipment and supplies 5154
Products or services (export): NACE-Code
Manufacture of instruments and appliances for measuring, checking, testing, navigating and other purposes, except industrial process control equipment 3320
Wholesale of other household goods 5147
Wholesale of hardware, plumbing and heating equipment and supplies 5154
Products or services (import): NACE-Code
Wholesale of other household goods 5147
Wholesale of hardware, plumbing and heating equipment and supplies 5154

46. Nabis, Ltd.

ADDRESS: ul. Borisenko, 8
246027, g. Gomel'
PHONE: 0232\794-170
FAX: 0232\794-170
E-MAIL: ppnabis@server.by
Products or services (manufactured): NACE-Code
Other wholesale 5170
Products or services (export): NACE-Code
Other wholesale 5170
Products or services (import): NACE-Code
Other wholesale 5170

47. Diamash-M Ltd., Foreign Enterprise

ADDRESS: ul. Serova, 4, k. 15
220024, g. Minsk
PHONE: 017\275-3125
FAX: 017\275-5845
E-MAIL: diamash@mail.ru
Products or services (manufactured): NACE-Code
WHOLESALE TRADE AND COMMISSION TRADE, EXCEPT OF MOTOR VEHICLES AND MOTORCYCLES 51
Wholesale of hardware, plumbing and heating equipment and supplies 5154
Wholesale of other machinery for use in industry, trade and navigation 5165
Products or services (export): NACE-Code
WHOLESALE TRADE AND COMMISSION TRADE, EXCEPT OF MOTOR VEHICLES AND MOTORCYCLES 51
Wholesale of hardware, plumbing and heating equipment and supplies 5154
Wholesale of other machinery for use in industry, trade and navigation 5165
Products or services (import): NACE-Code
WHOLESALE TRADE AND COMMISSION TRADE, EXCEPT OF MOTOR VEHICLES AND MOTORCYCLES 51
Wholesale of hardware, plumbing and heating equipment and supplies 5154
Wholesale of other machinery for use in industry, trade and navigation 5165

48. ASS, Additional liability company

ADDRESS: ul. Bochkina, 99a, k.1
246008, g. Gomel'
PHONE: 0232\781-319
FAX: 0232\781-318
Products or services (manufactured): NACE-Code
Wholesale of chemical products 5155
Wholesale of other intermediate products 5156
Products or services (export): NACE-Code

Wholesale of other intermediate products 5156
Products or services (import): NACE-Code
Wholesale of chemical products 5155
Wholesale of other intermediate products 5156

49. Donativa, Additional Liability Company

ADDRESS: a/ya 242
220116, g. Minsk
PHONE: 017\211-5843, 211-5841
FAX: 017\211-5841
E-MAIL: donativa@tut.by
Products or services (manufactured): NACE-Code
Sale, maintenance and repair of motorcycles and related parts and accessories 5040
Wholesale of other household goods 5147
Wholesale of metals and metal ores 5152
Products or services (export): NACE-Code
Sale, maintenance and repair of motorcycles and related parts and accessories 5040
Wholesale of other household goods 5147
Products or services (import): NACE-Code
Wholesale of other household goods 5147
Wholesale of metals and metal ores 5152

50. Aliansplast, ltd.

ADDRESS: ul. Il'inskogo, 47a
210001, g. Vitebsk
PHONE: 0212\363-041
FAX: 0212\365-165
E-MAIL: alliansplast@tut.by
Products or services (manufactured): NACE-Code
Manufacture of plastic packing 2522
Manufacture of other special purpose machinery nec 2956
Wholesale of other machinery for use in industry, trade and navigation 5165
Products or services (export): NACE-Code
Manufacture of plastic packing 2522
Manufacture of other special purpose machinery nec 2956
Wholesale of other machinery for use in industry, trade and navigation 5165
Products or services (import): NACE-Code
Manufacture of other special purpose machinery nec 2956
Wholesale of other machinery for use in industry, trade and navigation 5165

51. Dinamarket, Trade and Production Private Unitary Enterprise

ADDRESS: ul. Pionerskaya, 47
220020, g. Minsk
PHONE: 017\209-6620
FAX: 017\209-6621

E-MAIL: dinamarket@yandex.ru
Products or services (manufactured): NACE-Code
Manufacture of plastics in primary forms 2416
Manufacture of plastic plates, sheets, tubes and profiles 2521
Manufacture of builders' ware of plastic 2523
Wholesale of metals and metal ores 5152
Wholesale of wood and of construction materials 5153
Wholesale of hardware, plumbing and heating equipment and supplies 5154
Wholesale of chemical products 5155
Wholesale of other machinery for use in industry, trade and navigation 5165
Products or services (export): NACE-Code
Manufacture of plastics in primary forms 2416
Manufacture of plastic plates, sheets, tubes and profiles 2521
Manufacture of builders' ware of plastic 2523
Wholesale of hardware, plumbing and heating equipment and supplies 5154
Products or services (import): NACE-Code
Wholesale of metals and metal ores 5152
Wholesale of wood and of construction materials 5153
Wholesale of hardware, plumbing and heating equipment and supplies 5154
Wholesale of chemical products 5155
Wholesale of other machinery for use in industry, trade and navigation 5165

---

52. Yanina A.Shevchik, Private Enterpreneur

ADDRESS: ul. Tomina, 14a, k. 503
230026, g. Grodno
PHONE: 01522\69-652
Products or services (manufactured): NACE-Code
Wholesale of food, beverages and tobacco 513
Products or services (export): NACE-Code
Wholesale of food, beverages and tobacco 513
Products or services (import): NACE-Code
Wholesale of food, beverages and tobacco 513

---

53. Stroytemp, Trade Private Unitary Enterprise

ADDRESS: ul. k.Chornogo, 5a, k. 2
220012, g. Minsk
PHONE: 017\232-9082
FAX: 017\232-9082
Products or services (manufactured): NACE-Code
Wholesale of wood and of construction materials 5153
Products or services (export): NACE-Code
Wholesale of wood and of construction materials 5153
Products or services (import): NACE-Code
Wholesale of wood and of construction materials 5153

---

54. MDS-Holding, Production and Trade Unitary Enterprise

ADDRESS: ul. peredovaya, 15, k. 20
220037, g. Minsk
PHONE: 017\289-5849
FAX: 017\289-5859
E-MAIL: mds@it.org.by
Products or services (manufactured): NACE-Code
Wholesale of pharmaceutical goods 5146
Products or services (export): NACE-Code
Wholesale of pharmaceutical goods 5146
Products or services (import): NACE-Code
Wholesale of pharmaceutical goods 5146

55. Nikolay I. Kalchenko, Private Enterpreneur

ADDRESS: a/ya 368
222120, Minskaya obl., g. Borisov
PHONE: 029\615-1551, 0177\799-619
FAX: 0177\799-619
E-MAIL: nikolai@kalchenko.com
WEB SITE: www.kalchenko.com
Products or services (manufactured): NACE-Code
Manufacture of lighting equipment and electric lamps 3150
Products or services (export): NACE-Code
Manufacture of lighting equipment and electric lamps 3150
Products or services (import): NACE-Code
Manufacture of lighting equipment and electric lamps 3150

56. Belgazprombank, Belarusian-Russian Open Joint Stock Company

ADDRESS: ul. Pritytskogo, 60/2
220121, g. Minsk
PHONE: 017\259-4024
FAX: 017\259-4024
E-MAIL: bank@belgazptombank.by
WEB SITE: ww.belgazptombank.by
Products or services (manufactured): NACE-Code
Other monetary intermediation 6512
Financial leasing 6521
Other financial intermediation nec 6523
Activities auxiliary to financial intermediation nec 6713
Legal activities 7411
Business and management consultancy activities 7414
Other business activities nec 7484
Products or services (export): NACE-Code
Other monetary intermediation 6512
Financial leasing 6521
Other financial intermediation nec 6523

Activities auxiliary to financial intermediation nec 6713
Products or services (import): NACE-Code
Other monetary intermediation 6512
Financial leasing 6521
Other financial intermediation nec 6523

57. TIS-Magmet Production Assosiation Belprommetal, Closed Joint Stock Company

ADDRESS: ul. Krylenko, 5
212030, g. Mogilyov
PHONE: 0222\311-702
FAX: 0222-311-874
E-MAIL: mail@tis.belpak.mogilev.by
Products or services (manufactured): NACE-Code
Sale of motor vehicles 5010
Wholesale of metals and metal ores 5152
Wholesale of chemical products 5155
Wholesale of construction machinery 5162
Wholesale of other machinery for use in industry, trade and navigation 5165
Products or services (export): NACE-Code
Sale of motor vehicles 5010
Wholesale of metals and metal ores 5152
Wholesale of construction machinery 5162
Wholesale of other machinery for use in industry, trade and navigation 5165
Products or services (import): NACE-Code
Sale of motor vehicles 5010
Wholesale of metals and metal ores 5152
Wholesale of chemical products 5155
Wholesale of construction machinery 5162

58. Polpaper, Belarusian-Polish JV Ltd.

ADDRESS: a/ya 33, ul. Korzhenevskogo, 19, k. 405,
220108, g. Minsk
PHONE: 017\278-0784
FAX: 017\207-0290
Products or services (manufactured): NACE-Code
Wholesale of other machinery for use in industry, trade and navigation 5165
Products or services (export): NACE-Code
Wholesale of other machinery for use in industry, trade and navigation 5165
Products or services (import): NACE-Code
Wholesale of other machinery for use in industry, trade and navigation 5165

59. Konstal, Ltd.

ADDRESS: ul. Parkovaya, 16a
211440, Vitebskaya obl., Polotskiy r-on, g. Novopolotsk
PHONE: 0214\559-420

FAX: 0214\559-420
E-MAIL: konstal@tut.by
Products or services (manufactured): NACE-Code
Wholesale of non-agricultural intermediate products, waste and scrap 515
Wholesale of solid, liquid and gaseous fuels and related products 5151
Wholesale of chemical products 5155
Products or services (export):NACE-Code
Wholesale of non-agricultural intermediate products, waste and scrap 515
Wholesale of solid, liquid and gaseous fuels and related products 5151
Wholesale of chemical products 5155
Products or services (import):NACE-Code
Wholesale of solid, liquid and gaseous fuels and related products 5151

60. Ratenvest, Trading Private Unitary Enterprise

ADDRESS: ul. Khar'kovskaya, 2a, k. 4
220004, g. Minsk
PHONE: 017\246-7844
FAX: 017\246-7844
E-MAIL: zvezdochet1973@tut.by
Products or services (manufactured): NACE-Code
Sale of motor vehicle parts and accessories 5030
WHOLESALE TRADE AND COMMISSION TRADE, EXCEPT OF MOTOR VEHICLES AND MOTORCYCLES 51
Wholesale of household appliances and radio and television goods 5143
Wholesale of metals and metal ores 5152
Wholesale of machine tools for working metal and wood 5161
Wholesale of construction machinery 5162
Wholesale of other machinery for use in industry, trade and navigation 5165
Products or services (export):NACE-Code
Sale of motor vehicle parts and accessories 5030
WHOLESALE TRADE AND COMMISSION TRADE, EXCEPT OF MOTOR VEHICLES AND MOTORCYCLES 51
Wholesale of household appliances and radio and television goods 5143
Wholesale of construction machinery 5162
Products or services (import):NACE-Code
Sale of motor vehicle parts and accessories 5030
Wholesale of metals and metal ores 5152
Wholesale of machine tools for working metal and wood 5161
Wholesale of other machinery for use in industry, trade and navigation 5165

61. Belavtomazservice-Zapchast, Production and Trade Private Unitary Enterprise

ADDRESS: ul. P. Brovki, 15
220072, g. Minsk
PHONE: 017\289-2493
FAX: 017\289-2553
E-MAIL: ecadmin@jenty.by

Products or services (manufactured): NACE-Code
Sale of motor vehicle parts and accessories 5030
Products or services (export): NACE-Code
Sale of motor vehicle parts and accessories 5030
Products or services (import): NACE-Code
Sale of motor vehicle parts and accessories 5030

62. Vitebsk Plant of Polymeric Products, Open JSC

ADDRESS: pr. Frunze, 81
210602, g. Vitebsk
PHONE: 0212\249-916
FAX: 0212\261-817
Products or services (manufactured): NACE-Code
MANUFACTURE OF CHEMICALS AND CHEMICAL PRODUCTS 24
Manufacture of plastic plates, sheets, tubes and profiles 2521
Wholesale of other machinery for use in industry, trade and navigation 5165
Products or services (export): NACE-Code
MANUFACTURE OF CHEMICALS AND CHEMICAL PRODUCTS 24
Manufacture of plastic plates, sheets, tubes and profiles 2521
Wholesale of other machinery for use in industry, trade and navigation 5165
Products or services (import): NACE-Code
MANUFACTURE OF CHEMICALS AND CHEMICAL PRODUCTS 24
Wholesale of other machinery for use in industry, trade and navigation 5165

63. AMTengineering, JV Ltd

ADDRESS: ul. Kalinina, 7. k. 46/3
220012, g. Minsk
PHONE: 017\224-1274
FAX: 017\224-1274
E-MAIL: amtengine@infonet.by
WEB SITE: www.amtengine.com
Products or services (manufactured): NACE-Code
MANUFACTURE OF MACHINERY AND EQUIPMENT NEC 29
Manufacture of machine-tools 2940
Wholesale of machine tools for working metal and wood 5161
Research and experimental development on natural sciences and engineering 7310
Products or services (export): NACE-Code
MANUFACTURE OF MACHINERY AND EQUIPMENT NEC 29
Manufacture of machine-tools 2940
Research and experimental development on natural sciences and engineering 7310
Products or services (import): NACE-Code
MANUFACTURE OF MACHINERY AND EQUIPMENT NEC 29
Manufacture of machine-tools 2940

64. Tandem-Torg, Additional Liability Company

ADDRESS: ul. Lesnaya, 2-a, k. 6
223053, Minskaya obl., Minskiy r-on, d. Leskovka
PHONE: 017\232-9062
FAX: 017\232-9062
E-MAIL: egertonolga@rambler.ru
Products or services (manufactured): NACE-Code
Wholesale of grain, seeds and animal feeds 5121
Wholesale of fruit and vegetables 5131
Wholesale of meat and meat products 5132
Wholesale of dairy produce, eggs and edible oils and fats 5133
Wholesale of sugar and chocolate and sugar confectionery 5136
Wholesale of china and glassware, varnish, paint, wallpaper and cleaning materials 5144
Wholesale of wood and of construction materials 5153
Products or services (export): NACE-Code
Wholesale of grain, seeds and animal feeds 5121
Wholesale of fruit and vegetables 5131
Wholesale of meat and meat products 5132
Wholesale of dairy produce, eggs and edible oils and fats 5133
Wholesale of sugar and chocolate and sugar confectionery 5136
Wholesale of china and glassware, varnish, paint, wallpaper and cleaning materials 5144
Wholesale of wood and of construction materials 5153
Products or services (import): NACE-Code
Wholesale of grain, seeds and animal feeds 5121
Wholesale of sugar and chocolate and sugar confectionery 5136

---

65. Jawid, Private Unitary Production Enterprise

ADDRESS: ul. Vil'chkovskogo, 182 V
225320, Brestskaya obl., g. Baranovichi
PHONE: 0163\464-455, 463-819
FAX: 0163\464-455, 463-819
E-MAIL: jawid@mail.ru
WEB SITE: www.jawid.by
Products or services (manufactured): NACE-Code
Sawmilling and planing of wood, impregnation of wood 2010
Manufacture of chairs and seats 3611
Manufacture of other office and shop furniture 3612
Manufacture of other furniture 3614
Products or services (export): NACE-Code
Sawmilling and planing of wood, impregnation of wood 2010
Manufacture of chairs and seats 3611
Manufacture of other office and shop furniture 3612
Manufacture of other furniture 3614
Products or services (import): NACE-Code
Sawmilling and planing of wood, impregnation of wood 2010

---

66. Teoks, Additional Liability Company

ADDRESS: ul. Gurskogo, 30, k. 47
220015, g. Minsk
PHONE: 017\252-1122
FAX: 017\252-1122
E-MAIL: teoks@solo.by
Products or services (manufactured): NACE-Code
Wholesale of household appliances and radio and television goods 5143
Retail sale of furniture and lighting equipment 5244
Products or services (export): NACE-Code
Wholesale of household appliances and radio and television goods 5143
Products or services (import): NACE-Code
Wholesale of household appliances and radio and television goods 5143

67. Nikolay S. Vasilioglo

ADDRESS: ul. Sovetskaya, 61
225511, Brestskaya obl., Stolinskiy r-on, d. B. Vikorovichi
PHONE: 01655\24-200, 029\675-1470
FAX: 01655\22-442
Products or services (manufactured): NACE-Code
Wholesale of alcoholic and other beverages 5134
Non-specialized wholesale of food, beverages and tobacco 5138
Wholesale of wood and of construction materials 5153
Products or services (export): NACE-Code
Wholesale of alcoholic and other beverages 5134
Non-specialized wholesale of food, beverages and tobacco 5138
Wholesale of wood and of construction materials 5153
Products or services (import): NACE-Code
Wholesale of alcoholic and other beverages 5134
Non-specialized wholesale of food, beverages and tobacco 5138

68. MFL-Belaplast, Foreign Private Unitary Enterprise

ADDRESS: ul. Filimonova, 5
220037, g. Minsk
PHONE: 017\210-0756
FAX: 017\210-0756
E-MAIL: belaplast@tut.by
Products or services (manufactured): NACE-Code
Manufacture of plastic plates, sheets, tubes and profiles 2521
Manufacture of plastic packing 2522

Products or services (export): NACE-Code
Manufacture of plastic plates, sheets, tubes and profiles 2521
Manufacture of plastic packing 2522
Products or services (import): NACE-Code

Manufacture of plastic plates, sheets, tubes and profiles 2521

69. Bobruiskselmash, Republican Subsidiary Unitary Enterprise

ADDRESS: ul. Orlovskogo, 20
213823, Mogilyovskaya obl., g. Bobruysk
PHONE: 02251\24-066
FAX: 02251\24-066
E-MAIL: bobruiskselmash@bues.mogilev.by
WEB SITE: www.вobruiskselmash.by
Products or services (manufactured): NACE-Code
Manufacture of other agricultural and forestry machinery 2932
Manufacture of bodies (coachwork) for motor vehicles; manufacture of trailers and semi-trailers 3420
Products or services (export):NACE-Code
Manufacture of other agricultural and forestry machinery 2932
Manufacture of bodies (coachwork) for motor vehicles; manufacture of trailers and semi-trailers 3420
Products or services (import):NACE-Code
Manufacture of other agricultural and forestry machinery 2932
Manufacture of bodies (coachwork) for motor vehicles; manufacture of trailers and semi-trailers 3420

70. Belcotlokomplect, Closed Joint Stock Company

ADDRESS: ul. Lazo, 110
210033, g. Vitebsk
PHONE: 0212\240-439
FAX: 0212\242-042
E-MAIL: bkk@teplo.belpak.vitebsk.by
WEB SITE: www.belpak.vitebsk.by/boiler

Products or services (manufactured): NACE-Code
Manufacture of central heating radiators and boilers 2822
MANUFACTURE OF MACHINERY AND EQUIPMENT NEC 29
Wholesale of non-agricultural intermediate products, waste and scrap 515
Wholesale of hardware, plumbing and heating equipment and supplies 5154
Products or services (export):NACE-Code
Wholesale of non-agricultural intermediate products, waste and scrap 515
Wholesale of hardware, plumbing and heating equipment and supplies 5154
Products or services (import):NACE-Code
Wholesale of hardware, plumbing and heating equipment and supplies 5154

71. SVALX Foreign Enterprise

ADDRESS: ul.Pritytskogo, 2-1
220073, g. Minsk
PHONE: 017\220-8665

FAX: 017\220-8665
Products or services (manufactured): NACE-Code
Processing and preserving of fish and fish products 1520
Manufacture of other food products nec 1589
Products or services (export):NACE-Code
Processing and preserving of fish and fish products 1520
Manufacture of other food products nec 1589
Non-specialized wholesale of food, beverages and tobacco 5138
Products or services (import):NACE-Code
Processing and preserving of fish and fish products 1520
Manufacture of other food products nec 1589
Non-specialized wholesale of food, beverages and tobacco 5138

72. Beltsvetmet, Republican Production Unitary Enterprise

ADDRESS: ul.Denisovskaya, 33
220006, g. Minsk
PHONE: 017\221-2791
FAX: 017\221-0072
Products or services (manufactured): NACE-Code
Recycling of metal waste and scrap 3710
Products or services (export):NACE-Code
Recycling of metal waste and scrap 3710
Products or services (import):NACE-Code
Recycling of metal waste and scrap 3710

73. Lesbumsnab, Additional Liability Company

ADDRESS: ul.Mezhdunarodnaya, 29
246021, g. Gomel'
PHONE: 0232\585-200
FAX: 0232\584-859
E-MAIL: shevtsov@server.by
Products or services (manufactured): NACE-Code
Wholesale of china and glassware, varnish, paint, wallpaper and cleaning materials 5144
Wholesale of chemical products 5155
Wholesale of other intermediate products 5156
Products or services (export):NACE-Code
Wholesale of china and glassware, varnish, paint, wallpaper and cleaning materials 5144
Wholesale of other intermediate products 5156
Products or services (import):NACE-Code
Wholesale of china and glassware, varnish, paint, wallpaper and cleaning materials 5144
Wholesale of chemical products 5155
Wholesale of other intermediate products 5156

74. MELESHKEVICH Farming Enterprise

ADDRESS: Parkovyy per., 3
220131, Minskaya obl., Minskiy r-on, d. Syomkovo
PHONE: 017\261-7199, 261-2332
FAX: 017\261-7199
Products or services (manufactured): NACE-Code
Growing of cereals and other crops nec 0111
Growing of vegetables, horticultural specialities and nursery products 0112
Wholesale of agricultural raw materials and live animals 512
Products or services (export): NACE-Code
Growing of cereals and other crops nec 0111
Growing of vegetables, horticultural specialities and nursery products 0112
Wholesale of agricultural raw materials and live animals 512
Products or services (import): NACE-Code
Wholesale of agricultural raw materials and live animals 512

75. YVAMET Production and commercial Private Enterprise

ADDRESS: ul.Ol'shevskogo, 10
220073, g. Minsk
PHONE: 017\254-3350
FAX: 017\254-3350
Products or services (manufactured): NACE-Code
Wire drawing 2734
Manufacture of wire products 2873
Products or services (export): NACE-Code
Manufacture of wire products 2873
Products or services (import): NACE-Code

76. INOSAT, Scientific and Introductory Ltd.

ADDRESS: a/ya 211
220116, g. Minsk
PHONE: 017\206-6725
FAX: 017\206-6725
E-MAIL: inosat@nsys.by
Products or services (manufactured): NACE-Code
Manufacture of electricity distribution and control apparatus 3120
Products or services (export): NACE-Code
Products or services (import): NACE-Code
Manufacture of electricity distribution and control apparatus 3120

77. Grodno Regional Enterprise of Material and Technical Supply, Open Joint Stock Company

ADDRESS: st.Aul's
231750, Grodnenskaya obl., Grodnenskiy r-on, p/o Putrishki

PHONE: 0152\991-232
FAX: 0152\967-181, 755-679
Products or services (manufactured): NACE-Code
Sale of motor vehicle parts and accessories 5030
Wholesale of wood and of construction materials 5153
Wholesale of chemical products 5155
Wholesale of agricultural machinery and accessories and implements, including tractors 5166
Other wholesale 5170
Products or services (export): NACE-Code
Wholesale of agricultural machinery and accessories and implements, including tractors 5166
Other wholesale 5170
Products or services (import): NACE-Code
Sale of motor vehicle parts and accessories 5030
Wholesale of wood and of construction materials 5153
Wholesale of chemical products 5155
Wholesale of agricultural machinery and accessories and implements, including tractors 5166
Other wholesale 5170

78. KiS, Closed Joint Stock Company

ADDRESS: ul. Pravdy, 18, ofis 42
210015, g. Vitebsk
PHONE: 0212\253-148
FAX: 0212\372-702
Products or services (manufactured): NACE-Code
Manufacture of workwear 1821
Manufacture of other outerwear 1822
Wholesale of textiles 5141
Wholesale of other intermediate products 5156
Wholesale of other machinery for use in industry, trade and navigation 5165
Products or services (export): NACE-Code
Manufacture of workwear 1821
Manufacture of other outerwear 1822
Wholesale of textiles 5141
Wholesale of other intermediate products 5156
Products or services (import): NACE-Code
Wholesale of other intermediate products 5156
Wholesale of other machinery for use in industry, trade and navigation 5165

79. VtISZOS, Republican Production Subsidiary Enterprise

ADDRESS: ul.Kuprevicha, 10, k. 321, 409
220141, g. Minsk
PHONE: 017\263-6470
FAX: 017\285-8707

E-MAIL: vtl_szos@tut.by
Products or services (manufactured): NACE-Code
MANUFACTURE OF MACHINERY AND EQUIPMENT NEC 29
Adult and other education nec 8042
Products or services (export):NACE-Code
MANUFACTURE OF MACHINERY AND EQUIPMENT NEC 29
Products or services (import):NACE-Code
MANUFACTURE OF MACHINERY AND EQUIPMENT NEC 29

80. Omega Firm, Closed Joint Stock Company

ADDRESS: pr.Stroiteley, 11
210605, g. Vitebsk
PHONE: 0212\216-463
FAX: 0212\212-125
E-MAIL: gbn@omegav.belpak.vitebsk.by; gbn@omega.belpak.vitebsk.by
Products or services (manufactured): NACE-Code
Sale of motor vehicles 5010
WHOLESALE TRADE AND COMMISSION TRADE, EXCEPT OF MOTOR VEHICLES AND MOTORCYCLES 51
Wholesale of food, beverages and tobacco 513
Wholesale of clothing and footwear 5142
Wholesale of metals and metal ores 5152
Wholesale of wood and of construction materials 5153
Wholesale of hardware, plumbing and heating equipment and supplies 5154
Wholesale of other intermediate products 5156
Wholesale of machine tools for working metal and wood 5161
Wholesale of other machinery for use in industry, trade and navigation 5165
RETAIL TRADE, EXCEPT OF MOTOR VEHICLES AND MOTORCYCLES; REPAIR OF PERSONAL AND HOUSEHOLD GOODS 52
Products or services (export):NACE-Code
Sale of motor vehicles 5010
Wholesale of food, beverages and tobacco 513
Wholesale of metals and metal ores 5152
Wholesale of wood and of construction materials 5153
Wholesale of hardware, plumbing and heating equipment and supplies 5154
Wholesale of other intermediate products 5156
Wholesale of machine tools for working metal and wood 5161
Products or services (import):NACE-Code
Sale of motor vehicles 5010
Wholesale of food, beverages and tobacco 513
Wholesale of clothing and footwear 5142
Wholesale of other machinery for use in industry, trade and navigation 5165

81. ROLAN

ADDRESS: ul.Korzhenevskogo
220787, g. Minsk

PHONE: 017\277-7316
FAX: 017\278-4321
E-MAIL: trrlan@integral.minsk.by
Fishing, operation of fish hatcheries and fish farms; service activities incidental to fishing 50
WHOLESALE TRADE AND COMMISSION TRADE, EXCEPT OF MOTOR VEHICLES AND MOTORCYCLES 51
Wholesale of household goods 514
Other land passenger transport 6024
Other supporting land transport activities 6321
Products or services (export): NACE-Code
WHOLESALE TRADE AND COMMISSION TRADE, EXCEPT OF MOTOR VEHICLES AND MOTORCYCLES 51
Products or services (import): NACE-Code
WHOLESALE TRADE AND COMMISSION TRADE, EXCEPT OF MOTOR VEHICLES AND MOTORCYCLES 51

---

82. Viktoria KVC, Ltd.

ADDRESS: ul. Pobedy, 17-82
231300, Grodnenskaya obl., g. Lida
PHONE: 01561\22-678
FAX: 01561\26-784
E-MAIL: sslida@mail.ru
Products or services (manufactured): NACE-Code
Wholesale of household goods 514
Wholesale of clothing and footwear 5142
Wholesale of pharmaceutical goods 5146
Wholesale of wood and of construction materials 5153
Wholesale of hardware, plumbing and heating equipment and supplies 5154
Wholesale of chemical products 5155
Wholesale of other machinery for use in industry, trade and navigation 5165
Other land passenger transport 6024
Products or services (export): NACE-Code
Wholesale of wood and of construction materials 5153
Wholesale of other machinery for use in industry, trade and navigation 5165
Products or services (import): NACE-Code
Wholesale of household goods 514
Wholesale of clothing and footwear 5142
Wholesale of pharmaceutical goods 5146
Wholesale of wood and of construction materials 5153
Wholesale of hardware, plumbing and heating equipment and supplies 5154
Wholesale of chemical products 5155
Wholesale of other machinery for use in industry, trade and navigation 5165

---

83. Belcaps, Foreign Unitary Production Enterprise

ADDRESS: ul. Khutoryanskogo, 35a
246028, g. Gomel'
PHONE: 0232\569-870
FAX: 0232\569-862
E-MAIL: alcopack@alcopack.ru
Products or services (manufactured): NACE-Code
Manufacture of plastic plates, sheets, tubes and profiles 2521
Manufacture of plastic packing 2522
Manufacture of light metal packaging 2872

Products or services (export): NACE-Code
Manufacture of plastic plates, sheets, tubes and profiles 2521
Manufacture of plastic packing 2522
Manufacture of light metal packaging 2872
Products or services (import): NACE-Code
Manufacture of plastic packing 2522

---

84. LANT, Closed Joint Stock Company

ADDRESS: ul.Sovetskaya, 200
247500, Gomel'skaya obl., g. Rechitsa
PHONE: 02340\41-138
FAX: 02340\22-032
E-MAIL: lant@mail.gomel.by
Products or services (manufactured): NACE-Code
Manufacture of other kitchen furniture 3613
Wholesale of other household goods 5147
Wholesale of wood and of construction materials 5153
Products or services (export): NACE-Code
Manufacture of other kitchen furniture 3613
Wholesale of other household goods 5147
Wholesale of wood and of construction materials 5153
Products or services (import): NACE-Code
Wholesale of other household goods 5147

---

85. Melort, Belarusian-German JV Ltd.

ADDRESS: ul.Portovaya, 17
247760, Gomel'skaya obl., g. Mozyr'
PHONE: 02351\69-438
FAX: 02351\69-449
Products or services (manufactured): NACE-Code
Manufacture of metal structures and parts of structures 2811
Manufacture of locks and hinges 2863
Manufacture of fasteners, screw machine products, chain and springs 2874
Manufacture of lifting and handling equipment 2922
Other land passenger transport 6024
Products or services (export): NACE-Code

Manufacture of metal structures and parts of structures 2811
Manufacture of locks and hinges 2863
Manufacture of fasteners, screw machine products, chain and springs 2874
Manufacture of lifting and handling equipment 2922
Other land passenger transport 6024
Products or services (import): NACE-Code
Other land passenger transport 6024

86. Beltex Optik, Foreign Private Production Unitary Enterprise

ADDRESS: ul. Sovetskaya, 42
231300, Grodnenskaya obl., g. Lida
PHONE: 01561\29-570
FAX: 01561\29-570
E-MAIL: beltex@mail.lida.by
WEB SITE: www.sibiroptics.com
Products or services (manufactured): NACE-Code
Manufacture of television and radio receivers, sound or video recording or reproducing apparatus and associated goods 3230
Manufacture of optical instruments and photographic equipment 3340
Wholesale of non-agricultural intermediate products, waste and scrap 515
Wholesale of other machinery for use in industry, trade and navigation 5165
Products or services (export): NACE-Code
Manufacture of television and radio receivers, sound or video recording or reproducing apparatus and associated goods 3230
Manufacture of optical instruments and photographic equipment 3340
Wholesale of non-agricultural intermediate products, waste and scrap 515
Wholesale of other machinery for use in industry, trade and navigation 5165
Products or services (import): NACE-Code
Wholesale of other machinery for use in industry, trade and navigation 5165

87. BS Transit Trade, Belarusian-Russian JV Ltd.

ADDRESS: ul.Shosseynaya, 147
247210, Gomel'skaya obl., g. Zhlobin
PHONE: 02334\22-285
FAX: 02334\22-312
E-MAIL: bstt@foto.by
Products or services (manufactured): NACE-Code
Wholesale of food, beverages and tobacco 513
Wholesale of metals and metal ores 5152
Legal, accounting, book-keeping and auditing activities; tax consultancy; market research and public opinion polling; business and management consultancy; holdings 741
Market research and public opinion polling 7413
Products or services (export): NACE-Code
Wholesale of metals and metal ores 5152

Legal, accounting, book-keeping and auditing activities; tax consultancy; market research and public opinion polling; business and management consultancy; holdings 741
Market research and public opinion polling 7413
Products or services (import):NACE-Code
Wholesale of food, beverages and tobacco 513
Wholesale of metals and metal ores 5152

88. Aqualit, Closed Joint Stock Company

ADDRESS: ul. Kozlova, 6
220038, g. Minsk
PHONE: 017\235-8033, 235-1776
FAX: 017\235-3803
E-MAIL: aqualit1@brm.by
Products or services (manufactured): NACE-Code
Manufacture of taps and valves 2913
Manufacture of other general purpose machinery nec 2924
Manufacture of instruments and appliances for measuring, checking, testing, navigating and other purposes, except industrial process control equipment 3320
Products or services (export):NACE-Code
Manufacture of taps and valves 2913
Manufacture of other general purpose machinery nec 2924
Manufacture of instruments and appliances for measuring, checking, testing, navigating and other purposes, except industrial process control equipment 3320
Wholesale of hardware, plumbing and heating equipment and supplies 5154
Products or services (import):NACE-Code
Manufacture of taps and valves 2913
Manufacture of other general purpose machinery nec 2924
Manufacture of instruments and appliances for measuring, checking, testing, navigating and other purposes, except industrial process control equipment 3320
Wholesale of hardware, plumbing and heating equipment and supplies 5154

89. Remcomp, Foreign Private Production Unitary Enterprise

ADDRESS: ul. Pushkina, 62
247250, Gomel'skaya obl., g. Rogachyov
PHONE: 02339\24-849
FAX: 02339\14-320
E-MAIL: info@remeza.com
WEB SITE: www.remeza.com
Products or services (manufactured): NACE-Code
MANUFACTURE OF FABRICATED METAL PRODUCTS, EXCEPT MACHINERY AND EQUIPMENT 28
Manufacture of locks and hinges 2863
Manufacture of pumps and compressors 2912
Products or services (export):NACE-Code

MANUFACTURE OF FABRICATED METAL PRODUCTS, EXCEPT MACHINERY AND EQUIPMENT 28
Manufacture of locks and hinges 2863
Manufacture of pumps and compressors 2912
Products or services (import):NACE-Code
Manufacture of pumps and compressors 2912

---

90. Dmitry G. Pchelnikov, Individual Enterprneur

ADDRESS: v/g Kolodishchi, d.224, k.56
223051, Minskaya obl., Minskiy r-on, p. Kolodishchi
PHONE: 017\508-2835
FAX: 017\508-2835
E-MAIL: direktor@iss-krater.com
WEB SITE: www.iss-krater.com
Products or services (manufactured): NACE-Code
Wholesale of other machinery for use in industry, trade and navigation 5165
Software consultancy and supply 7220
Data processing 7230
Data base activities 7240
Market research and public opinion polling 7413
Advertising 7440
Products or services (export):NACE-Code
Wholesale of other machinery for use in industry, trade and navigation 5165
Products or services (import):NACE-Code
Wholesale of other machinery for use in industry, trade and navigation 5165

---

91. Tayur, Ltd.

ADDRESS: ul. Serafimovicha, 2/2
230029, g. Grodno
PHONE: 0152\720-768
FAX: 0152\720-768
Products or services (manufactured): NACE-Code
CONSTRUCTION 45
Wholesale on a fee or contract basis 511
Retail sale in non-specialized stores 521
Other land passenger transport 6024
Products or services (export):NACE-Code
Wholesale on a fee or contract basis 511
Retail sale in non-specialized stores 521
Other land passenger transport 6024
Products or services (import):NACE-Code
Wholesale on a fee or contract basis 511
Retail sale in non-specialized stores 521

---

92. AVERSEV, Additional Liability Company

ADDRESS: ul. Bogdanovicha, 129a, k. 30
220123, g. Minsk
PHONE: 017\234-2412
FAX: 017\234-2412, 234-3714
E-MAIL: office@aversev.com
WEB SITE: www.aversev.com
Products or services (manufactured): NACE-Code
Publishing of books, brochures, musical books and other publications 2211
Products or services (export):NACE-Code
Publishing of books, brochures, musical books and other publications 2211
Products or services (import):NACE-Code
Publishing of books, brochures, musical books and other publications 2211

93. TETA, Education and Production Enterprise

ADDRESS: ul. Dunina-Martsinkevicha, 4, korp. 2, k. 1-7
220092, g. Minsk
PHONE: 017\207-2493
FAX: 017\207-2492
Products or services (manufactured): NACE-Code
Sale of motor vehicle parts and accessories 5030
Wholesale of other machinery for use in industry, trade and navigation 5165
Other wholesale 5170
Products or services (export):NACE-Code
Wholesale of other machinery for use in industry, trade and navigation 5165
Other wholesale 5170
Products or services (import):NACE-Code
Sale of motor vehicle parts and accessories 5030
Wholesale of other machinery for use in industry, trade and navigation 5165
Other wholesale 5170

94. Krichevsk mezhraybaza, Unitary Trade Enterprise

ADDRESS: Mstislavskoe shosse, 3
213500, Mogilyovskaya obl., g. Krichev
PHONE: 02241\57-037
FAX: 02241\57-766
Products or services (manufactured): NACE-Code
Wholesale of food, beverages and tobacco 513
Wholesale of household goods 514
Products or services (export):NACE-Code
Wholesale of food, beverages and tobacco 513
Wholesale of household goods 514
Products or services (import):NACE-Code
Wholesale of food, beverages and tobacco 513
Wholesale of household goods 514

95. Belarusian Oil Trade House, Republican Branch Unitary Enterprise

ADDRESS: pr-t Dzerzhinskogo, 73
220116, g. Minsk
PHONE: 017\271-9552
FAX: 017\271-9552, 271-9813
E-MAIL: bntd@iptel.by
Products or services (manufactured): NACE-Code
WHOLESALE TRADE AND COMMISSION TRADE, EXCEPT OF MOTOR VEHICLES AND MOTORCYCLES 51
Wholesale of meat and meat products 5132
Wholesale of dairy produce, eggs and edible oils and fats 5133
Non-specialized wholesale of food, beverages and tobacco 5138
Wholesale of solid, liquid and gaseous fuels and related products 5151
Wholesale of chemical products 5155
Wholesale of other intermediate products 5156
Products or services (export): NACE-Code
Wholesale of meat and meat products 5132
Wholesale of dairy produce, eggs and edible oils and fats 5133
Non-specialized wholesale of food, beverages and tobacco 5138
Wholesale of solid, liquid and gaseous fuels and related products 5151
Wholesale of chemical products 5155
Wholesale of other intermediate products 5156
Products or services (import): NACE-Code
Wholesale of solid, liquid and gaseous fuels and related products 5151

96. Firm Malvina, Belarusian-Cypriot JV Open Joint Stock Company

ADDRESS: ul. Mayakovskogo, 111
220028, g. Minsk
PHONE: 017\221-0050
FAX: 017\221-0050
E-MAIL: malvina@infonet.by
WEB SITE: www.malvina.by.com

Products or services (manufactured): NACE-Code
Manufacture of games and toys 3650
Products or services (export): NACE-Code
Manufacture of games and toys 3650
Products or services (import): NACE-Code
Manufacture of games and toys 3650

97. Isakidis Granites Ltd, Foreign Private Enterprise

ADDRESS: a/ya 27
223017, Minskaya obl., Minskiy r-on, p. Gatovo
PHONE: 017\210-5796, 503-5430
FAX: 017\210-5795
E-MAIL: isakidis_granites@tut.by

Products or services (manufactured): NACE-Code
Quarrying of stone for construction 1411
Cutting, shaping and finishing of stone 2670
Other building completion 4545
Products or services (export):NACE-Code
Cutting, shaping and finishing of stone 2670
Products or services (import):NACE-Code
Quarrying of stone for construction 1411
Cutting, shaping and finishing of stone 2670

---

98. Anatoliy V. Sazonov, Private Enterpreneur

ADDRESS: ul. Orlovskaya, 51, k.87
224031, g. Brest
PHONE: 0162\414-104
FAX: 017\210-3895
Products or services (manufactured): NACE-Code
Sale of motor vehicle parts and accessories 5030
Products or services (export):NACE-Code
Sale of motor vehicle parts and accessories 5030
Products or services (import):NACE-Code
Sale of motor vehicle parts and accessories 5030

---

99. Raznotrade, Foreign Production and Trade Private Unitary Enterprise

ADDRESS: ul. Belorusskaya, 51 k.207
224025, g. Brest
PHONE: 0162\242-056
FAX: 0162\242-024
E-MAIL: iprazn@rambler.ru
Products or services (manufactured): NACE-Code
Wholesale of perfume and cosmetics 5145
Products or services (export):NACE-Code
Wholesale of perfume and cosmetics 5145
Products or services (import):NACE-Code
Wholesale of perfume and cosmetics 5145

---

100. BestPack, Belarusian-American JV Ltd.

ADDRESS: per. Domashevskiy, 9 of. 2
220036, g. Minsk
PHONE: 017\286-2625, 286-1757
FAX: 017\286-2625
E-MAIL: bestpack@tut.by
WEB SITE: www.bestpack.by.com
Products or services (manufactured): NACE-Code
Manufacture of plastic plates, sheets, tubes and profiles 2521
Wholesale of other intermediate products 5156

Wholesale of other machinery for use in industry, trade and navigation 5165
Products or services (export): NACE-Code
Wholesale of other machinery for use in industry, trade and navigation 5165

Products or services (import): NACE-Code
Wholesale of other intermediate products 5156
Wholesale of other machinery for use in industry, trade and navigation 5165
01. Milkimport, Additional Liability Company

ADDRESS: ul. Gorodetskaya, 44, k. 193
22125 , g. Minsk
PHONE: 017\283-4667. 228-5466
FAX: 017\283-5698, 283-4667
E-MAIL: milkimport@mail.ru
WEB SITE: www.milkimport.ru
Products or services (manufactured): NACE-Code
Wholesale of dairy produce, eggs and edible oils and fats 5133
Products or services (export): NACE-Code
Wholesale of dairy produce, eggs and edible oils and fats 5133
Products or services (import): NACE-Code
Wholesale of dairy produce, eggs and edible oils and fats 5133

# IMPORTANT GOVERNMENT AND BUSINESS CONTACTS

## SELECTED GOVERNMENT CONTACTS

**President: Aleksandr Lukashenko**

Head of Presidential Administration: Mikhail Myasnikovich

Chairman, Supreme Soviet: Semyon Sharetsky
220016, Minsk
Ul. K. Marxa, 38
Tel: 172/ 296-004

Acting Prime Minister: Syarhey Linh
220010, Minsk
House of Government

First Deputy Minister: Pyotr Prokopovich
Deputy Prime Minister: Vladzimir Harkun
Deputy Prime Minister: Vasil Dalhalyow
Deputy Prime Minister: Valeryy Kokaraw
Deputy Prime Minister: Vladzimir Rusakevich

Ministry of Agriculture and Food: Vasily Leonov
220031, Minsk
Ul. Kirova, 15
Fax: 172/ 275-388

Ministry of Communications and Information Technology: Vladimir Goncharenko
220050, Minsk
Prospekt F. Skoriny, 10
Fax: 172/ 260-848

Ministry of Construction : Gennadiy Navitsky
220050, Minsk
Ul. K. Marxa, 3
Tel.: 172/ 272-422

Ministry of Culture & Publishing: Aleksandr Sosnovsky
220010, Minsk
Ul. Sovetskaya, 9
Fax: 172/ 209-125

Ministry of Defense Alexander Tchumakov
220003, Minsk
Ul. Kommunisticheskaya, 1
Tel: 172/ 330-352, 273-671

Ministry of Economy Vladimir Shimov
220000, Minsk
10 Sovetskaya St.
Fax: 172/296-944

Ministry of Education: Vasiliy Strazhov
220010, Minsk
Ul. Sovetskaya, 9
Fax: 172/ 208-057

Ministry of Energy: Valentin Gerasimov
220677, Minsk
Ul. K. Marxa, 14
Fax: 172/ 298-468

Ministry of Finance: Pavel Dik
220010, Minsk
Ul. Sovetskaya, 11
Fax: 172/ 296-640

Ministry of Foreign Affairs: Ivan Antanovich
220030, Minsk
Ul. Lenina, 19
Fax: 172/ 274-521

Ministry for Foreign Economic Relations: Mikhail Marinich
Minsk, 220010
House of Government/
Sovetskaya ul. 10
Fax: 172/ 296-335

Ministry of Forestry: Valentin Zorin
220039, Minsk
Ul. Chkalova, 6
Fax: 172/ 244-183

Ministry of Health: Igor Zelenkevich
220010, Minsk
Ul. Myasnikova, 39
House of Government
Fax: 172/ 296-297

Ministry of Housing and
Communal Services: Boris Batura
220640, Minsk
Ul. Bersona, 16
Fax: 172/ 200-297

Ministry of Justice: Gennady Vorontsov
220084, Minsk
Ul. Kollektornaya, 10
Fax: 172/ 209-684

Ministry of Natural Resources
& Environmental Protection: Mikhail Rusyy
220855, Minsk
Ul. Kazintsa, 4
Fax: 172/ 260-084

Ministry of Social Security: Olga Dargel
220010, Minsk
Ul. Sovetskaya, 9
Fax: 172/ 296-990

Ministry of State Property
& Privatization: Vasily Novak
220010, Minsk
Ul. Myasnikova, 39
Tel: 172/ 768-178, 205-260

Ministry of Transport: Aleksandr Lukashev
220612, Minsk
Ul. Lenina, 17
Tel: 172/ 27 16 42
Fax: 172/ 271-981

Ministry of Industry
220033 Minsk
Partizansky Prospekt 2/4
Tel: 172/20 61 37
Fax: 172/27 39 24

### SELECTED STATE COMMITTEES

State Committee on Customs
220029, Minsk
Kommunisticheskaya ul, 11
Tel: 172/ 33 23 16
Fax: 172/34 68 93

State Committee on Energy
220084, Minsk
Ul. Karla Marksa 14
Fax: 172/ 229-8355

## IMPORTANT GOVERNMENT CONTACTS

### MINISTRIES

Ministry of Justice
Minister : Oleg L. Slizhevskiy
Phone: 8 (017) 200-86-87, 200-97-55
Address: 220004, r. Minsk , Kollektornaya Str., 10

Email: kanc@minjust.by
Website: http://www.minjust.by/en

Ministry of Economy
Minister : Nikolay G. Snopkov
Phone: 8 (017) 200-87-67
Fax: 8 (017) 200-37-77
Address: 220050, r. Minsk , Bersona Str., 14

Email: minec@economy.gov.by
Website: http://www.economy.gov.by/en

Ministry of Information
Minister : Akexander Karliukevich
Phone: 8 (017) 203-92-31
Fax: 8 (017) 203-34-35
Address: 220004, г. Minsk , Pobediteley Ave., 11

Email: info@mininform.gov.by
Website: http://www.mininform.gov.by

Ministry of Defence
Minister: Andrey A. Ravkov
Phone: 8 (017) 297-11-19
Fax: 8 (017) 297-28-47
Address: 220034, г. Minsk, Communisticheskaya Str., 1

Email: mod@mod.mil.by
Website: http://www.mod.mil.by/news_eng.html

Ministry of Forestry
Minister : Mikhail M. Amelyanovich
Phone: 8 (017) 200-46-01
Fax: 8 (017) 200-44-97
Address: 220039, г. Minsk , Myasnikova Str., 39

Email: info@komleschoz.org
Website: http://www.mlh.by/en/forestry/resources.html

Ministry of Health
Minister : Valeriy A. Malashko
Phone: 8 (017) 222-60-33
Fax: 8 (017) 222-46-27
Address: 220048, г. Minsk , Myasnikova Str., 39

Website: http://minzdrav.gov.by/en/

Ministry of Agriculture and Food
Minister : Leonid K. Zayats
Phone: 8 (017) 327-37-51
Fax: 8 (017) 327-42-96
Address: 220050, г. Minsk , Kirov Str., 15

Email: kanc@mshp.minsk.by
Website: http://mshp.minsk.by

Ministry of Sport and Tourism

Minister : Sergei Kovalchuk
Phone: 8 (017) 327-76-21
Address: 220050, r. Minsk , Kirov Str., 8/2

Email: office@mst.by
Website: http://www.mst.by/en

Ministry of Communications and Informatization
Minister : Sergei P. Popkov
Phone: 8 (017) 287-87-06
Fax: 8 (017) 327-21-57
Address: 220050, r. Minsk , Nezavisimosti Ave., 10

Email: mpt@mpt.gov.by
Website: http://www.mpt.gov.by/en/

Ministry of Labour and Social Protection
Minister : Irina A. Kostevich
Phone: 8 (017) 306-37-90
Fax: 8 (017) 306-38-84
Address: 220004, r. Minsk , Pobediteley Ave., 23/2

Email: mlsp@mintrud.gov.by
Website: http://www.mintrud.gov.by
Ministry of Emergency Situations
Minister : Vladimir A. Vashchenko
Phone: 8 (017) 203-94-28, 203-88-00
Fax: 8 (017) 203-77-81
Address: 220050, r. Minsk , Revolutionnaya Str., 5

Email: mcs@infonet.by
Website: http://112.by/

Ministry of Foreign Affairs
Minister : Vladimir V. Makei
Phone: 8 (017) 327-29-22
Fax: 8 (017) 210-42-50, 327-45-21
Address: 220030, r. Minsk , Lenin Str., 19

Email: mail@mfabelar.gov.by
Website: http://www.mfa.gov.by/en/

Ministry of Transport and Communications
Minister : Anatoly A. Sivak
Phone: 8 (017) 334-11-52
Fax: 8 (017) 292-83-91
Address: 220029, r. Minsk , Chicherin Str., 21

Email: mail@mintrans.by
Website: http://www.mintrans.gov.by/eng/index

Ministry of Education
Minister : Igor V. Karpenko
Phone: 8 (017) 327-47-36
Address: 220010, r. Minsk , Sovetskaya Str., 9

Email: root@minedu.unibel.by
Website: http://edu.gov.by/

Ministry of Culture
Minister : Yuriy Bondar
Phone: 8 (017) 203-75-74
Fax: 8 (017) 203-90-45
Address: 220004, r. Minsk , Pobediteley Ave., 11

Website: http://kultura.by/en

Ministry of Finance
Minister: Vladimir V. Amarin
Phone: 8 (017) 222-61-37
Fax: 8 (017) 222-45-93
Address: 220010, r. Minsk, Sovetskaya Str., 7

Email: minfin@minfin.gov.by
Website: http://www.minfin.gov.by/

Ministry of Industry
Minister : Dzmitry S. Katsiarynich
Phone: 8 (017) 223-93-96
Fax: 8 (017) 328-30-48
Address: 220033, r. Minsk , Partizansky Ave., 2/4

Email: minprom1@ntc.niievm.minsk.by
Website: http://www.minprom.gov.by/eng/welcome

Ministry of Housing and Communal Services
Minister : Alexandr A. Terekhov
Phone: 8 (017) 200-15-45; 200-31-85
Fax: 8 (017) 200-87-08; 200-55-31
Address: 220030, r. Minsk , Bersona Str., 16

Website: http://www.mjkx.gov.by

Ministry on Taxes and Dues
Minister: Vladimir N. Poluyan

Phone: 8 (017) 229-79-72; 229-79-36; горячая линия: 229-79-29; Phone доверия: 328-53-53
Address: 220010, г. Minsk , Sovetskaya Str., 9

Website: http://www.nalog.gov.by/

Ministry of Antimonopoly Regulation and Trade
Minister : Vladimir V. Koltovich
Phone: 8 (017) 327-48-02 (приёмная); 200-92-02 (общественная приёмная)
Address: 220050, г. Minsk , Kirov Str., 8/1

Email: mail@mart.gov.by
Website: http://www.mintorg.gov.by/index.php?lang=en

Ministry of Internal Affairs
Minister : Igor A. Shunevich
Phone: 8 (017) 218-78-95, деж. 218-79-09
Address: 220030, г. Minsk , Gorodskoy Val Str., 4

Website: http://mvd.gov.by

Ministry of Energy
Minister: Vladimir N. Potupchik
Phone: 8 (017) 218-21-02
Fax: 8 (017) 218-24-68
Address: 220030, г. Minsk, K. Marx Str., 14

Email: minsecretary@min.energo.net.by
Website: http://www.minenergo.gov.by/en

Ministry of Natural Resources and Environmental Protection
Minister: Andrey M. Kovhuto
Phone: 8 (017) 200-66-91
Address: 220048, г. Mins, Kollektornaya Str., 10

Email: minproos@mail.belpak.by
Website: http://minpriroda.gov.by/en

Ministry of Architecture and Construction
Minister : Tchorny Anatoli B.
Phone: 8 (017) 327-26-42; 327-19-34
Fax: 8 (017) 200-74-24
Address: 220048, г. Minsk , Myasnikova Str., 39

Website: http://www.mas.by/

## STATE COMMI*TTEES

State Committee on Standardization

Chairman : Victor V. Nazarenko
Phone: 8 (017) 233-52-13
Fax: 8 (017) 233-25-88
Address: 220053, г. Minsk , Starovilensky Trakt, 93

Email: belst@gosstandart.gov.by
Website: http://gosstandart.gov.by/en-US/

State Military and Industrial Committee
Chairman : Sergey P. Gurulev
Phone: 8 (017) 280-91-00
Fax: 8 (017) 280-90-81
Address: 220600, г. Minsk , Nezavisimosti Ave. , 115

Website: http://www.vpk.gov.by/en/

State Committee on Science and Technologies
Chairman: Shumilin Alexander G.
Phone: 8 (017) 284-07-60
Fax: 8 (017) 284-02-79
Address: 220072, г. Minsk , Akademicheskaya Str., 1

Email: gknt@gknt.org.by
Website: http://gknt.org.by/opencms/opencms/en/index.html

National Statistical Committee of the Republic of Belarus (Belstat)
Chairman: Inna V. Medvedeva
Phone: 8 (017) 367-52-00
Fax: 8 (017) 367-22-04
Address: 220070, г. Minsk , Partizanskiy Ave., 12

Email: belstat@belstat.gov.by
Website: http://belstat.gov.by/en/

State Committee on Property
Chairman : Andrey A. Gaev
Phone: 8 (017) 288-10-19
Fax: 8 (017) 288-27-25
Address: 220005, г. Minsk , Krasnozvezdny Ln., 12

Email: info@gki.gov.by
Website: http://www.gki.gov.by/

State Security Committee
Chairman : Valery P. Vakulchik
Phone: 8 (017) 219-94-01, 219-92-21
Fax: 8 (017) 226-00-38
Address: 220030, г. Minsk, Nezavisimosti Ave., 17

Website: http://kgb.by/en/

State Border Committee
Chairman: Anatoliy P. Lappo
Phone: 8 (017) 216-26-12
Fax: 8 (017) 227-70-03
Address: 220050, г. Minsk , Volodarskogo Str., 24

Email: post@gpk.gov.by
Website: http://gpk.gov.by/

State Customs Committee
Chairman : Yuri A. Senko
Phone: 8 (017) 218-91-04, 218-90-00
Fax: 8 (017) 218-91-97
Address: 220007, г. Minsk, Mogilyovskaya Str., 45/1

Email: gtk@customs.gov.by
Website: http://customs.gov.by/en

Investigation Committee of the Republic of Belarus
Chairman: Ivan D. Noskevich
Phone: 8 (017) 222-32-72, 389-50-02 (Оперативно-дежурная служба (круглосуточно))
Fax: 290-35-48
Address: 220034, г. Minsk, Pervomayskaia Str., 7

Website: http://sk.gov.by/en/

## REGIONAL ADMINISTRATIVE BODIES

Brest Oblast Executive Committee
Chairman: Anatoly V. Lis
Phone: 8 (0162)21-22-37
Fax: 21-96-66
Address: 224005, г. Brest, Lenin Str., 11

Email: contact@brest-region.by
Website: http://brest-region.gov.by/index.php/en/

Gomel Oblast Executive Committee
Chairman: Vladimir A. Dvornik
Phone: 8 (0232)75-45-00
Fax: 75-45-26
Address: 246050, г. Gomel, Lenin Ave., 2

Website: WWW: http://www.gomel-region.by/en/

Для обращений граждан и юридических лиц
Email: oblisp-uip@mail.gomel.by

Grodno Oblast Executive Committee
Chairman: Vladimir V. Kravtsov
Phone: 8 (0152)72-31-90; 73-55-66 (запись на прием)
Address: 230023, г. Grodno, Ozheshko Str., 3

Website: http://www.region.grodno.by/en

Для обращений граждан и юридических лиц
Email: Groblisp@mail.grodno.by

Minsk City Executive Committee
Chairman: Andrei V. Shorets
Phone: 8 (017)218-00-01
Address: 220030, г. Minsk, Nezavisimosti Ave., 8

Website: WWW: http://minsk.gov.by/en/

Minsk Oblast Executive Committee
Chairman: Semyon B. Shapiro
Phone: 8 (017)500-41-44
Address: 220030, г. Minsk, Engels Str., 4

Website: http://www.minsk-region.gov.by/en/

Mogilev Oblast Executive Committee
Chairman: Vladimir V. Domanevsky
Phone: 8 (0222)32-80-59
Address: 212030, г. Mogilev, Pervomayskaya Str., 71

Website: http://region.mogilev.by/en/

Vitebsk Oblast Executive Committee
Chairman: Nicolay N. Sherstnev
Phone: 8 (0212)42-57-57
Fax: 42-57-81
Address: 210010, г. Vitebsk, Gogol Str., 6

Website: http://www.vitebsk-region.gov.by/en/

## BELARUS CHAMBER OF COMMERCE OFFICES

**Information Services**

- Exchange of business and commercial information with chambers of commerce of the CIS and other countries worldwide, and import/export promoting organizations.

- Collection, processing and dissemination of business information in foreign economic and business activities in the Republic of Belarus and abroad.
- Publication and dissemination of "Business in the Republic of Belarus" catalog and the Belarusian CCI bulletin "Mercury".
- Monitoring the sources of business and commercial information within the Republic of Belarus and abroad.
- Establishment and maintenance of the Uniform Information Systems of Belarusian CCI.

**Foreign Trade Services**

- Assist enterprises and organizations in establishing cooperation in science, technology and industry, setting up joint ventures, and development of other forms foreign economic cooperation.
- Promote export of goods, identification of new resources, products and services and their involvement in the foreign trade turnover.
- Assist enterprises and companies in drawing up business plans, contracts, protocols of intentions, and other foreign economic documents.
- Organize visits of foreign delegations and individual representatives of the foreign business circles to the Republic of Belarus on behalf of the Chamber's Members, business meetings and negotiations.
- Look for foreign partners in trade and cooperation.
- Organize and conduct of Economy Days, business missions, presentations of foreign and Belarusian companies and enterprises, symposia and conferences on foreign trade matters both in the Republic of Belarus and abroad.
- Make and maintain business connections between the Belarusian CCI and the International Chamber of Commerce, foreign commerce-and-industry and economic chambers as well as CCI representation offices abroad and mixed CCIs.

## MINSK BRANCH

**General Information**

The history of the Minsk Branch of the Belarusian Chamber of Commerce and Industry goes back to 1 January 1970 when the Minsk Regional Office of Commodity Examination was established by resolution of the Presidium of the All-Union Chamber of Commerce and Order No. 157 of the BSSR Department of the All-Union Chamber of Commerce of 26 December 1969. The Office staff was 30 employees. Primary line of activity of the Minsk Regional Branch of the Chamber of Commerce and Industry of BSSR was expertise of quality, quantity and completeness of goods, equipment of domestic and foreign produce and raw material.

Since the year 2000, the Minsk Branch of the Belarusian Chamber of Commerce and Industry was transformed into a Minsk Branch of the Belarusian Chamber of Commerce and Industry Unitary Enterprise for Services. The Minsk Region is a territory of great economic potentialities and promising future. It attracts foreign investors. At present there have been registered more than 1800 enterprises with foreign participation (more than half of which are joint ventures) and they continue to grow in number. Foreign companies and joint ventures have been established with participation of investors from more than 60 countries.

Minsk Branch of the Belarusian Chamber of Commerce and Industry UE focuses on implementation of interests of BelCCI Members in the Minsk Region in foreign economic activity, increase of exports of products, works and services, attraction of foreign investments, practical assistance to enterprises in export/import operations.

Work is underway towards strengthening and expansion of cooperation with the regional chambers of commerce and industry in CIS and distant foreign countries. At present the Minsk Branch has concluded Agreements on Cooperation with 103 chambers of commerce and industry, of which 77 are with the chambers of commerce and industry in CIS.

Members of the Minsk and Minsk Region Branch of BelCCI are about 800 enterprises and organizations of various ownership, among which 25% are state-owned enterprises and 75% are private enterprises.

Minsk Branch of the Belarusian Chamber of Commerce and Industry UE employs about 200 regular employees and more than 300 nonstaff employees. Subject to its Charter registered with the Minsk City Executive Committee on 22.06.2000 under Registration No. 0012178, the Minsk Branch of the Belarusian Chamber of Commerce and Industry UE is allowed to render services of more than 50 types.

**Address:**
ul. Ya. Kolasa, 65
220113, Minsk
Telephone: +375 17 266-04-73, fax: +375 17 266-26-04
E-mail: secret@mdbcci.belpak.minsk.by
Web-site: http://www.tppm.by

### Organization Structure

**Foreign economic cooperation department**
Telephone: +375 17 266-06-73

**Information - Exhibition center**
Telephone: +375 17 262-54-18

**Advertising bureau**
Telephone: +375 17 266-04-72

**Translation bureau**
Telephone: +375 17 266-00-81, 266-00-82

**Expertise and equipment certification bureau**
Telephone: +375 17 266-04-70, 266-06-71

**Manufactured goods expertise bureau**
Telephone: +375 17 266-65-42

**Foodstuff expertise and certification bureau**

**Household goods expertise and certification bureau**

Telephone: +375 17 266-00-71, 266-06-61

Telephone: +375 17 266-04-71, 266-14-90

**Department of Information's technologies**
Telephone: +375 17 266-89-91

Regional Branches

**Borisov branch**
ul. 8 marta, 27
222120, Borisov
Telephone: +375 1777 3-31-19, fax: 3-27-65

**Nesvizh branch**
ul. Sovetskaya, 4
222620, Nesvizh
Telephone: +375 1770 5-44-31

**Dzerzhinsk branch**
ul. Furmanova, 2
222720, Dzerzhinsk
Telephone\fax: +375 1716 6-56-97

**Slutsk branch**
ul. Lenina, 183
223610, Slutsk
Telephone\fax: +375 1795 5-62-29

**Molodechno branch**
ul. Galitskogo, 8
222310, Molodechno
Telephone\fax: +375 1773 5-35-74

**Soligorsk branch**
ul. Zaslonova, 56
223710, Soligorsk
Telephone: +375 1710 5-47-19, fax: 5-47-10

**Business Region" Exhibition**

For more than five years the Minsk Branch of the Belarusian Chamber of Commerce and Industry UE has been running "Business Region" permanent exhibition. It is aimed primarily to assist enterprises of various ownership that have been operating in the Minsk region in looking for business partners and introduction of goods into the market.

Exhibition of catalogs of the leading exporters in Belarus is an integral part of the "Business Region" exhibition. Summary information on enterprises participating in the exhibition is presented in the "Minsk and Minsk Region: Exported Products and Services" catalog, which is regularly distributed between chambers of commerce and industry in neighboring and distant countries as well as traveling events arranged by the Branch.

The exhibition is provided with modern European equipment. Exhibiting enterprises on regularly rearrange and refill the display. Information tablets installed in each show display specify location of enterprise, contact points and nomenclature of products.

Currently, the Business Region exhibition displays "Minsk" FEZ, Dzerzhinsk garment factory "ELIZ", "Keramin" JSC, "Minsk Horizont Plant" state-owned enterprise, "LeGrand" LLC JV, Minsk Porcelain Works, JSC; "Minsk Watch-Making Factory", JSC; "Belorussian Wallpaper" JSC; "Borisov Motor-and-Tractor Equipment Plant", JSC; "Polimiz" LLC;

"Rudensk" JSC; NPO INTEGRAL, Borisov Instrument-Making Plant; "BelKhudKeramika" JSC; Minsk Varnish-and-Paint Plant; "Kristall" Wines and Spirits Plant; 'Krynitsa" company; "BelReaKhim" RUP PS as well as a number of foreign firms and companies interested in the Belorussian market.

The "Business Region" exhibition is used both as a place for promotion of goods produced in the Minsk region and for business meetings and negotiations between potential partners.

Due to eye-catching display of products and high attendance of the exhibition, Minsk Varnish-and-Paint Plant has succeeded to fund buyers in France, Czech Republic, Krasnojarsk, and Komi Republic. The "BelReaKhim" state-owned enterprise has established partnership with enterprises in the Moscow, Leningrad and Volgograd regions. Due to assistance on the part of the "Business Region" exhibition "Kalchenko & Co" company that produces lighting equipment entered into contract with the Management of the Metropolitan Railway in Progress for delivery of searchlight projectors. The "Termoplast" plant in Minsk supplies its products to the Omsk region. The Dzerzhinsk garment factory "ELIZ" has succeeded to fins partners in Voronezh, Omsk, and Saratov. The "Belkas" enterprise in Molodechno has established contacts with businessmen in the Tver, Smolensk and Leningrad Regions. Due to participation in the Exhibition, "Mpis" - Polish enterprise – has found partners for cooperation and established a joint venture "Polifas".

For recent years the Exhibition was attended by representatives of business circles of Russia from the Sverdlovsk, Penza, Kirov, Omsk, Smolensk, Saransk, Ryazan, Samara, and Chelyabinsk regions, Republic of Mordovia and other. Among those who attended the Exhibition were representative of business circles of France, Italy, Poland, Slovakia, and Palestine.

The "Business Region" permanent exhibition has become an important link in international cooperation and contributor to export potential of the Minsk region.

## BREST BRANCH

### General Information

The history of the Brest Branch goes back to the year of 1962 when a representation office of the All-Union Chamber of Commerce was opened at the Brest-Central Station of the Belarusian Railway. In 1964 the Representation office was transformed into the Brest Region Commodity Examination Bureau under the Byelorussian Branch of the All-Union Chamber of Commerce. In 1979 it was transformed into the Brest Branch of the Chamber of Commerce and Industry of the Byelorussian SSR.

At present the unitary enterprise "Brest Branch of the Belarusian Chamber of Commerce and Industry" has been implementing the aims and tasks of its founder, i.e. the Belarusian Chamber of Commerce and Industry, in its region.

Many-sided activity carried out by the Unitary Enterprise has its specific features attributed to location of the Brest region and the city of Brest at the junction of state borders of Belarus, Poland and Ukraine. This is a very important transport and trade crossroad. The pioneer free economic zone "Brest" as well as the establishment and development of an Euro-region "Bug" exert primary control over operation of the Enterprise.

The "Belovezhskaya Pushcha" National Park is also located in the territory of the Brest region. This is the oldest forest preserve in Europe placed on the World Heritage List and given the status of a Biosphere Reserve by UNESCO's resolution.

In its activity the Enterprise closely cooperates with governmental bodies and first of all with the Committee for economic and marketing relations, with the regional territorial committee for business and investment, administration of FEZ "Brest" and other organizations.

The Enterprise maintains and develops cooperation with regional chambers of commerce in Poland, Ukraine, Russia, Hungary, Czech Republic, Slovakia, Lithuania, and Kazakhstan. They have concluded 42 agreements on cooperation with them. Business relations with Bialo-Podlaska CC, Polish-Belarusian CCI, Volyn CCI, Kaunas CCI, Debrecen CC are especially close which makes it easier for the Enterprise to attain its objectives.

**Address:**
ul. Kuybysheva, 14
224016, Brest
Telephone +375 162 23-24-00, fax: +375 162 23-48-54
E-mail: box@tppbrs.belpak.brest.by

## Organization Structure

**Foreign economic cooperation department**
Telephone:+375 162 23-74-80

**Foodstuffs expertise bureau**
Telephone: +375 162 23-18-30

**Expertise, certification and declaration bureau**
Telephone: +375 162 23-48-97, 23-48-54

**Manufactured goods expertise bureau**
Telephone: +375 162 25-93-45

Regional Branches

**Baranovichi Branch**
ul. Sovetskaya, 59
225320, Baranovichi
Telephone/Fax: +375 163 45-25-77

**Luninets Branch**
ul. Krasnaya, 175
225650, Luninets
Telephone: +375 1647 2-54-20

**Bereza Branch**
ul. Masterov, 8
225210, Bereza
Telephone: +375 1643 4-27-50, 4-28-19

**Pinsk Branch**
ul. Sovetskaya, 8
225710, Pinsk
Telephone: +375 1653 2-27-41, 2-51-92, fax: 2-33-35
E-mail: box@beltpp.belpak.brest.by

**Ivatsevichi Branch**
ul. Zavodskaya, 4
225250, Ivatsevichi
Telephone: +375 1645 2-29-33, 3-52-73

**Kobrin Branch**
ul. Suvorova, 27
225860, Kobrin
Telephone: +375 1642 2-14-06

**Prujany Branch**
ul. Sovetskaya, 8
225140, Prujany
Telephone: +375 1632 2-06-85

## VITEBSK BRANCH

### General Information

On 5 June 1963, an examination office of the Byelorussian Department of the All-Union Chamber of Commerce was established by resolution of the Council of Ministers of the BSSR on the basis of the Commodity Examination Bureau under the Trade Administration of the Vitebsk Region Executive Committee. When the Republic of Belarus restored sovereignty, the examination office was transformed into the Vitebsk Branch of the Belarusian Chamber of Commerce and Industry. Since July 2000 the Vitebsk Branch of the Belarusian Chamber of Commerce and Industry is a unitary enterprise of the Belarusian Chamber of Commerce and Industry.

At present, the Enterprise is a major division of the Belarusian Chambers of Commerce and Industry which services about 140 Members of the Chamber as well as other economic entities in the city of Vitebsk, the Vitebsk region and the FEZ "Vitebsk".

The Enterprise has its branch and representation offices in Polotsk, Novopolotsk, Orsha, Lepel, and Novolukoml. The Enterprise and its structural units employ 57 regular highly-skilled specialists that offer services in the areas supported by the Belarusian Chamber of Commerce and Industry, and about 30 nonstaff employees for specific services.

The Enterprise maintains close relations with regional chambers of commerce and industry in Russia, Ukraine, Baltic States and Moldova. Twenty four agreements on cooperation have been concluded with the said chambers. The Enterprise cooperates successfully with local authorities in the Vitebsk region. They have concluded agreements with the Vitebsk City Executive Committee, Committee for Economic and Marketing Relations under the Vitebsk City Executive Committee, the Vitebsk Region Territorial Committee for Business and Investment, Administration of FEZ "Vitebsk", the Vitebsk Regional Council of Manufacturers and Employers and other organizations.

Due to its geographical location, the Vitebsk Branch of the Belarusian Chamber of Commerce and Industry focuses on the development of foreign economic cooperation with the neighboring regions of the Russian Federation. They have established and have been developing successfully relations with the "Central Russia" Association of Chambers of Commerce and Industry. They have been maintaining close cooperation with the CCIs of the Smolensk, Pskov and Tver regions.

As a result of their joint effort interregional exhibitions "Republic of Belarus is Your Partner" are regularly conducted in Smolensk. Similar exhibitions "Golden Autumn –99" and "Vitebsk Spring-2000" were conducted in Tver and Vitebsk, respectively.

**Address:**
ul. Kosmonavtov, 4
210001, Vitebsk
Telephone: +375 212 36-30-52
Fax: +375 212 36-46-74
E-mail: ccivi@mail.ru
vitebsk@cci.by

- **Organization structure**

**Foreign economic cooperation department**
Telephone: +375 212 37-22-70, 36-26-00

**Expertise and certification bureau**
Telephone: +375 212 36-32-47, 36-33-10

Regional Branches

**Polotsk Branch**
ul. Scoriny, 14
211400, Polotsk
Telephone: +375 2144 4-32-82, 6-09-24
Fax: +375 2144 9-10-47

**Novopolotsk Branch**
ul. Parkovaya, 16, к.2
211440, Novopolotsk
Telephone: +375 2144 5-87-75

**Orsha Branch**
ul. Mira, 11
211030, Orsha
Telephone/fax: +375 2161 2-45-03

**Lepel Branch**
pl. Svobody, 10
211180, Lepel
Telephone: +375 2132 4-38-64

**Novolukoml Branch**
Novolukoml'skiy zavod keramzitovogo graviya
211162, Tchashnikskiy r-on, g. Novolukoml
Telephone: +375 2133 3-78-41, 3-72-92

## GOMEL BRANCH

**General Information**

The Unitary Enterprise Gomel Branch of BelCCI as an integral part of the Belarusian Chamber of Commerce and Industry is operating in the territory of the Gomel region. Its aim is the development of regional economy and its integration in the world economy, establishment of market infrastructure, creation of favorable conditions for business, and broadening trade and economic relations between the Gomel region and other countries.

The Gomel Branch is one of the eldest regional branches of the BelCCI. It was established in the year 1953. The Branch includes four subunits in Mozyr, Rechitsa, Zhlobin and Svetlogorsk and two representation offices in Zhitkovich and Rogachev. The Branch employs more than 70 regular high-skilled specialists that offer various services. Among them is examination and certification, exhibition activity, business education, translation/interpretation, legal support to foreign-economic activity, and information service.

The Branch stands up for business community interests before power structures, render assistance in the development of foreign relations, trade, market research, raising prestige and popularity of companies, product promotion for the BelCCI Member companies in the external market.

The Branch unites more than 220 enterprises, organizations, firms, and private undertakers that represent the public and private sectors of the economy as well as foreign and mixed capital. Chamber Members account for more than 80% of industrial output in the region. The Gomel Branch offers a full range of services that is traditional for CCI to Chamber Members and other businessmen.

The Branch maintains close relations with 46 regional chambers of commerce and industry in Russia, Ukraine, Moldova, Kazakhstan and distant foreign countries, cooperates with them in such areas as information exchange on foreign economic legislation, business offers of parties, support in the arrangement of exhibitions, fairs, presentations, business missions, assistance to businessmen in making contacts.

**Address:**
ul. Pervomayskaya, 21
246000, Gomel
Telephone: +375 232 55-03-90; fax: 55-82-58
E-mail: cci@mail.gomel.by
Web-site: http://www.cci.gomel.by

- **Organization Structure**

**Foreign economic relations department**
Telephone: +375 232 72-18-61
Fax: +375 232 55-82-58

**Translation bureau**
Telephone: +375 232 55-93-97

**Certification and declaration department**
Telephones: +375 232 572-18-66, 55-61-55, 55-76-82

**Expertise and certification department**
Telephone: +375 232 53-13-56, 72-18-65

Regional Branches

**Zhlobin Branch**
ul. Bartashova, 26
247210, Zhlobin
Telephone: +375 2334 2-24-05
E-mail: ccizhlobin@tut.by

**Rogachev Branch**
ul. Pushkina, 69
247250, Rogachev
Telephone: +375 2339 2-25-96

**Mozir' Branch**
bulvar Druzhby, 10
247760, Mozir'
Telephone/fax: +375 2351 5-19-56
E-mail: ccimozyr@tut.by

**Svetlogorsk Branch**
ul. Zelenaya, 10
247400, Svetlogorsk
Telephone/fax: +375 2342 2-01-95
E-mail: ccisvetlogorsk@tut.by

**Rechitsa Branch**
ul. K. Marksa, 22
247500, Rechitsa
Telephone: +375 2340 2-30-90
E-mail: cciretchitsa@tut.by

**Zhitkovitchi Branch**
ul.K.Marksa, 80
Zhitkovitchi
Telephone: +375 2353 2-45-88

## GRODNO BRANCH

### General Information

The history of the Grodno Branch goes back to the year of 1963. Then the enterprise was established and ran as a structural unit of the Byelorussian Branch of the All-Union Chamber of Commerce. Its activity aimed to examination of commodities, raw materials and equipment.

The Unitary Enterprise Grodno Branch of the Belarusian Chamber of Commerce and Industry is located in an ancient Belorussian city of Grodno close to the Belarus/Poland border. Traditional East-West transport routes transit the city. The Grodno region carries on cooperation with the Euroregion "Neman".

At present the enterprise is an integral structure existing in the organization-legal form of a unitary enterprise includes 5 (five) regional subsidiaries. The Grodno Branch employs more than 30 high-skilled specialists who render services to members of the Grodno-region Chamber and other economic entities in the region.

The enterprise has been accredited as a certification authority for food and vegetable products with the National System Gosstandart and issues certificates of conformity with respect to safety and consumer properties. Moreover, the enterprise has been granter a permit for licensing by ministries and department of the Republic of Belarus.

The Grodno Branch and its subsidiary in the town of Lida offer legal services. We have accumulated a fairly wide experience in interaction with foreign partners. Over many years we have been carrying cooperation with Polish organizations, namely, with the East Economic Company and the Center of Fairs and Eastern Market Promotion (Warszawa - Bialostok), Polish-Lithuanian Chamber of Economy (Suwalki), the Business School (Bialostok), Bialostok Province Development Fund for implementation of a European Union research and training project under the CREDO program aimed to the development of business in the Poland/Belarus border area.

The Enterprise maintains and develops ties with diplomatic missions of various states: Consulate-General of the Republic of Poland in Grodno, Trade Delegation of the Slovak Republic in the Republic of Belarus, Consulate-General of the Republic of Belarus in Bialostok, the Trade Adviser Office under the Polish Embassy in the Republic of Belarus. Also it has been cooperating with chambers of commerce and industry of the Russian Federation (Tambov, Bryansk, Smolensk), Ukraine (Lvov, Chernigov, Lutsk and Rovno) and Lithuania (Kaunas).

Under concluded agreements on cooperation, they distribute commercial information and commercial offers between economic entities of any ownership in the Grodno region and foreign partners, look for partners for mutually beneficial cooperation.

They often visit the Polish town of Bialostok for participation in exhibitions and fairs arranged by the Center of Fairs and Eastern Market Promotion.

**Address:**
ul. Sovetskaya, 23
230023, Grodno
Telephone: +375 152 44-90-70, fax: +375 17 210-81-06
E-mail: anat@grocci.belpak.grodno.by

- **Organization Structure**

**Foreign economic relation department**
Telephone: +375 152 47-36-12, 47-20-04

**Expertise and certification bureau**
Telephone: +375 152 72-18-24, 44-42-64

Regional Branches

**Volkovysk branch**
ul. Dzerzhinskogo, 3
231900, Volkovysk
Telephone\fax: +375 1512 2-39-06

**Oshmyany branch**
kvartal Stroiteley, 5, office 19
231100, Oshmyany
Telephone: +375 1593 2-18-28

**Lida Branch**
231300, Lida, Sovetskaya str., 43
Telephone\fax: +375 1561 2-62-32

**Slonim branch**
ul. Krasnoarmeyskaya, 17a
231800, Slonim
Telephone\fax: +375 1562 2-14-91

**Novogrudok branch**
ul. 1 May, 2
231400, Novogrudok
Telephone\fax: +375 1597 2-17-45

## MOGILEV BRANCH

### General Information

On 15 June 1963, an examination office of the Byelorussian Department of the All-Union Chamber of Commerce was established by resolution of the Council of Ministers of the BSSR on the basis of the Commodity Examination Bureau under the Trade Administration of the Mogilev Region Executive Committee. When the Republic of Belarus restored sovereignty, the examination office was transformed into the Mogilev Branch of the Belarusian Chamber of Commerce and Industry. Since July 2000 the Mogilev Branch of the Belarusian Chamber of Commerce and Industry is a unitary enterprise of the Belarusian Chamber of Commerce and Industry.

At present, the Enterprise is a major division of the Belarusian Chambers of Commerce and Industry, which services about 130 Members of the Chamber as well as other economic entities in the city of Mogilev and the Mogilev region.

The Enterprise has its branch and representation offices in Bobruisk, Osipovichi, Krichev and Klimovichi. The Enterprise and its structural units employ more than 40 regular highly-skilled specialists that offer services in the areas supported by the Belarusian Chamber of Commerce and Industry, and about 8 nonstaff employees for specific services.

The Enterprise maintains close relations with regional chambers of commerce and industry in Russia, Ukraine, Baltic States and Moldova. Nineteen agreements on cooperation have been concluded with the said chambers. The Enterprise cooperates successfully with local authorities in the Mogilev region, the Mogilev Region Territorial Committee for Business and Investment, the Mogilev Association of Manufacturers and Employers and other organizations.

Due to its geographical location, the Mogilev Branch of the Belarusian Chamber of Commerce and Industry focuses on the development of foreign economic cooperation with the neighboring regions of the Russian Federation. They have established and have been successfully developing relations with the “Central Russia” Association of Chambers of Commerce and Industry. They have been maintaining close cooperation with the CCIs of the Smolensk region.

As a result of their joint effort interregional exhibitions “Republic of Belarus is Your Partner” are regularly conducted in Smolensk. Similar exhibition “Golden Autumn –99” was conducted in Tver. Also a specialized exhibition “Mogilevstroiprogress” is traditionally conducted in Mogilev.

**Address:**
Dom Sovietov, office 802
212030, Mogilev
Telephone/fax: +375 222 22-54-21
E-mail: palata@torgprom.belpak.mogilev.by

- **Organization Structure**

**Foreign economic relation department**
Telephone: +375 222 25-22-60

**Department of certification of quality**
Telephone: +375 222 22-04-90

**Certification and expertise department**
Telephone: +375 222 25-22-60, 22-53-96

Regional Branches

**Bobruysk branch**
ul. K. Marksa, 22/20
213826, Bobruysk
Telephone/fax: +375 2251 7-38-70

**Krichev branch**
ul. Sovetskaya, 36
213500, Krichev
Telephone/fax: +375 2241 2-15-09

**Klimovichi branch**
ul. Naberezhnaya, 10
213600, Klimovichi
Telephone: +375 2244 2-21-72, 2-21-83

**Osipovichi branch**
ul. Leninskaya, 88, office 60
213760, Osipovichi
Telephone/fax: +375 2235 2-44-47

## INTERNATIONAL ARBITRATION COURT

Address:
pr-t Masherova, 23, korp. 1, kab. 706
220004, Minsk
Telephone: 375 17 223-28-46, 223-53-85
Fax: 375 17 223-28-46

## BELPATENTSERVICE

Ulitsa Ya. Kolassa, 65, Minsk, BELARUS
P.O. Box 217, 220113
Phone/fax: +375 17 285-78-93
E-mail: patent@cci.by
Web-site: http://www.belpatentservice.org

## EXHIBITION COMPANY "BELINTEREXPO – BELARUSIAN INTERNATIONAL EXHIBITIONS" JOINT TO THE BELARUSIAN CHAMBER OF COMMERCE AND INDUSTRY

| | |
|---|---|
| Address: | 14, Masherov Ave., Minsk, 220035 |
| Tel.: | +375 17 226-9938 |
| Fax: | +375 17 226-9168, 226-9143 |
| E-mail: | fairdept@cci.by |
| Director | |
| Tel.: | +375 17 226-9938 |
| Deputy Director | |
| Tel.: | +375 17 226-9143 |
| Fairs Department (abroad) | |

| | |
|---|---|
| Tel./fax: | +375 17 226-9142, 250-2092 |
| Fairs Department (in Belarus) | |
| Tel./fax: | +375 17 226-9143, 226-9422 |
| Accounts Department | |
| Tel.: | +375 17 226-9187 |

## REPRESENTATIVE OFFICE OF BELCCI IN GERMANY AND COUNTRIES OF WESTERN EUROPE

Messe-Allee 2, Raum 309a D-04356, Leipzig
Phone: 8-10-49 341\603 1704,
Fax: 8-10-49 341\603 1705
E-mail: hikbelarus@t-online.de

**Representative:** Serenkov Viktor Valentinovitch

## REPRESENTATIVE OFFICES ABROAD

China

Office 1503, Guangming Building, Liangmagiao Road, Chaoyang Distrikt, Beijing, China.
Post code: 100016
Phone: 8-10-8610\64678822 ext. 1503;
Phone/Fax: 64624219

**Representative:** Nitievskij Albert Bronislavovich

Estonia

Estonia, Talin, Fosforiidi 13 EE0030
Phone: 8-10-372\6006087, 6006119, 6006048, 6006079
Fax: 8-10-372\6006101, 6006081
GSM: 8-10-372\5051886
E-mail: info@tureks.ee

**Representative:** Bugaev Michail Mar'yanovich

Hungary

Hungary, Budapesht 1147, Egreshshi 8
Phone: 8-10-361\468-3566,
Fax: 8-10-361\468-3571
GSM: 8-10 36 20\974-4403
E-mail: bytrade@axelero.hu

**Representative:** Peter Lator

Italy

Via Arzeron, 4 45011 Adria (RO) Italia
Phone/Fax: 8-10-39\0426-41506
GSM 8-10-39\338 8660 885; (8-10-39) 340 480 22 78
E-mail: samousenko@iol.it

**Representative:** Samusenko Natalia Vsevolodovna

Netherlands

Zwolsestraat 190 2587 WB The Hague Netherlands
Тел. 8-10-3170\30-60-120,
факс 8-10-3170\30-60-225
E-mail: victor@gourov.demon.nl

**Representative:** Gurov Victor Alexandrovich

Russian Federation

**South federal district**

Russian Federation, 344064,
Rostov-on-Don, Radiatornyj alleyway 8,
Phone: 8-107 8632\95-8289, 77-4186, 77-4783
Fax: 8-107 8632\77-4601

**Representative:** Taranenko Yurij Stepanovich

**Privolzhsky federal district**

Russian Federation, Nizhegorodskaya oblast,
Dzerzhinsk, Chkalova avenue, 17a - 71
Phone: 8-107 8312\77-5496
GSM: (8-910)793-27-99
Fax: 8-107 8312\77-5586
E-mail: kaa@yarmarka.ru

**Representative:** Koropchenko Alexander Anatoljevich

**Belgorodskaya, Bryanskaya, Voronezhskaya, Kurskaya, Lipetskaya, Orlovskaya, Ryazanskaya, Tambovskaya, Tulskaya oblast (part of Central Federal district)**

Russian Federation, Voronezh,
Lenin avenue, 174, P.O. Box 394722
Phone: 8-107-0732\23-0333 (in Voronezh)
8-107-095\921-24-11 (in Moscow)
GSM: 8-910\4292627

**Representative:** Verbitsky Vladimir Viktorovich

Sweden

Box 223, SE-35105 VA x JO, Sweden
Phone: 4647048811, 4647048809,
Fax: 4647048807

**Representative:** Uchaev Yurij Albertovich

Turkey

Han Sokak No 13\1 ve 06700 Ankara
Phone: 0312 4463042
Fax: 8-10-903-12-4460150

**Representative:** Volchok Tatsiana Il'yinichna

For additional information send your request to the Department of Foreign Economic Co-operation:

Fax: 017\226-91-41
E-mail: interdept@cci.by

**JOINT CHAMBERS**

Belarusian-Polish CCI

pt-t Masherova, 14, off. 10
220035, Belarus, Minsk
Telephone: 017\226-91-41
Fax: 017\226-98-60

## OTHER USEFUL CONTACTS

Chamber of Commerce and Industry of the Republic of Belarus
Chairman: Vladimir Lesun
220600, Minsk, Prospekt Masherova, 14
Fax: 172/ 29--936
Tel: 172/ 269-937

Belarusian Science and Industry Association
Director of Overseas Economic Relations: Vladimir Sobolev
220030, Minsk, Ul. Lenina, 19
Fax: 172/ 271-529

National Bank of Belarus
Acting Chair: Mykolai Kuzmich
220008 Minsk, 20 F. Skorina Ave
Tel: 172/ 274-479, 270-946, 276-431
Fax: 172/ 276-431

Union of Entrepreneurs of the Republic of Belarus
President: Vladimir Karyagin
220050, Minsk, Ul. Internatsionalnaya, 13
Tel: 172/ 271-483
Fax: 172/ 271-596

Union of Cooperatives of Belarus
220034, Minsk, Per. Voyskovy, 12
Tel: 172/ 391-063
Fax: 172/ 391-290

Union of Entrepreneurs and Lessees of Belarus
220079 Minsk, Ul. Bersona, 16
Tel: 172/ 203-114
Fax: 172/ 270-342

Belarus Computer-Aided Business Information System
Director: Leonid Gruzdilovich
220676, Minsk, Masherov, 7
Tel: 172/ 233-495
Fax: 172/ 209-125

National Brokers Guild of the Republic of Belarus
President: Alexander Yelovik
220030, Minsk, K. Marx St., 40
Tel: 172/ 274-075
Fax: 172/ 278-995

## SELECTED BUSINESS CONTACTS FOR BELARUS[3]

U.S. Embassy/Minsk
Ambassador: The Honorable Daniel V. Speckhard
Deputy Chief of Mission: Mr. George Krol
Political/Economic Officer: Mr. Anthony Godfrey
Political/Commercial Officer: Ms. Anne L. Carson

Minsk Location: #46 Starovilenskaya
Mailing Address: U.S. Embassy Minsk
Department of State
Washington, D.C. 20521-7010
Tel: 375-172/ 347-761
Fax: 375-172/ 347-853

Embassy of Belarus in the US
Ambassador: The Honorable Valery Tsepkalo
Commercial Counselor: Mr. Eugene Bogomazov

[3] Please note: It is reported that local telephone numbers in Minsk which used to begin with 293 and 296 have been changed to begin with 223 and 226, respectively.

Address: Embassy of the Republic of Belarus
1619 New Hampshire Ave., NW
Washington, D.C. 20009
Tel: 202/986-1604
Fax: 202/986-1805

European Bank for Reconstruction and Development (EBRD
Allan Popoff, Resident Representative
ul. Sovetskaya 7, 6th Floor
220050 Minsk
Tel: 375-172/ 201-537
Fax: 375-172/ 207-668

Export-Import Bank
U.S. Toll Free Number: 1 (800 565-EXIM
Worldwide Number: 202/565-3946

Overseas Private Investment Corporation (OPIC
Mr. James Gale
1100 New York Ave., NW
Washington, DC 20527-0001
Tel: 202/ 336-8629
Fax: 202/ 408-5145

U.S. Department of Agriculture
Grant Pettrie, Area Manager
Foreign Agricultural Service
14th and Independence Ave., SW, Rm 4524
Washington, DC 20250-1000
Tel: 202/720-5319
Fax: 202/690-0251

U.S. Trade and Development Agency (TDA
Dan Stein, Regional Director
Tanya Shamson, Country Manager
SA-16, Room 309
Washington, DC 20532-1602
Tel: 703/875-4357
Fax: 703/875-4009

Western NIS Enterprise Fund
Scott Carlson, President &CEO
11 West 39th Street, 11th floor
New York, NY 10018
Tel: 212/556-9320
Fax: 212/556-9321

# SUPPLEMENTS

## BUSINESS LAWS

- On the Entrepreneurship in the Republic of Belarus - Law of the Republic of Belarus of May 28, 1991
- On Foreign Investments on the Territory of the Republic of Belarus - Law of the Republic of Belarus of November 14, 1991
- On Commodity Exchanges - Law of the Republic of Belarus of March 13, 1992
- On Counteraction of Monopolistic Activities and Promotion of Competition - Law of the Republic of Belarus of December 10, 1992
- On Veterinary - Law of the Republic of Belarus of December 2, 1994
- On Standardization - Law of the Republic of Belarus of September 5, 1995
- On Ensuring the Uniformity of Measurements - Law of the Republic of Belarus of September 5, 1995
- On Certification of Products, Works and Services - Law of the Republic of Belarus of September 5, 1995
- On Advertising - Law of the Republic of Belarus of February 18, 1997
- On State Regulation of Alcoholic Products Output and Turnover - Law of the Republic of Belarus of July 20, 1998
- On Financial and Industrial Groups - Law of the Republic of Belarus of June 4, 1999
- On Tourism - Law of the Republic of Belarus of November 25, 1999

- On the Creation and Activities of the Economic Groups in the Republic - Decree of the President of the Republic of Belarus [1] 482 of November 27, 1995
- On State Support of the Development and Export of the Information Technologies - Decree of the President of the Republic of Belarus [1] 234 of May 3, 2001

- On Legal Treatment of Foreign Investments From Member-States of the Commonwealth of Independent States - Ordinance of the President of the Republic of Belarus [1] 13 of August 5, 1998
- On the Regulation of State Registration and Liquidation (Termination of Activities) of Economic Entities - Ordinance of the President of the Republic of Belarus [1] 11 of March 16, 1999

- On Peculiarities of Establishment of Foreign Enterprises on the Territory of the Republic of Belarus - Decision of the Government of the Republic of Belarus [1] 97 of February 24, 1992
- On the Procedure of Referring the Products (Works, Services) of Foreign Companies and Joint Ventures Existing on the Territory of the Republic of Belarus to the Own Made Production - Decision of the Government of the Republic of Belarus [1] 421 of July 10, 1992
- On Approval of the List of Products of Particular Importance the Council of Ministers of the Republic of Belarus is Entitled to Reduse the Profit Tax Rate by 50 Percent for Any Enterprise with Foreign Investments Manufacturing them for a Period of Three Year - Decision of the Government of the Republic of Belarus [1] 345 of May 26, 1993

- **On the List of Lines of Activities Subject to Special Permit (License) and Bodies to Issue Such Permits (Licences) - Decision of the Government of the Republic of Belarus [1] 456 of August 21, 1995**
- **On Introduction of Mandatory Certification of All Types of Alcoholic and Tobacco Goods in the Republic of Belarus - Decision of the Government of the Republic of Belarus [1] 260 of April 16, 1996**
- **On the Procedure of Opening and Operation of Representations of Foreign Companies and Organizations in the Republic of Belarus - Decision of the Government of the Republic of Belarus [1] 929 of July 22, 1997**

## U.S. MERCHANDISE TRADE WITH BELARUS

84 MACHINERY
24 TOBACCO
98 SPECIAL OTHER
85 ELECTRICAL MACHINERY
30 PHARMACEUTICAL PRODUCTS
61 KNIT APPAREL
90 OPTIC,NT
87 VEHICLES, NOT RAILWAY
39 PLASTIC
59 IMPREGNATD TEXT FABRICS
57 TEXTILE FLOOR COVERINGS
41 HIDES AND SKINS
69 CERAMIC PRODUCTS
38 MISC. CHEMICAL PRODUCTS
94 FURNITURE AND BEDDING
52 COTTON+YARN,FABRIC
76 ALUMINUM
20 PRESERVED FOOD
96 MISCELLANEOUS MANUFACT
56 WADDING,FELT,TWINE,ROPE
60 KNIT,CROCHETED FABRICS
44 WOOD 0
09 SPICES,COFFEE AND TEA
58 SPCL WOVEN FABRIC,ETC
43 FURSKIN+ARTIFICIAL FUR
51 ANIMAL HAIR+YARN,FABRC
54 MANMADE FILAMENT,FABRIC
27 MINERAL FUEL, OIL ETC0.035
48 PAPER,PAPERBOARD
49 BOOK+NEWSPAPR;MANUSCRPT
63 MISC TEXTILE ARTICLES
34 SOAP,WAX,ET;DENTAL PREP
03 FISH AND SEAFOOD
62 WOVEN APPAREL
55 MANMADE STAPLE FIBERS
25 SALT;SULFUR;EARTH,STONE

95 TOYS AND SPORTS EQUIPMT
70 GLASS AND GLASSWARE
22 BEVERAGES
28 INORG CHEM;RARE ERTH MT
88 AIRCRAFT,SPACECRAFT
33 PERFUMERY,COSMETIC,ETC
21 MISCELLANEOUS FOOD
73 IRON/STEEL PRODUCTS
82 TOOL,CUTLRY, OF BASE MTL
32 TANNING,DYE,PAINT,PUTTY
89 SHIPS AND BOATS
53 OTHER VEG TEXTILE FIBER
50 SILK;SILK YARN,FABRIC
40 RUBBER
71 PRECIOUS STONES,METALS
68 STONE,PLASTR,CEMENT,ETC
91 CLOCKS AND WATCHES
92 MUSICAL INSTRUMENTS
83 MISC ART OF BASE METAL
86 RAILWAY;TRF SIGN EQ
35 ALBUMINS;MOD STRCH;GLUE
37 PHOTOGRAPHIC/CINEMATOGR
42 LEATHR ART;SADDLRY;BAGS
02 MEAT
10 CEREALS
12 MISC GRAIN,SEED,FRUIT
15 FATS AND OILS
18 COCOA
23 FOOD WASTE; ANIMAL FEED
29 ORGANIC CHEMICALS

## U.S. IMPORTS FROM BELARUS

62 WOVEN APPAREL
31 FERTILIZERS
53 OTHER VEG TEXTILE FIBER
72 IRON AND STEEL
55 MANMADE STAPLE FIBERS
29 ORGANIC CHEMICALS
28 INORG CHEM;RARE ERTH MT
54 MANMADE FILAMENT,FABRIC
70 GLASS AND GLASSWARE
84 MACHINERY
92 MUSICAL INSTRUMENTS
87 VEHICLES, NOT RAILWAY
61 KNIT APPAREL
90 OPTIC,NT 8544;MED INSTR
51 ANIMAL HAIR+YARN,FABRC
57 TEXTILE FLOOR COVERINGS

40 RUBBER
44 WOOD
99 O SPECL IMPR PROVISIONS

85 ELECTRICAL MACHINERY
97 ART AND ANTIQUES
98 SPECIAL OTHER
38 MISC. CHEMICAL PRODUCTS
49 BOOK+NEWSPAPR; MANUSCRPT
39 PLASTIC
26 ORES,SLAG,AS
73 IRON/STEEL PRODUCTS
25 SALT;SULFUR;EARTH,STONE
63 MISC TEXTILE ARTICLES
65 HEADGEAR
95 TOYS AND SPORTS EQUIPMT
68 STONE,PLASTR,CEMENT,ETC
37 PHOTOGRAPHIC/CINEMATOGR
94 FURNITURE AND BEDDING
30 PHARMACEUTICAL PRODUCTS
71 PRECIOUS STONES,METALS
75 NICKEL+ARTICLES THEREOF
33 PERFUMERY,COSMETIC,ETC
60 KNIT,CROCHETED FABRICS
69 CERAMIC PRODUCTS
59 IMPREGNATD TEXT FABRICS
58 SPCL WOVEN FABRIC,ETC
52 COTTON+YARN,FABRIC
42 LEATHR ART;SADDLRY;BAGS
43 FURSKIN+ARTIFICIAL FUR
35 ALBUMINS;MOD STRCH;GLUE
04 DAIRY,EGGS,HONEY,ETC
14 OTHER VEGETABLE
22 BEVERAGES
74 COPPER+ARTICLES THEREOF
81 OTHER BASE METALS, ETC.
96 MISCELLANEOUS MANUFACT
82 TOOL,CUTLRY, OF BASE MTL
83 MISC ART OF BASE METAL

## BASIC TITLES FOR BELARUS

***IMPORTANT!***

***All publications are updated annually!***

***Please contact IBP, Inc. at ibpusa3@gmail.com for the latest ISBNs and additional information***

| TITLE |
|---|
| Belarus A "Spy" Guide - Strategic Information and Developments |
| Belarus A Spy" Guide" |

| TITLE |
|---|
| Belarus Banking & Financial Market Handbook |
| Belarus Banking & Financial Market Handbook |
| Belarus Business and Industrial Directory |
| Belarus Business and Industrial Directory |
| Belarus Business and Investment Opportunities Yearbook |
| Belarus Business and Investment Opportunities Yearbook |
| Belarus Business and Investment Opportunities Yearbook Volume 1 Strategic Information and Opportunities |
| Belarus Business and Investment Opportunities Yearbook Volume 2 Leading Export-Import, Business, Investment Opportunities and Projects |
| Belarus Business Intelligence Report - Practical Information, Opportunities, Contacts |
| Belarus Business Intelligence Report - Practical Information, Opportunities, Contacts |
| Belarus Business Law Handbook - Strategic Information and Basic Laws |
| Belarus Business Law Handbook - Strategic Information and Basic Laws |
| Belarus Business Law Handbook - Strategic Information and Basic Laws |
| Belarus Business Law Handbook - Strategic Information and Basic Laws |
| Belarus Business Law Handbook Volume 1 Strategic Information and Basic Laws |
| Belarus Business Law Handbook Volume 2 Investment and Trade Laws Volume 2 Investment and Trade Laws |
| Belarus Business Success Guide - Basic Practical Information and Contacts |
| Belarus Company Laws and Regulations Handbook |
| Belarus Company Laws and Regulations Handbook - Strategic Information and Basic Laws |
| Belarus Constitution and Citizenship Laws Handbook - Strategic Information and Basic Laws |
| Belarus Country Study Guide - Strategic Information and Developments |
| Belarus Country Study Guide - Strategic Information and Developments |
| Belarus Country Study Guide - Strategic Information and Developments Volume 1 Strategic Information and Developments |
| Belarus Country Study Guide Volume 1 Strategic Information and Developments |
| Belarus Country Study Guide Volume 1 Strategic Information and Developments - Everything you need to know about the country - Geography, history, politics, economy, business, etc. |
| Belarus Criminal Laws, Regulations and Procedures Handbook - Strategic Information, Regulations, Procedures |
| Belarus Customs, Trade Regulations and Procedures Handbook |
| Belarus Customs, Trade Regulations and Procedures Handbook |
| Belarus Diplomatic Handbook - Strategic Information and Developments |
| Belarus Diplomatic Handbook - Strategic Information and Developments |
| Belarus Ecology & Nature Protection Handbook |
| Belarus Ecology & Nature Protection Handbook |
| Belarus Ecology & Nature Protection Laws and Regulation Handbook |
| Belarus Electoral, Political Parties Laws and Regulations Handbook - Strategic Information, Regulations, Procedures |
| Belarus Energy Policy, Laws and Regulation Handbook |
| Belarus Export-Import Trade and Business Directory |
| Belarus Export-Import Trade and Business Directory |
| Belarus Fishing and Aquaculture Industry Handbook - Strategic Information, Regulations, Opportunities |
| Belarus Foreign Policy and Government Guide |
| Belarus Foreign Policy and Government Guide |
| Belarus Government and Business Contacts Handbook |
| Belarus Government and Business Contacts Handbook |
| Belarus Immigration Laws and Regulations Handbook - Strategic Information and Basic Laws |

| TITLE |
| --- |
| Belarus Industrial and Business Directory |
| Belarus Industrial and Business Directory |
| Belarus Insolvency (Bankruptcy) Laws and Regulations Handbook - Strategic Information and Basic Laws |
| Belarus Internet and E-Commerce Investment and Business Guide - Strategic and Practical Information: Regulations and Opportunities |
| Belarus Internet and E-Commerce Investment and Business Guide - Strategic and Practical Information: Regulations and Opportunities |
| Belarus Investment and Business Guide - Strategic and Practical Information |
| Belarus Investment and Business Guide - Strategic and Practical Information |
| Belarus Investment and Business Guide - Strategic and Practical Information |
| Belarus Investment and Business Guide - Strategic and Practical Information |
| Belarus Investment and Business Guide Volume 1 Strategic and Practical Information |
| Belarus Investment and Business Guide Volume 2 Business, Investment Opportunities and Incentives |
| Belarus Investment and Business Profile - Basic Information and Contacts for Succesful investment and Business Activity |
| Belarus Investment and Trade Laws and Regulations Handbook |
| Belarus Investment, Trade Strategy and Agreements Handbook - Strategic Information and Basic Agreements |
| Belarus Labor Laws and Regulations Handbook - Strategic Information and Basic Laws |
| Belarus Labor Laws and Regulations Handbook - Strategic Information and Basic Laws |
| Belarus Land Ownership and Agriculture Laws Handbook |
| Belarus Mineral & Mining Sector Investment and Business Guide - Strategic and Practical Information |
| Belarus Mineral & Mining Sector Investment and Business Guide - Strategic and Practical Information |
| Belarus Mining Laws and Regulations Handbook |
| Belarus President Alexander LUKASHENKO Handbook |
| Belarus President Alexander LUKASHENKO Handbook |
| Belarus Privatization Programs and Regulations Handbook |
| Belarus Privatization Programs and Regulations Handbook |
| Belarus Recent Economic and Political Developments Yearbook |
| Belarus Recent Economic and Political Developments Yearbook |
| Belarus Recent Economic and Political Developments Yearbook |
| Belarus Starting Business (Incorporating) in....Guide |
| Belarus Tax Guide Volume 1 Corporate and Business Taxation |
| Belarus Tax Guide Volume 1 Strategic Information and Basic Regulations |
| Belarus Tax Guide Volume 2 Personal Taxation |
| Belarus Taxation Laws and Regulations Handbook |
| Belarus Telecom Laws and Regulations Handbook |
| Belarus Telecommunication Industry Business Opportunities Handbook |
| Belarus Telecommunication Industry Business Opportunities Handbook |
| Belarus Transportation Policy and Regulations Handbook |
| Belarus: Doing Business and Investing in Belarus Guide |
| Belarus: How to Invest, Start and Run Profitable Business in Belarus Guide - Practical Information, Opportunities, Contacts |
| Belarus: US Assistance to Belarus Handbook |

## BASIC LAWS AND REGULATIONS AFFECTING BUSINESS[4]

| COUTRY | LAW TITLE |
|---|---|
| Belarus | Banking Code of the Republic of Belarus |
| Belarus | Civil Code of the Republic of Belarus Part I |
| Belarus | Civil Code of the Republic of Belarus Part II |
| Belarus | Civil Code of the Republic of Belarus Part III |
| Belarus | Civil Code of the Republic of Belarus Part IV |
| Belarus | Civil Code of the Republic of Belarus Part V |
| Belarus | Civil Code of the Republic of Belarus Part VI |
| Belarus | Code of the Republic of Belarus on Land Part I |
| Belarus | Code of the Republic of Belarus on Land Part II |
| Belarus | Code of the Republic of Belarus on Land Part III |
| Belarus | Constitution of the Republic of Belarus |
| Belarus | Criminal Code of the Republic of Belarus Part I |
| Belarus | Criminal Code of the Republic of Belarus Part II |
| Belarus | Criminal Code of the Republic of Belarus Part III |
| Belarus | Criminal Code of the Republic of Belarus Part IV |
| Belarus | Criminal Code of the Republic of Belarus Part V |
| Belarus | Criminal Code of the Republic of Belarus Part VI |
| Belarus | Electoral Code Of The Republic Of Belarus |
| Belarus | Investment Code |
| Belarus | Investment Code of the Republic of Belarus |
| Belarus | Law of the Republic of Belarus on Copyright and Contiguous Rights (of January 2003) |
| Belarus | Law of the Republic of Belarus On Export Control |
| Belarus | Law Of The Republic Of Belarus On Free Economic Zones |
| Belarus | Law of the Republic of Belarus on Geographic Indications (of October 2004) |
| Belarus | Law of the Republic of Belarus on Patents, on Inventions, Industrial Models and Industrial Designs (of October 2004). |
| Belarus | Law of The Republic Of Belarus on The Constitutional Court Of The Republic Of Belarus |
| Belarus | Law on Advertising |
| Belarus | Law on Amending Certain Codes of the Republic of Belarus to Increase Liability for Human Trafficking and Other Related Offences (2005) |
| Belarus | Law on Auditing activities |
| Belarus | Law on Banks And Banking In The Republic Of Belarus |
| Belarus | Law on Child's Rights |
| Belarus | Law on Citizenship (1991) |

[4] For ordering tests of specific laws in English or French, Please contact Global Investment Center USA at ibpusa3@gmail.com

| | |
|---|---|
| Belarus | Law on Communications |
| Belarus | Law on Copyright And Contiguous Rights |
| Belarus | Law on Counteraction to Monopolistic Activities and Promotion of Competition |
| Belarus | Law on Enterprises in the Republic of Belarus Part I |
| Belarus | Law on Enterprises in the Republic of Belarus Part II |
| Belarus | Law on Environmental Protection (1992) |
| Belarus | Law on External Labor Migration |
| Belarus | Law on Financial and Industrial Groups |
| Belarus | Law on Financial Industrial Groups |
| Belarus | Law on Foreign Investment |
| Belarus | Law on Gatherings, Meetings, Street Processions, Demonstrations and Picketing |
| Belarus | Law on Geographic Names |
| Belarus | Law on Immigration (1998) |
| Belarus | Law on Immovable property tax |
| Belarus | Law on Income Tax |
| Belarus | Law on Insolvency and Bankruptcy |
| Belarus | Law on Insurance |
| Belarus | Law on International Arbitration Court (Tribunal) |
| Belarus | Law on Legal Protection of Topology of Integrated Circuits |
| Belarus | Law on Legal Status of Foreign Citizens and Persons without Citizenship in the Republic of Belarus (1993, as amended 2000) |
| Belarus | Law on Mass Actions (1997 as amended 2006) |
| Belarus | Law on Measures To Fight Organized Crime And Corruption |
| Belarus | Law on Natural Monopolies |
| Belarus | Law on Patents for industrial models |
| Belarus | Law on Patents for inventions |
| Belarus | Law on Patents on Inventions, Industrial Models and Industrial Designs |
| Belarus | Law on payments for land |
| Belarus | Law on Political Parties |
| Belarus | Law on President (1995 as amended 2006) |
| Belarus | Law on Protection Of The Environment |
| Belarus | Law on protection of the Environment |
| Belarus | Law on protection of the right of consumers |
| Belarus | Law on Protection of the rights of the consumers |
| Belarus | Law on Public Associations (1994 as amended 2005) |
| Belarus | Law on Real Estate Tax |
| Belarus | Law on Refugees (2003) |
| Belarus | Law on Sanitary and Epidemic Well-Being of Population |
| Belarus | Law on Securities and Stock exchange |
| Belarus | Law on Social care |

| | |
|---|---|
| Belarus | Law on State Statistics |
| Belarus | Law on Taxes and duties collected by the Republic of Belarus |
| Belarus | Law on Taxes On Incomes And Profits Of Enterprises, Amalgamations, Organizations |
| Belarus | Law on the Central Commission on Holding Elections and Republican Referenda |
| Belarus | Law on the Constitutional Court |
| Belarus | Law on the Customs Tariff |
| Belarus | Law On The Fight Against Terrorism (3 January 2002, no. 77-?) |
| Belarus | Law on the Freedom of Religion and Religious Organizations |
| Belarus | Law on the Legal Status of Aliens and Stateless Persons (1993 as amended 2000) |
| Belarus | Law on the National Bank of In The Republic Of Belarus |
| Belarus | Law on the press and other mass media |
| Belarus | Law on Tourism |
| Belarus | Law on Trademarks and Service marks |
| Belarus | Law on Trade-Unions |
| Belarus | Law on Value-added Tax |
| Belarus | On Measures to Prevent Legalization of Illegally Acquired Proceeds and financing of terrorist activity |
| Belarus | On Prevention of Disablement and Rehabilitation of Invalids |
| Belarus | Plant Variety Patent Law, 1995 |
| Belarus | Tax Code of the Republic of Belarus (General part) |

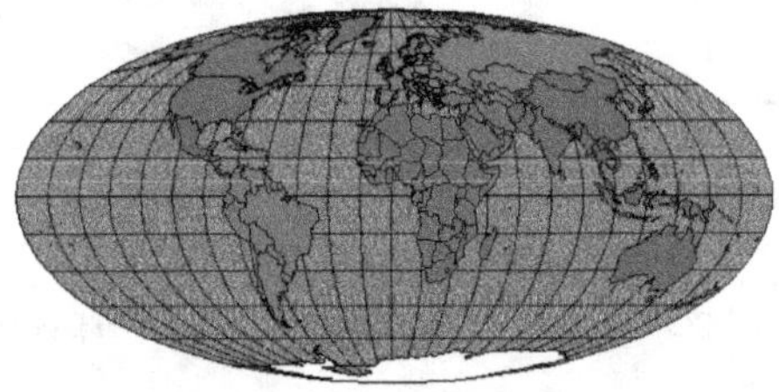

# WORLD RECENT ECONOMIC AND POLITICAL DEVELOPMENT YEARBOOK LIBRARY

## Price: $99.95 Each

| TITLE |
|---|
| Afghanistan Recent Economic and Political Developments Yearbook |
| Aland Recent Economic and Political Developments Yearbook |
| Albania Recent Economic and Political Developments Yearbook |
| Algeria Recent Economic and Political Developments Yearbook |
| Andorra Recent Economic and Political Developments Yearbook |
| Angola Recent Economic and Political Developments Yearbook |
| Anguilla Recent Economic and Political Developments Yearbook |
| Antigua and Barbuda Recent Economic and Political Developments Yearbook |
| Antilles (Netherlands) Recent Economic and Political Developments Yearbook |
| Argentina Recent Economic and Political Developments Yearbook |
| Armenia Recent Economic and Political Developments Yearbook |
| Aruba Recent Economic and Political Developments Yearbook |
| Australia Recent Economic and Political Developments Yearbook |
| Austria Recent Economic and Political Developments Yearbook |
| Azerbaijan Recent Economic and Political Developments Yearbook |
| Bahamas Recent Economic and Political Developments Yearbook |
| Bahrain Recent Economic and Political Developments Yearbook |
| Bangladesh Recent Economic and Political Developments Yearbook |
| Barbados Recent Economic and Political Developments Yearbook |
| Belarus Recent Economic and Political Developments Yearbook |
| Belgium Recent Economic and Political Developments Yearbook |
| Belize Recent Economic and Political Developments Yearbook |
| Benin Recent Economic and Political Developments Yearbook |
| Bermuda Recent Economic and Political Developments Yearbook |
| Bhutan Recent Economic and Political Developments Yearbook |
| Bolivia Recent Economic and Political Developments Yearbook |
| Bosnia and Herzegovina Recent Economic and Political Developments Yearbook |
| Botswana Recent Economic and Political Developments Yearbook |
| Brazil Recent Economic and Political Developments Yearbook |
| Brunei Recent Economic and Political Developments Yearbook |
| Bulgaria Recent Economic and Political Developments Yearbook |
| Burkina Faso Recent Economic and Political Developments Yearbook |
| Burundi Recent Economic and Political Developments Yearbook |
| Cambodia Recent Economic and Political Developments Yearbook |
| Cameroon Recent Economic and Political Developments Yearbook |
| Canada Recent Economic and Political Developments Yearbook |
| Cape Verde Recent Economic and Political Developments Yearbook |
| Cayman Islands Recent Economic and Political Developments Yearbook |
| Central African Republic Recent Economic and Political Developments Yearbook |
| Chad Recent Economic and Political Developments Yearbook |

**For additional analytical, business and investment opportunities information,
Please contact Global Investment & Business Center, USA
at (202) 546-2103. Fax: (202) 546-3275. E-mail: rusric@erols.com**

| TITLE |
| --- |
| Chile Recent Economic and Political Developments Yearbook |
| China Recent Economic and Political Developments Yearbook |
| Colombia Recent Economic and Political Developments Yearbook |
| Comoros Recent Economic and Political Developments Yearbook |
| Congo Recent Economic and Political Developments Yearbook |
| Congo, Democratic Republic Recent Economic and Political Developments Yearbook |
| Cook Islands Recent Economic and Political Developments Yearbook |
| Costa Rica Recent Economic and Political Developments Yearbook |
| Cote d'Ivoire Recent Economic and Political Developments Yearbook |
| Croatia Recent Economic and Political Developments Yearbook |
| Cuba Recent Economic and Political Developments Yearbook |
| Cyprus Recent Economic and Political Developments Yearbook |
| Czech Republic Recent Economic and Political Developments Yearbook |
| Denmark Recent Economic and Political Developments Yearbook |
| Djibouti Recent Economic and Political Developments Yearbook |
| Dominica Recent Economic and Political Developments Yearbook |
| Dominican Republic Recent Economic and Political Developments Yearbook |
| Ecuador Recent Economic and Political Developments Yearbook |
| Egypt Recent Economic and Political Developments Yearbook |
| El Salvador Recent Economic and Political Developments Yearbook |
| Equatorial Guinea Recent Economic and Political Developments Yearbook |
| Eritrea Recent Economic and Political Developments Yearbook |
| Estonia Recent Economic and Political Developments Yearbook |
| Ethiopia Recent Economic and Political Developments Yearbook |
| Falkland Islands Recent Economic and Political Developments Yearbook |
| Faroes IslandsRecent Economic and Political Developments Yearbook |
| Fiji Recent Economic and Political Developments Yearbook |
| Finland Recent Economic and Political Developments Yearbook |
| France Recent Economic and Political Developments Yearbook |
| Gabon Recent Economic and Political Developments Yearbook |
| Gambia Recent Economic and Political Developments Yearbook |
| Georgia Recent Economic and Political Developments Yearbook |
| Germany Recent Economic and Political Developments Yearbook |
| Ghana Recent Economic and Political Developments Yearbook |
| Gibraltar Recent Economic and Political Developments Yearbook |
| GlobalRecent Economic and Political Developments Yearbook |
| Greece Recent Economic and Political Developments Yearbook |
| Greenland Recent Economic and Political Developments Yearbook |
| Grenada Recent Economic and Political Developments Yearbook |
| Guam Recent Economic and Political Developments Yearbook |
| Guatemala Recent Economic and Political Developments Yearbook |
| Guernsey Recent Economic and Political Developments Yearbook |
| Guinea Recent Economic and Political Developments Yearbook |
| Guinea-Bissau Recent Economic and Political Developments Yearbook |
| Guyana Recent Economic and Political Developments Yearbook |
| Haiti Recent Economic and Political Developments Yearbook |
| Honduras Recent Economic and Political Developments Yearbook |
| Hungary Recent Economic and Political Developments Yearbook |
| Iceland Recent Economic and Political Developments Yearbook |
| India Recent Economic and Political Developments Yearbook |

| TITLE |
| --- |
| Indonesia Recent Economic and Political Developments Yearbook |
| InternationalRecent Economic and Political Developments Yearbook |
| Iran Recent Economic and Political Developments Yearbook |
| Iraq Recent Economic and Political Developments Yearbook |
| Ireland Recent Economic and Political Developments Yearbook |
| Israel Recent Economic and Political Developments Yearbook |
| Italy Recent Economic and Political Developments Yearbook |
| Jamaica Recent Economic and Political Developments Yearbook |
| Japan Recent Economic and Political Developments Yearbook |
| Jersey Recent Economic and Political Developments Yearbook |
| Jordan Recent Economic and Political Developments Yearbook |
| Kazakhstan Recent Economic and Political Developments Yearbook |
| Kenya Recent Economic and Political Developments Yearbook |
| Kiribati Recent Economic and Political Developments Yearbook |
| Korea, North Recent Economic and Political Developments Yearbook |
| Korea, South Recent Economic and Political Developments Yearbook |
| KosovoRecent Economic and Political Developments Yearbook |
| KurdistanRecent Economic and Political Developments Yearbook |
| Kuwait Recent Economic and Political Developments Yearbook |
| Kyrgyzstan Recent Economic and Political Developments Yearbook |
| Laos Recent Economic and Political Developments Yearbook |
| Latvia Recent Economic and Political Developments Yearbook |
| Lebanon Recent Economic and Political Developments Yearbook |
| Lesotho Recent Economic and Political Developments Yearbook |
| Liberia Recent Economic and Political Developments Yearbook |
| Libya Recent Economic and Political Developments Yearbook |
| Liechtenstein Recent Economic and Political Developments Yearbook |
| Lithuania Recent Economic and Political Developments Yearbook |
| Luxembourg Recent Economic and Political Developments Yearbook |
| Macao Recent Economic and Political Developments Yearbook |
| Macedonia,Recent Economic and Political Developments Yearbook |
| Madagascar Recent Economic and Political Developments Yearbook |
| MadeiraRecent Economic and Political Developments Yearbook |
| Malawi Recent Economic and Political Developments Yearbook |
| Malaysia Recent Economic and Political Developments Yearbook |
| Maldives Recent Economic and Political Developments Yearbook |
| Mali Recent Economic and Political Developments Yearbook |
| Malta Recent Economic and Political Developments Yearbook |
| Man Recent Economic and Political Developments Yearbook |
| Marshall Islands Recent Economic and Political Developments Yearbook |
| Mauritania Recent Economic and Political Developments Yearbook |
| Mauritius Recent Economic and Political Developments Yearbook |
| Mayotte Recent Economic and Political Developments Yearbook |
| Mexico Recent Economic and Political Developments Yearbook |
| Micronesia Recent Economic and Political Developments Yearbook |
| Moldova Recent Economic and Political Developments Yearbook |
| Monaco Recent Economic and Political Developments Yearbook |
| Mongolia Recent Economic and Political Developments Yearbook |
| Monserrat Recent Economic and Political Developments Yearbook |
| Morocco Recent Economic and Political Developments Yearbook |

| TITLE |
| --- |
| Mozambique Recent Economic and Political Developments Yearbook |
| Myanmar Recent Economic and Political Developments Yearbook |
| Namibia Recent Economic and Political Developments Yearbook |
| Nauru Recent Economic and Political Developments Yearbook |
| Nepal Recent Economic and Political Developments Yearbook |
| Netherlands Recent Economic and Political Developments Yearbook |
| New Caledonia Recent Economic and Political Developments Yearbook |
| New Zealand Recent Economic and Political Developments Yearbook |
| Nicaragua Recent Economic and Political Developments Yearbook |
| Niger Recent Economic and Political Developments Yearbook |
| Nigeria Recent Economic and Political Developments Yearbook |
| Niue Recent Economic and Political Developments Yearbook |
| Northern Mariana Islands Recent Economic and Political Developments Yearbook |
| Norway Recent Economic and Political Developments Yearbook |
| OffshoreRecent Economic and Political Developments Yearbook |
| Oman Recent Economic and Political Developments Yearbook |
| Pakistan Recent Economic and Political Developments Yearbook |
| Palau Recent Economic and Political Developments Yearbook |
| Palestine Recent Economic and Political Developments Yearbook |
| Panama Recent Economic and Political Developments Yearbook |
| Papua New Guinea Recent Economic and Political Developments Yearbook |
| Paraguay Recent Economic and Political Developments Yearbook |
| Peru Recent Economic and Political Developments Yearbook |
| Philippines Recent Economic and Political Developments Yearbook |
| Pitcairn Islands Recent Economic and Political Developments Yearbook |
| Poland Recent Economic and Political Developments Yearbook |
| Polynesia French Recent Economic and Political Developments Yearbook |
| Portugal Recent Economic and Political Developments Yearbook |
| Qatar Recent Economic and Political Developments Yearbook |
| Romania Recent Economic and Political Developments Yearbook |
| Russia Recent Economic and Political Developments Yearbook |
| Rwanda Recent Economic and Political Developments Yearbook |
| Saint Kitts and Nevis Recent Economic and Political Developments Yearbook |
| Saint Lucia Recent Economic and Political Developments Yearbook |
| Saint Vincent and The Grenadines Recent Economic and Political Developments Yearbook |
| Samoa (American) A Recent Economic and Political Developments Yearbook |
| Samoa (Western) Recent Economic and Political Developments Yearbook |
| San Marino Recent Economic and Political Developments Yearbook |
| Sao Tome and Principe Recent Economic and Political Developments Yearbook |
| Saudi Arabia Recent Economic and Political Developments Yearbook |
| Scotland Recent Economic and Political Developments Yearbook |
| Senegal Recent Economic and Political Developments Yearbook |
| SerbiaRecent Economic and Political Developments Yearbook |
| Seychelles Recent Economic and Political Developments Yearbook |
| Sierra Leone Recent Economic and Political Developments Yearbook |
| Singapore Recent Economic and Political Developments Yearbook |
| Slovakia Recent Economic and Political Developments Yearbook |
| Slovenia Recent Economic and Political Developments Yearbook |
| Solomon Islands Recent Economic and Political Developments Yearbook |
| Somalia Recent Economic and Political Developments Yearbook |

| TITLE |
| --- |
| South Africa Recent Economic and Political Developments Yearbook |
| Spain Recent Economic and Political Developments Yearbook |
| Sri Lanka Recent Economic and Political Developments Yearbook |
| St. Helena Recent Economic and Political Developments Yearbook |
| St. Pierre & Miquelon Recent Economic and Political Developments Yearbook |
| Sudan Recent Economic and Political Developments Yearbook |
| Suriname Recent Economic and Political Developments Yearbook |
| Swaziland Recent Economic and Political Developments Yearbook |
| Sweden Recent Economic and Political Developments Yearbook |
| Switzerland Recent Economic and Political Developments Yearbook |
| Syria Recent Economic and Political Developments Yearbook |
| Taiwan Recent Economic and Political Developments Yearbook |
| Tajikistan Recent Economic and Political Developments Yearbook |
| Tanzania Recent Economic and Political Developments Yearbook |
| Thailand Recent Economic and Political Developments Yearbook |
| Togo Recent Economic and Political Developments Yearbook |
| Tonga Recent Economic and Political Developments Yearbook |
| Trinidad and Tobago Recent Economic and Political Developments Yearbook |
| Tunisia Recent Economic and Political Developments Yearbook |
| Turkey Recent Economic and Political Developments Yearbook |
| Turkmenistan Recent Economic and Political Developments Yearbook |
| Turks & Caicos Recent Economic and Political Developments Yearbook |
| Tuvalu Recent Economic and Political Developments Yearbook |
| Uganda Recent Economic and Political Developments Yearbook |
| Ukraine Recent Economic and Political Developments Yearbook |
| United Arab Emirates Recent Economic and Political Developments Yearbook |
| United Kingdom Recent Economic and Political Developments Yearbook |
| United States Recent Economic and Political Developments Yearbook |
| Uruguay Recent Economic and Political Developments Yearbook |
| Uzbekistan Recent Economic and Political Developments Yearbook |
| Vanuatu Recent Economic and Political Developments Yearbook |
| Vatican City Recent Economic and Political Developments Yearbook |
| Venezuela Recent Economic and Political Developments Yearbook |
| Vietnam Recent Economic and Political Developments Yearbook |
| Virgin Islands, British Recent Economic and Political Developments Yearbook |
| Wake Atoll Recent Economic and Political Developments Yearbook |
| Wallis & Futuna Recent Economic and Political Developments Yearbook |
| Western Sahara Recent Economic and Political Developments Yearbook |
| Yemen Recent Economic and Political Developments Yearbook |
| Zambia Recent Economic and Political Developments Yearbook |
| Zimbabwe Recent Economic and Political Developments Yearbook |

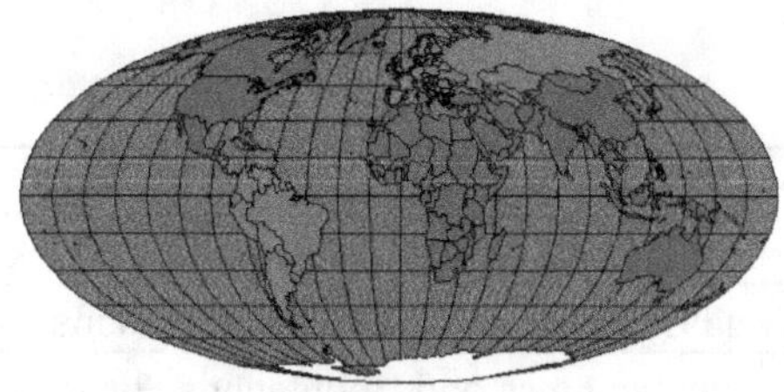

# GLOBAL IMMIGRATION AND CITIZENSHIP LAWS AND REGULATIONS HANDBOOK LIBRARY

**Price: $149.95 Each**

1. Albania Immigration and Citizenship Laws and Regulations Handbook
2. Algeria Immigration and Citizenship Laws and Regulations Handbook
3. Andorra Immigration and Citizenship Laws and Regulations Handbook
4. Angola Immigration and Citizenship Laws and Regulations Handbook
5. Antigua & Barbuda Immigration and Citizenship Laws and Regulations Handbook
6. Antilles (Netherlands) Immigration and Citizenship Laws and Regulations Handbook
7. Argentina Immigration and Citizenship Laws and Regulations Handbook
8. Armenia Immigration and Citizenship Laws and Regulations Handbook
9. Australia Immigration and Citizenship Laws and Regulations Handbook
10. Austria Immigration and Citizenship Laws and Regulations Handbook
11. Azerbaijan Immigration and Citizenship Laws and Regulations Handbook
12. Bahamas Immigration and Citizenship Laws and Regulations Handbook
13. Bangladesh Immigration and Citizenship Laws and Regulations Handbook
14. Barbados Immigration and Citizenship Laws and Regulations Handbook
15. Belarus Immigration and Citizenship Laws and Regulations Handbook
16. Belgium Immigration and Citizenship Laws and Regulations Handbook
17. Belize Immigration and Citizenship Laws and Regulations Handbook
18. Bermuda Immigration and Citizenship Laws and Regulations Handbook
19. Bolivia Immigration and Citizenship Laws and Regulations Handbook
20. Bosnia and Herzegovina Immigration and Citizenship Laws and Regulations Handbook
21. Botswana Immigration and Citizenship Laws and Regulations Handbook
22. Brazil Immigration and Citizenship Laws and Regulations Handbook
23. Brunei Immigration and Citizenship Laws and Regulations Handbook
24. Bulgaria Immigration and Citizenship Laws and Regulations Handbook
25. Cambodia Immigration and Citizenship Laws and Regulations Handbook
26. Cameroon Immigration and Citizenship Laws and Regulations Handbook
27. Canada Immigration and Citizenship Laws and Regulations Handbook
28. Cayman Islands Immigration and Citizenship Laws and Regulations Handbook
29. Chile Immigration and Citizenship Laws and Regulations Handbook
30. China Immigration and Citizenship Laws and Regulations Handbook
31. Colombia Immigration and Citizenship Laws and Regulations Handbook
32. Comoros Immigration and Citizenship Laws and Regulations Handbook
33. Cook Islands Immigration and Citizenship Laws and Regulations Handbook
34. Costa Rica Immigration and Citizenship Laws and Regulations Handbook
35. Croatia Immigration and Citizenship Laws and Regulations Handbook

---

**For additional analytical, business and investment opportunities information,
Please contact Global Investment & Business Center, USA
at (202) 546-2103. Fax: (202) 546-3275. E-mail: rusric@erols.com**

| |
|---|
| 36. Cuba Immigration and Citizenship Laws and Regulations Handbook |
| 37. Cyprus Immigration and Citizenship Laws and Regulations Handbook |
| 38. Czech Republic Immigration and Citizenship Laws and Regulations Handbook |
| 39. Denmark Immigration and Citizenship Laws and Regulations Handbook |
| 40. Dominica Immigration and Citizenship Laws and Regulations Handbook |
| 41. Dominican Republic Immigration and Citizenship Laws and Regulations Handbook |
| 42. Dubai Immigration and Citizenship Laws and Regulations Handbook |
| 43. Ecuador Immigration and Citizenship Laws and Regulations Handbook |
| 44. Egypt Immigration and Citizenship Laws and Regulations Handbook |
| 45. El Salvador Immigration and Citizenship Laws and Regulations Handbook |
| 46. Equatorial Guinea Immigration and Citizenship Laws and Regulations Handbook |
| 47. Estonia Immigration and Citizenship Laws and Regulations Handbook |
| 48. Falkland Islands Immigration and Citizenship Laws and Regulations Handbook |
| 49. Fiji Immigration and Citizenship Laws and Regulations Handbook |
| 50. Finland Immigration and Citizenship Laws and Regulations Handbook |
| 51. France Immigration and Citizenship Laws and Regulations Handbook |
| 52. Georgia Immigration and Citizenship Laws and Regulations Handbook |
| 53. Germany Immigration and Citizenship Laws and Regulations Handbook |
| 54. Gibraltar Immigration and Citizenship Laws and Regulations Handbook |
| 55. Greece Immigration and Citizenship Laws and Regulations Handbook |
| 56. Grenada Immigration and Citizenship Laws and Regulations Handbook |
| 57. Guam Investment & Business Guide |
| 58. Guatemala Immigration and Citizenship Laws and Regulations Handbook |
| 59. Guernsey Immigration and Citizenship Laws and Regulations Handbook |
| 60. Guyana Immigration and Citizenship Laws and Regulations Handbook |
| 61. Haiti Immigration and Citizenship Laws and Regulations Handbook |
| 62. Honduras Immigration and Citizenship Laws and Regulations Handbook |
| 63. Hungary Immigration and Citizenship Laws and Regulations Handbook |
| 64. Iceland Immigration and Citizenship Laws and Regulations Handbook |
| 65. India Immigration and Citizenship Laws and Regulations Handbook |
| 66. Indonesia Immigration and Citizenship Laws and Regulations Handbook |
| 67. Iran Immigration and Citizenship Laws and Regulations Handbook |
| 68. Iraq Immigration and Citizenship Laws and Regulations Handbook |
| 69. Ireland Immigration and Citizenship Laws and Regulations Handbook |
| 70. Israel Immigration and Citizenship Laws and Regulations Handbook |
| 71. Italy Immigration and Citizenship Laws and Regulations Handbook |
| 72. Jamaica Immigration and Citizenship Laws and Regulations Handbook |
| 73. Japan Immigration and Citizenship Laws and Regulations Handbook |
| 74. Jersey Immigration and Citizenship Laws and Regulations Handbook |
| 75. Jordan Immigration and Citizenship Laws and Regulations Handbook |
| 76. Kazakhstan Immigration and Citizenship Laws and Regulations Handbook |
| 77. Kenya Immigration and Citizenship Laws and Regulations Handbook |
| 78. Kiribati Immigration and Citizenship Laws and Regulations Handbook |

| |
|---|
| 79. Korea, North Immigration and Citizenship Laws and Regulations Handbook |
| 80. Korea, South Immigration and Citizenship Laws and Regulations Handbook |
| 81. Kuwait Immigration and Citizenship Laws and Regulations Handbook |
| 82. Kyrgyzstan Immigration and Citizenship Laws and Regulations Handbook |
| 83. Laos Immigration and Citizenship Laws and Regulations Handbook |
| 84. Latvia Immigration and Citizenship Laws and Regulations Handbook |
| 85. Lebanon Immigration and Citizenship Laws and Regulations Handbook |
| 86. Libya Immigration and Citizenship Laws and Regulations Handbook |
| 87. Liechtenstein Immigration and Citizenship Laws and Regulations Handbook |
| 88. Lithuania Immigration and Citizenship Laws and Regulations Handbook |
| 89. Luxemburg Immigration and Citizenship Laws and Regulations Handbook |
| 90. Macao Immigration and Citizenship Laws and Regulations Handbook |
| 91. Macedonia, Republic Immigration and Citizenship Laws and Regulations Handbook |
| 92. Madagascar Immigration and Citizenship Laws and Regulations Handbook |
| 93. Malaysia Immigration and Citizenship Laws and Regulations Handbook |
| 94. Malta Immigration and Citizenship Laws and Regulations Handbook |
| 95. Man Immigration and Citizenship Laws and Regulations Handbook |
| 96. Mauritius Immigration and Citizenship Laws and Regulations Handbook |
| 97. Mauritius Immigration and Citizenship Laws and Regulations Handbook |
| 98. Mexico Immigration and Citizenship Laws and Regulations Handbook |
| 99. Micronesia Immigration and Citizenship Laws and Regulations Handbook |
| 100. Moldova Immigration and Citizenship Laws and Regulations Handbook |
| 101. Monaco Immigration and Citizenship Laws and Regulations Handbook |
| 102. Mongolia Immigration and Citizenship Laws and Regulations Handbook |
| 103. Morocco Immigration and Citizenship Laws and Regulations Handbook |
| 104. Myanmar Immigration and Citizenship Laws and Regulations Handbook |
| 105. Namibia Immigration and Citizenship Laws and Regulations Handbook |
| 106. Netherlands Immigration and Citizenship Laws and Regulations Handbook |
| 107. New Caledonia Immigration and Citizenship Laws and Regulations Handbook |
| 108. New Zealand Immigration and Citizenship Laws and Regulations Handbook |
| 109. Nicaragua Immigration and Citizenship Laws and Regulations Handbook |
| 110. Nigeria Immigration and Citizenship Laws and Regulations Handbook |
| 111. Northern Mariana Islands Immigration and Citizenship Laws and Regulations Handbook |
| 112. Norway Immigration and Citizenship Laws and Regulations Handbook |
| 113. Pakistan Immigration and Citizenship Laws and Regulations Handbook |
| 114. Panama Immigration and Citizenship Laws and Regulations Handbook |
| 115. Peru Immigration and Citizenship Laws and Regulations Handbook |
| 116. Philippines Immigration and Citizenship Laws and Regulations Handbook |
| 117. Poland Immigration and Citizenship Laws and Regulations Handbook |
| 118. Portugal Immigration and Citizenship Laws and Regulations Handbook |
| 119. Romania Immigration and Citizenship Laws and Regulations Handbook |
| 120. Russia Immigration and Citizenship Laws and Regulations Handbook |
| 121. Samoa (American) Investment & Business Guide |

| |
|---|
| 122. Samoa (Western) Immigration and Citizenship Laws and Regulations Handbook |
| 123. Saudi Arabia Immigration and Citizenship Laws and Regulations Handbook |
| 124. Scotland Immigration and Citizenship Laws and Regulations Handbook |
| 125. Singapore Immigration and Citizenship Laws and Regulations Handbook |
| 126. Slovakia Immigration and Citizenship Laws and Regulations Handbook |
| 127. Slovenia Immigration and Citizenship Laws and Regulations Handbook |
| 128. South Africa Immigration and Citizenship Laws and Regulations Handbook |
| 129. Spain Immigration and Citizenship Laws and Regulations Handbook |
| 130. Sri Lanka Immigration and Citizenship Laws and Regulations Handbook |
| 131. St. Helena Immigration and Citizenship Laws and Regulations Handbook |
| 132. Sudan Immigration and Citizenship Laws and Regulations Handbook |
| 133. Suriname Immigration and Citizenship Laws and Regulations Handbook |
| 134. Sweden Immigration and Citizenship Laws and Regulations Handbook |
| 135. Switzerland Immigration and Citizenship Laws and Regulations Handbook |
| 136. Syria Export Import & Business Directory |
| 137. Taiwan Immigration and Citizenship Laws and Regulations Handbook |
| 138. Tajikistan Immigration and Citizenship Laws and Regulations Handbook |
| 139. Thailand Immigration and Citizenship Laws and Regulations Handbook |
| 140. Tunisia Immigration and Citizenship Laws and Regulations Handbook |
| 141. Turkey Immigration and Citizenship Laws and Regulations Handbook |
| 142. Turkmenistan Immigration and Citizenship Laws and Regulations Handbook |
| 143. Uganda Immigration and Citizenship Laws and Regulations Handbook |
| 144. Ukraine Immigration and Citizenship Laws and Regulations Handbook |
| 145. United Arab Emirates Immigration and Citizenship Laws and Regulations Handbook |
| 146. United Kingdom Immigration and Citizenship Laws and Regulations Handbook |
| 147. United States Immigration and Citizenship Laws and Regulations Handbook |
| 148. Uruguay Immigration and Citizenship Laws and Regulations Handbook |
| 149. US Immigration and Citizenship Laws and Regulations Handbook |
| 150. Uzbekistan Immigration and Citizenship Laws and Regulations Handbook |
| 151. Venezuela Immigration and Citizenship Laws and Regulations Handbook |
| 152. Vietnam Immigration and Citizenship Laws and Regulations Handbook |
| 153. Serbia Immigration and Citizenship Laws and Regulations Handbook |

www.ingramcontent.com/pod-product-compliance
Lightning Source LLC
LaVergne TN
LVHW080038210926
848481LV00011B/3229